H. E. Bates was born in 190
Northamptonshire and was educated at
Kettering Grammar School. His first
novel, *The Two Sisters*, was published when
he was twenty and in the next fifteen years
he acquired a distinguished reputation for
his stories about English country life, the
best of which are collected in *Country Tales*
(1938).

During the Second World War he was
commissioned to write short stories of
RAF life by the Air Ministry. He produced
two best-selling collections, *The Greatest
People in the World* (1942) and *How Sleep the
Brave* (1943), under the pseudonym
'Flying Officer X', and under his own
name wrote the enormously successful *Fair
Stood the Wind for France* (1944).

In the 1950's he began to write the
popular Larkin family novels, starting
with *The Darling Buds of May* (1958). His
autobiography originally appeared in
three parts: *The Vanished World* (1969), *The
Blossoming World* (1971) and *The World in
Ripeness* (1972). *The Blossoming World* and
The World in Ripeness are reissued here in
one paperback volume.

H. E. Bates was awarded the C.B.E. in
1973 and died in January 1974. He
married in 1931, had four children and
lived most of his life in Kent.

H. E. Bates

THE RIPENING WORLD

A Writer's Autobiography
containing The Blossoming World
and The World in Ripeness

Illustrated by John Ward

Robinson Publishing
London

Robinson Publishing
11 Shepherd House
Shepherd Street
London W1Y 7LD

First published in Great Britain by
Michael Joseph Ltd in two volumes
as The Blossoming World *(1971) and*
The World in Ripeness *(1972)*

Printed by Wm. Collins & Sons Ltd., Glasgow

THE BLOSSOMING WORLD

I

On a damp, grey morning in the first week of January 1926 I boarded the 8.40 train from Wellingborough, bound for London's St Pancras. I was five months short of my 21st birthday. I had already written two novels, several one-act plays, a number of short stories, a batch of verse, almost all of it very bad, and a radio play. The occasion of that damp New Year journey imprints itself firmly on memory as one both momentous and exciting but touched, at the same time, with a certain apprehension. I was in fact on my way to meet my first publisher, Jonathan Cape, his partner and their reader, whose name I did not know, in the semi-hallowed precincts of Bloomsbury.

The great drab glass dome of London's St Pancras station, that towering château of Victorian Gothic, has often seemed to me to be very like the massive wingspread of a giant eagle brooding with smoke-blackened wings over the restless nest of platforms, trains and travellers below. It has also sometimes seemed to be, as eagles often are, both a symbol and a monument: symbol of a departed and lamented era of railway steam and a monument to an area, also departed, but utterly unlamented, of what were once some of London's most squalid and putrefying slums. The entire area of what now consists of one of London's three great railway termini serving the Midlands and the North was formerly a sink of rotting slums, thieves' kitchens, gin-houses and prostitution whose squalor and contagion were evidently a combination of the London of Fielding and Dickens at its worst. There are some who see in the half-ecclesiastical mass of St Pancras, with the faded splendour of its once great staircases, grill-rooms and dining-rooms, a certain nobility. But for me it has long had that monumental broodiness, an air of steamy, smoky shadow.

St. Pancras Station

It was by no means my first visit to London and St Pancras. On the way southward for summer holidays I had often stopped for refreshment of some sort with my parents at the huge, smoky, steamy station. To enter the grill-room in those days was like going into a palace. There was everywhere an air of opulence and grandeur, of palms and brass, of marble and mahogany. A huge black-hooded grill, its charcoal glowing scarlet, was presided over by men in white tunics and chefs' white hats. Chops, steaks, cutlets, sausages were all laid out in readiness for your selection, to be grilled to your taste. Sirloins of beef, legs of lamb, saddles of mutton reposed under the gleaming silver domes of trolleys, to be produced for the delectation of customers by conjuring carvers armed with steels and knives. The head waiters wore frock coats. The napkins and tablecloths were almost brittle with starchiness. The carpets had a deep plushiness almost royal. The feeling about everything was one of splendid amplitude. I have a haunting memory of delicious apricot tarts; another of my father casually tipping porters; still another of my father holding easy discourse with waiters not as if he had sprung from the painful poverty of a little Midland boot-and-shoe town, as in fact he had, but as if he had been moving in the elevated circles of St Pancras station restaurant and its counterparts all his life. Splendidly, almost embarrassingly at ease in this world, he guided us through lunch before at last escorting us to the fresh grandeur of a taxi that would take us across town to another station, so that we could embark on the third lap of our journey to the seaside.

And this, it must be remembered, was a railway restaurant; the great Midland Railway, in its proud maroon livery, had a similar restaurant in every station of any importance from London to Edinburgh. The traveller of those days was not to be treated like cattle. Today it is an undisputed fact that if in Switzerland you are in doubt as to where to eat, the wise course is at once to seek out the railway station, the Bahnhof Buffet; it is incontestable that you can hardly eat better than at the large Swiss station restaurants, a state of affairs just as true of France, for which the celebrated *Guide Michelin* issues a special guide for *Restaurants à la Gare.*

But on that morning in early January 1926 I had no time to linger in what were still St Pancras' opulent rooms; nor had I any money for taxis. I set off, in fact, to walk through Bloomsbury's Squares to Charing Cross Road and its bookshops. Opposite St Pancras there still stood the old grimy King's Theatre, at which, only a year or so later, you could get into a season of Shaw plays for as little, if memory serves me correctly, as a shilling a time. There were still trams in the streets and still open-top buses. London still had its wintry cloak of mist and soot through the gloom of which the naked, spotted trunks of plane-trees in the Squares stood like elephantine creatures, brooding and waiting. I stopped somewhere, I think at an A.B.C., and got myself a cup of coffee. The morning was raw; and it was not only the plane-trees that were brooding. There was also a greater, darker brooding, its roots social and political, in the air. The year was to be eventful, in fact, not for the publication of a certain young novelist's *The Two Sisters*, but for the General Strike, a circumstance hardly opportune for the publishing world or any other. Half the nation looked ill-dressed, lost, underfed, if not emaciated. But happily the path of youth, in my case at any rate, was single-minded; and though I had already expressed my bitterness at the cankering poverty and dole-queues of the twenties in a searing one-act play, *The Last Bread*, I had really no time, that morning, to do my own brooding on social injustice and social inequality. I had to meet for the first time my publishers, Jonathan Cape, and their reader, in order to discuss a contract which was to offer me a fortune of £25 and further to discuss some few points of criticism in my MS. that 'our reader' had raised.

I had a couple of hours to fill before my luncheon appointment in Bedford Square. Memory isn't always sharp over a distance of more than forty years but there is little doubt, I think, that I spent most of that morning in Charing Cross Road, with its double lane of book-shops. I was book-mad; I suffered from the chronic and ever increasing disease of reading. I could scarcely have read more at a university than I did on my own account; moreover my particular syllabus was my own. That morning therefore I was again searching for my own chosen idols, Turgenev, Tchehov, Maupassant, Crane, Donne and various others, and with an almost total lack of success that by now had become a commonplace. Charing Cross Road, dingy, seedy, depressed both architecturally and in atmosphere, has always seemed to me to be the oddest place to have become, whether by accident or design, the Mecca of bookshops. It also wears a slight air of shame: accounted for perhaps by the fact that it stands on the very door-step of the notorious Seven Dials, through which even as late as the years immediately before the First World War it was hardly safe for the respectably dressed citizen to walk with impunity, and further by the fact that, in 1926 at any rate, almost every other

30
Jonathan Cape
30 Bedford
Square

shop was an emporium for contraceptives, together with pills and potions for the promotion of male vigour, other restoratives, probably of the same concoction, for the restitution and rejuvenation of lost potency and immoral books of dubious authorship calculated similarly to stimulate or restore the sexual appetite by means of words. It was also notorious for that particular sort of shop which is always *Closing Down Stock Must be Cleared Regardless of Cost. Great Sacrifice:* the sacrifice always being made, of course, by the meek lamb who, licking the steam off the window, falls at last for the 22-carat gold, 50-jewelled watch at twenty-five shillings that is displayed before his very eyes in the window. It is a trap I myself know only too well, having fallen into it headlong, not on that January morning, but on a summer afternoon that same year, when I at last decided to plunge for a window-bargain 22-carat gold, 50-jewelled wrist-watch at twenty-two shillings and ended up in the clutches of two Jewish gentlemen whose gripping attentions reminded me of the words of the hymnal *Oh! Love that will not let me go,* except that they eventually did let me go, short of a fiver and the possessor of a gun-metal watch that had probably been stolen anyway.

Such was the innocence of the young man who finally found his way to that most beautiful of London's Squares, part of the vast inheritance of the Bedfordshire dukedom: the elegant, plane-tree shrouded, Adam-built Bedford Square. At No. 30 I was greeted by a young receptionist who appeared to be scarcely less than a goddess – a singularly distinguishing feature of the Cape regime of the twenties and thirties was the remarkable propensity on the part of Jonathan Cape himself for filling his offices with marvellously attractive young ladies, some of whom I adored and all of whom had to be remarkably quick-footed in the presence of the master – who seemed to be more than slightly taken aback by the arrival of an author looking not much more than a schoolboy.

I was duly taken, by the young goddess, up the magnificent Adam staircase to Cape's own equally splendid Adam room on the first floor. I fancy Jonathan was also no little surprised at my own extreme youthfulness. As I have already indicated in Vol. I of this work my sex, as the author of *The Two Sisters*, a novel of young female love, had been the subject of some argument and discussion among Cape, his partner Wren Howard, who presently joined us, and 'our reader', whom I was yet to meet. The ultimate majority opinion among them had been that I was a girl: a decision resulting in my being addressed, by letter, as 'Miss Bates'. This trifling mistake I had put right by confessing to being a 'mere male', which still didn't prevent both Cape and Wren Howard from peering at me rather as if I *ought* to have been a girl, firmly masculine though I was.

Cape was tallish and dark, Wren Howard spruce, military-like and fair. Cape had laid the ground-work of his publishing career as a traveller in, I think, the firm of Duckworth. Wren Howard was a specialist, and a very good one, indeed in some ways revolutionary, in typography. Both were shrewd. I will not give offence to their memory by saying that they were also mean; let it merely be said that they were not notable for a glowing generosity. That they seemed almost royally generous to me on that drab January morning does not alter the point. When you first rapturously kiss a beautiful girl you do not pause to wonder if she has holes in her stockings or has forgotten to change her knickers overnight. Similarly I was not disposed to be concerned, that morning, with the parsimonious nature, or otherwise, of publishers. That they were publishers, and were about to be my publishers, was enough. I should add here to the credit side of both men that they had succeeded, in the space of a mere five or six years, in producing the best-looking books in the entire London publishing world, an achievement for which undoubtedly the flair and taste of Wren Howard were in large degree responsible. Their books were a delight to the eye and a joy to handle. What was more, the distinguished wrappers held behind them a collection of authors, many of them American, of parallel distinction: Louis Bromfield, Sherwood Anderson, Dorothy Canfield, Hemingway, Eugene O'Neill, Sinclair Lewis, Manuel Komroff,

Kay Boyle and Sarah Orne Jewett on the American side; A. E. Coppard, Liam O'Flaherty, Pauline Smith, Martin Armstrong, Laurence Housman, Doughty and others of much distinction on the English. It was a matter of extreme and intense pride to me to join such a company, representing as it did a scintillating segment of the golden age of the twenties and thirties, an age beside which all too many of the productions of the fifties and sixties look like the cast-offs of a flea-bitten rag-bag.

After we had been joined by a young man from the editorial department, Gilchrist Thompson, we all went off to lunch in order to meet 'our reader', as to whose identity I had still no clue. On the way to Charlotte Street, a mere five minutes or so away, I walked with Cape, who among other things asked if I had read Eugene O'Neill and when I replied that I hadn't at once promised to send me copies of the American's plays, a promise duly kept, thus introducing me to an author whom another American once called 'our greatest playwright – unfortunately'.

In Charlotte Street we reached the *Etoile*, a restaurant long celebrated not only for its cuisine but as a meeting place for literary men, and happily carrying on in the same tradition today. My few excursions into the station restaurant at St Pancras constituted almost my entire experience of the world of eating in London and I was in consequence no little overwhelmed by the *Etoile's* continental menu and atmosphere. I felt nervous and out of my depth. I was confused by the offerings on the menu and eventually got out of the problem of what to order by ordering what everyone else did, namely *minestrone* and *escalope de veau* and *spaghetti*. Even then I was so utterly uncertain of myself and everything else that when the offering of *parmesan* cheese was finally made I had no idea whatever as to what it was for and had to be shown, like a child, by Gilchrist Thompson.

It was somewhere about the time of my innocent struggle with the *parmesan* that there walked into the restaurant an arresting and extraordinary figure. I have already described

L'Etoile
Charlotte Street

this moment and this figure in terms* on which I do not think I can possibly improve and I now therefore quote myself:

'There came into the restaurant a semi-patriarchal, semi-diabolical figure in a floppy cloak-like overcoat, a grey scarf wound round his neck like a python, and a preposterously small felt hat. He had grey hair, grey jowl-like cheeks that quivered ponderously like the gills of an ancient turkey, and he appeared to have lost himself completely. He appeared also to be an extraordinarily clumsy person; he was something over six feet tall and big-boned in proportion, but he was in fact extraordinarily agile (as I shall show later) for so large a man. His thick-lensed glasses gave him an appearance that was in that moment, and remained for me for a long time afterwards, quite frightening. He staggered about for some moments like a great bear unable to recall the steps of a dance he had just begun, and then hung up his coat, hat, scarf and walking stick on the hat stand. He then smoothed his hair with his hands, gave several painful snorts of breath through his mouth as if the whole procedure had winded him completely, and advanced towards us.

'I stood up, hypnotised and terrified by this enormous and grizzly figure, and as I shook hands there was in the air a faint smell of herbal cigarettes and a weird glint of myopic eyes.

' "Mr Edward Garnett," someone said and I could have fainted.'

Just as it is characteristic of youth that youth's immaturities are rarely self-evident, so youth is inclined to see as old, or even ancient, anyone over fifty. If Edward Garnett were alive today he would be exactly one hundred. When I met him on that first devastating occasion in Charlotte Street he would therefore have been only fifty-eight, or five years younger than I am as I write these words. Yet such was the gap between fifty-eight and twenty that the words 'patriarchal', 'grizzly' and 'ancient turkey' seem, even in far retrospect, to be accurate

* *Edward Garnett: a Memoir* by H. E. Bates (Parrish 1950) out of print.

and just descriptions. They are not of course exactly so, but this was the eye of youth observing, and this is the man youth saw: a man apparently so absent and unworldly and clumsy that as he sat down at the restaurant he immediately performed the sort of act so characteristic of him. Stretching out his hand for the *parmesan* cheese he let the sleeve of his jacket fall into the *minestrone*: without, of course, having the faintest notion that he

had done so. Rather in the same way he brought his gaze to bear on Cape, Wren Howard, Gilchrist Thompson and myself as if slightly bewildered by the fact that we were there at all.

If Garnett had been dressed in city morning coat, pin-stripe trousers, bowler-hat, grey neck-tie and pearl tie-pin his effect on me that January day would have been no less impressive than it was. If Cape had previously informed me that I was going to meet as 'our reader' John Galsworthy, Desmond MacCarthy, Gerald Gould, A. E. Housman or Hilaire Belloc I should have been suitably impressed but by no means awed, still less bowled over. I had read them all; some I viewed with respect, some with admiration. But my meeting with Edward Garnett may well be likened to that of a cub-reporter of an earlier generation finding himself in the presence, for the first time, of Dickens or Hardy. Garnett had already been, though he did not know it, one of many formative influences on me. I had read and eagerly digested his prefaces to his wife's, Constance Garnett's, translations of Turgenev; and together the prefaces and translations had made on me an immense and guiding impression. Today, as I turn back to them and similarly to Garnett's critical assessments of Tchehov, D. H. Lawrence, Stephen Crane, Sarah Orne Jewett, Henry Lawson, Sherwood Anderson, Robert Frost and many others I find no reason for doubting either their rightness or perspicacity. Garnett, if I had been asked to make a literary choice, would have been the man I most wanted to meet in a generation when literary figures were by no means small.

Of the general pattern of conversation at lunch that January day I now remember little. It is the impressions of conversation after lunch, when Cape and his partners had returned to Bedford Square and I was left alone with Garnett, the coffee and the herbal cigarettes, that remain indelible to this day. This conversation consisted mostly of catechisms on Garnett's part and answers, some eager, some diffident, on my own. How had *The Two Sisters* come to be written? Was it autobiographical? Or a work totally of imagination? Had I written anything else? If so, what else? Stories, poems, plays? What, above all, did I read?

I believe it was Garnett's turn to be astonished when I let out a list of my gods: Tchehov, Turgenev, Tolstoy, Ibsen, Maupassant, Crane, Conrad, Gorki, Bierce, Flaubert. Conrad alone, perhaps, produced no astonishment in him, since he had already rightly detected his influence on *The Two Sisters'* every page. But his astonishment at the rest was enough to cause him to inquire what university I had been to? Since, like me, he had been to no university himself but had, again like me, provided and pursued his own literary syllabus, my reply of 'None' delighted him as much as the list of my gods. Now and then, as I gave my answers to his many catechisms, the oyster-like myopic eyes rolled, the herbal cigarette ash dropped all over the waistcoated bosom, and the red, loose, pouting lips let forth a juicy and approving 'Yes, yes.' He had also much approval, with some reservations, for *The Two Sisters*. It was remarkably perceptive, most poetic; an achievement, for a young man, of no mean kind. The influence of Conrad was, of course, clearly discernible, though not necessarily obtrusive, as he afterwards confessed. But would *they* understand it? That was the point. There was the rub. Would *they* recognise the quality of so youthful yet perceptive a work? He was clearly highly dubious of their wit to do so and was generously insistent, throughout the rest of the meal, that he write a preface to it in order to guide them from the dark errors of their ways.

They were the critics; the philistines. It is hard to say whether Garnett had a lower opinion of the average literary critic of his day or of the general public; but on balance I would settle for the critics. 'They don't *know*, you see, Bates, they don't *know*.' Indeed they didn't know; nor, of the greater part of them, can it be said that they know today. The tendency to behave like a wasp, irately stinging everyone in sight; the propensity to bumble useless as a bee; the illusion that speculation is criticism; the pretension to self-glorification; the manifest use of clichés and jargon while condemning them in others; the sheer love of wounding for wounding's sake, so evident in literature ever since its Edinburgh inception inspired Byron to the wrath of *English Bards and Scots Reviewers:* all these are as much part of the contemporary literary snob-pit as they were of Garnett's day. 'They don't *know*, you see, Bates, they don't *know*,' was Garnett's often repeated, scornful, mournful truth, to which he might well have added that of Ibsen, who perhaps of all 19th century writers suffered more than any other from the obtuse 'slings and arrows of outrageous fortune' and sheer purblind bigotry: 'there has never yet been a memorial to a critic'. Indeed there never has.

So we talked that day until nearly four o'clock; until we were the only persons, except for the last few tired waiters, left in the restaurant; until at last Garnett, hitherto oblivious of the fact that our presence was becoming something of an embarrassment, became aware of the situation and decided we must go. Outside, in Charlotte Street, I have described my progress with him as being rather like that of 'a spaniel puppy without a collar trotting by a shaggy and lumbering sheep-dog whose wind was not very good and whose eyes were not what they had been'; and I see no reason to alter the description today. As we came to say good-bye, somewhere near Bedford Square, he shook my hand affectionately and made me reiterate my promise to send him every manuscript I had written, stories, plays or poems, as soon as possible, and this I declared I would do. One of his gods that I hadn't mentioned, and who had so far escaped me, was W. H. Hudson. He promised in turn to send me Hudson's little masterpiece of a story *El Ombú*, adding his fervent praise of the new offering. It was characteristic of him that he left it in a restaurant the following day.

My response to Garnett's request for MSS. must have been extraordinarily prompt and his own reaction to them hardly less so. It was in fact only January 4th when in the characteristically generous and unselfish way that marked his entire approach to creative as opposed to destructive criticism he was already writing his first letter to me, praising some of the stories I had sent him, lightly rejecting others. It was also characteristic of him that he could be practical too:

I am sending 'Once' to Mr Middleton Murry and hope that he will take it for 'The Adelphi'. It is beautifully rendered, the woman's absorption in the baby and the man's absorption in both, and the Bank Holiday travel – all is beautifully felt.

'Encore' is almost as good . . . If you could cut the sketch down to say 12 pages and send it to me again, I think we might try 'The Criterion' or some other magazine.

The poem 'Clamour' I am sending to 'The Nation' and I only hope that this editor will think as highly of it as I do. But people are often insensitive to the genuine thing.

'The Flame' shows that you have mastered this form of the short sketch. It is beautifully felt and written. You must do others in this style – terse, with not a word thrown away. I will send it somewhere.

'The Unbelievers' is a very good idea and has some excellent passages . . . but it is 'romantic' or romanticized. Later on you can re-write it, but not now.

'Possession' is also unreal . . . 'Defeat' is very well written but here again the atmosphere and accessories are too romantic . . . 'The Lady Poverty' has charm but there is a 'stock' element in it . . . It's not up to your level.

And so on, characteristically: criticism both creative and constructive, sound advice, practical advice; already a pursuit, on behalf of myself and my stories, of celebrated editors.

The response of some of these was also prompt. Within a few days Leonard Woolf had accepted *The Flame* for *The Nation*; presently he was sending me books to review. Small wonder that I was carried away by elation: an elation rather tempered by the fact that I had neglected to tell Garnett that I had already entered *The Flame* for a short story competition run by Robert Lynd for *The Daily News*, never really dreaming that it would gain a prize. It didn't in fact gain a prize but was accepted for publication almost on the very day that Leonard Woolf gave it his blessing; a state of affairs that had to be rapidly adjusted in favour of *The Nation*.

It is scarcely surprising that after the momentous experience of meeting Garnett in London I returned to my native Northamptonshire, its boot factories, its rigid nonconformity and its harsh, barren red brick, in a mood of rarefied elation which the news from Leonard Woolf and Middleton Murry rarefied still further; nor was it surprising, since I was still so very young, that this elation should also have been tinged with a certain pride which, though some considerable distance from actual conceit, may well have been misconstrued as aloofness. Indeed I was, and felt, aloof.

It might well be truer to say that I felt very alone, though not lonely. I had no one, with the exception of an old school-friend, Harry Byrom, now at King's College London and whom I rarely saw except during vacations, and my old English master, Edmund Kirby, with whom to share my new-found exultations. I did not speak of my writing much, if at all, to my parents. Even Madge, whom I was eventually to marry, seemed to cast some doubt on the truth of the fact that I was about to publish a book; but then she too was very young and could at that time claim no acquaintance with the world of authors and authorship, a defect that the ensuing years were to do much to remedy.

My life, in fact, divided itself into two parts: the one in which I played football, went with Madge to dances and cinemas, was mildly social and so on; the other in which I retired for hours at a time like a brooding young hermit to the little box-room my parents had now given me as a study and from which I escaped for occasional relaxation for long solitary walks into the countryside, there to brood also, hardly seeing a soul with whom to pass the time of day, almost my only company the stark black elms so characteristic of that scarcely inspiring Midland winter landscape. That I was not lonely in doing all this and that I can still endure hours of being alone without any hint of being beset or oppressed by loneliness may well be due to the fact that, in the summer of 1911, in that glorious year that has been called the *Annus Mirabilis*, when I was six, I fell victim to a stroke of physical ill-fortune.

On a beautiful hot Saturday afternoon in July that year I was taken to a garden party. Again I am sure that it was, pictorially at any rate, a cross somewhere between a painting by Renoir and some pages out of *A la Recherche du Temps Perdu*: gay sunshades, mutton-leg sleeves, sweeping skirts, straw boaters, bright blazers, the ribboned hair of little girls; scarlet geraniums, blue lobelia and yellow calceolarias, that most hideous of Edwardian horticultural clashes, in the flower beds; gloxinias of purple and wine-red trumpeting behind the glass of conservatories; and then madeira cake and doughnuts and raspberries and cream for tea. On the raspberries and cream I gorged so piggishly that I was warned over and over again that I should pay for it. And pay for it I did.

Next morning, Sunday, I woke to find myself generously covered with bright raspberry-red spots. I also felt singularly unwell. This, I was told, was the clear result of my unheeding Saturday sins; the raspberries were leaving their mark on me. The joke, however, was short-lived. Presently my head was aching; then it was no longer a head but the piston of a steam engine, wildly bumping; soon I was in a half-trance, partly light-headed, only vaguely aware of mundane events, the victim of a strange feeling of groping intoxication, a fearful impression of floating helplessly away.

The doctor arrived to diagnose scarlet fever: not surprisingly, since the town was being swept by an epidemic and a girl in the next street had already died. I do not recall any anxiety of any kind about my dying also, but only of being put to bed in an enormous brass four-poster, from which I eventually emerged to a sentence, (unheard-of in these present days) of eight weeks' solitary imprisonment. It is wholly for this reason that the summer of 1911, the *Annus Mirabilis*, remains so indelibly imprinted on my memory. I saw its great beauty only from the windows of my bedroom. Not that I was utterly solitary. School-friends came to play street games with me under the window; I blew bubbles from a clay pipe and watched the diaphanous balloons float away over the roofs of the boot factories in the crystalline summer air; and in the evenings my father came and sat with me and puffed, for the one and only time in his life, at cigarettes of a particularly nasty brand in the fond belief that the resulting smoke would kill germs, a belief fully in accordance with another notion prevalent about the turn of the century, namely that smells and odours obnoxious would inevitably result in complaints that were 'catching'.

Scarlet fever is not among the most aesthetic of diseases; nor, any longer, is it a killing one in the way that it was fifty years, and even less, ago. But I duly went through the unpicturesque process of 'peeling' and survived. And it was during all this that I learned, I think, to be alone and above all not to mind being alone. This, perhaps, is one of the compensations of illness: that the enforced detachment of it acts as a sort of balm. Another is that illness tends to magnify trivialities, so that little things, a soap-bubble floating over roofs in the sunshine, voices in the street, the finger tendrils of a Virginia creeper grasping the raw red brick of a wall, become things of fascination and importance. I used to watch, all that summer, the way the Virginia creeper grew: up and along the walls and out of sight along the next door houses and the walls of the boot factory and slowly, like tiny fingers drawing an invisible body up from drowning somewhere at the foot of the wall, over the window sill. In that way I am perfectly sure I first learned, and even liked, to be alone. It is perhaps also from this cause that some part of my temperament was shaped, so that my present doctor tells me that I am the most philosophical patient he has ever known.

Thus was I able easily to adjust myself to the solitude of the little box-room that I converted into a study, furnishing it with an old Victorian arm-chair, a table, a bureau and presently a few book-shelves. Like a contemplative snail I retired, sometimes from eight o'clock in the morning to eight at night, into my self-constructed shell. In a town built round a single industry the day's hard time-table is inexorably fixed. At half past seven every morning the factory hooters and whistles wailed, preceded for some minutes before by the sound of workers' running feet and then followed by the clatter of odd stragglers through the sudden silence that meant they had 'missed a quarter'. At precisely the same hour you heard the factory engines start up, bang, chuff-pause-chuff, pause, bang, chuff-chuff-chuff and so into steady rhythm. Thereafter a great silence spread over the town's grey slate roofs and with it a curious sense of guilt: a feeling that *you* too ought to have been working, a prisoner until half past twelve behind factory bars. At that hour the factory hooters and whistles wailed again;

wild streams of workers, many still struggling into jackets, disgorged from factory doors like released prisoners, running and cycling in all directions as if at the start of a mad marathon. At half past one the hooters and whistles wailed again; the silence and the accompanying sense of guilt spread and brooded once more over the town, not to be broken until a quarter past five.

I should add to this 'if all went well'. But in the mid-twenties all was not well. The slump lay on the country, and most severely on one-trade towns such as Rushden, like a dark disease. Dole queues were long; three-on three-off was almost a blessing when compared with long weeks of shut-down, sometimes bankruptcy. The quick war-time fortunes were everywhere dissipating; under the demoralising blight of short-time, vain hope and utter idleness, war-veterans wandered lamely from house to house pushing or carrying baskets of shoe-laces, polishes, brushes, cheap underwear, buttons, dusters, safety pins. An occasional gypsy knocked on the door, clothes' basket full of pegs, household bits and pieces crudely made, sometimes with some cure-all mysteriously concocted ('It'll put you right, dearie, it will in no time. Any old rags to spare, dearie? Something you don't want, dearie, eh? It'll put you right, dearie, I'll tell you. You're lucky, dearie. You're lucky. You've got a lucky face, dearie. I can see that. God bless you. A lucky face.') My mother, like my grandfather, never refused gypsies. Whether they got to know her as a soft touch I never knew but they used to come back, year in, year out, with the old moaning, droning, pleading back-door whine, the sure cure-all for everything, the well-acted eternal promise, the eternal 'God-bless-you-dearie,' for eternal good luck.

But it needed more than gypsy-wished good luck to see a worker through the barren ways of the mid-twenties and perhaps for this reason I counted my own good luck, precariously secluded though I was in my self-made snailshell, as God-sent, yet another example of the hand of 'the divinity that shapes our ends'. I could surely be forgiven if I felt that I was lucky. An advance of twenty-five pounds on my first novel, five guineas for a story, three guineas for another, two guineas for a review: riches, luck indeed. In addition to all this the B.B.C. had accepted for broadcasting a one-act play *Loyalties*, for which I got the staggering sum of ten guineas. I had also sent my angry-young-man broadside, *The Last Bread*, to the Labour Publishing Company, run by E. N. and Monica Ewer, and that too had been accepted, though without advance, and was presently to be published at a shilling, thus becoming my first published book, preceding *The Two Sisters* by a month or two.

Presently, also at the instigation of Edward Garnett, I was sending stories to *The Manchester Guardian*, whose perceptive literary editor Allan Monkhouse ran a back-page short story of about 1000 words every day of the week in that then great newspaper; and to *The New Statesman* and *The Bermondsey Book*, the latter one part of a project, *The Bermondsey Centre*, designed to give some sort of hope to a particularly blighted corner of a blighted world. Whether it was the godsend to the poor of Bermondsey that it was intended to be I never quite knew, but *The Manchester Guardian* was a godsend, and in more ways than one, to me. To write a short story of 1000 words may appear to be as easy, on the face of it, as one of those tricks with three or four matches that are sometimes presented to you, but that, in practice, turn out to be vastly more demanding. The task of pruning down a story to Monkhouse's desired length was an exercise both admirable and exhausting. It took me, lesson by lesson, through the exacting art of making one word do the work of two, and even sometimes of three or four. So great was my devotion to that particular lesson in fact that I was presently able, in one instance at any rate, to become master instead of pupil.

Among the few writing friends I had at that time were a group of local newspaper reporters who used to meet, mid-mornings, at an old Temperance Hotel-cum-café for coffee: a decaying, fusty, shabby haunt complete with bubbling hot water geysers, marble-topped tables, aspidistras, a general odour of stale tea and cabbage and an air of half-sanctified lassitude not so very far removed from my childhood Sunday schools. Here I sometimes used to join the reporters for a morning half an hour or so. I was induced to see in one of them, a rather podgy, groping fellow, a picture of myself as I might have been if I hadn't mercifully sacked myself at a tender age from the squalid local office of *The Northampton Chronicle:* not so much a man as a cypher, not so much a writer as a shabby collector of shabby facts for a shabby weekly, a scribbler for ever in pursuit of shattering events at bazaars, garden parties, fêtes, council meetings, funerals, weddings, police courts. While I continued to thank God I had so early made an escape from that kind of life sentence I felt an increasing pity for my older, podgy, slaving friend. He too was striving to write short stories, but with a total, dismal, stultifying lack of success. When it began to appear that I had contributed, so young, to *The Nation*, *The New Statesman*, *The Adelphi* and *The Manchester Guardian* he was moved, one morning, to ask if I would read what he diffidently called 'one of his efforts'.

It was a sprawling, fleshy, verbose thing, stuffed with clichés, of some 1700 words. I read through it, over coffee, on the marble-topped table. The eye already guided by Garnett and made keener by the demands of Monkhouse then proceeded to take its podgy author through it, word by word, performing surgery on sentence after sentence as with a scalpel. I think, as he saw his many precious words mercilessly cut like diseased tissue and thrown out, he was near to despair; I even suspected he might well have thought I was merely showing off. But when the operation was at last over he seemed to revive a little under my assurance that the whole piece now had both air and shape and might be printable. 'Send it to Monkhouse,' I advised, 'at the *Manchester Guardian*,' which he duly did: to enter, a week later, for the first time, the joyous realms of acceptance.

If this incident and the various successful experiences that led up to it prompt the conclusion that my life was now all roses and honey let me at once dispel it. The elation of first success is not for ever. But of one thing I was positively, stubbornly, unremittingly certain: I was never going to be, ever, come hell or high water, anything but a writer. I would never, God being my helper, take another job. But youth, as George Moore has pointed out, 'goes forth singing', and no doubt I was, as he has also said, 'lapped in the evanescent haze of the edge of the wood, the enchantment of a May morning'. As to how deep the wood would be or that the May morning would surely lose its first innocence and evanescence I did not bother to think. I did not pause to examine the questions that I was about to take up a profession that offered no certainty of employment or reward; no steady office hours, no fixed salary, no promotion, no holidays with pay; that can promise no pension, no superannuation scheme or redundancy pay, as they are now fancifully called; that provides no trade union for the protection or promotion of those employed; that accepts criticism, though often libellous, mischievous and capable of injuring the livelihood of the criticised, as 'fair' and 'in the public interest'; a curious world in which a writer's reputation, however great or profitable, cannot be sold as 'a going concern', with 'goodwill', in the open market, as a business manufacturing soap-powders or soda-water can be; where authors' copyrights pass into the public domain 'at 10% thirty years after an author's death and wholly, for free, after fifty years'; where one copy of an author's books can be read a hundred, two hundred, five hundred times at a so-called 'free' public library, while the author himself draws the royalty, somewhere perhaps between a shilling and half-a-crown, for the sale of only one copy; a profession mostly if not wholly unorganised, with no 'pressure groups' to pursue its interests in high places; and where, well within living memory, it was the practice for publishers to give 'a baker's dozen' for all copies sold, thus depriving the author of his due royalties on one dozen of every gross of his sales.

No; I never once thought of these things. Blindly and happily youthful, I simply went forth singing.

II

The subsequent publication of *The Two Sisters* (which after 45 years is still in print) inspired in me no sense of elation. My guess is that for the most part artists, whether writers, painters, sculptors or musicians, feel only a sense of cold detachment from their work once it has, so to speak, passed from the privacy of their possession into the public domain. This may express itself further in sheer embarrassment, even revulsion; in the most self-critical it may well emerge as hatred. I myself, though not expressly hating *The Two Sisters*, was simply aware to a highly painful degree of its many faults; I could scarcely bring myself to open its pages, beautifully printed as they were in the celebrated Cape image, still less to read it. I do not now recall that I even bought another copy to add to the traditional half dozen free ones that an author receives; perhaps I did; I recall only a sort of guilty embarrassment compulsive enough to make me want to forget my first curious and not altogether coherent exercise in fiction.

As if to confirm my own doubts and guilt the first review was a bad one. Several subsequent ones were no better. A few others were of such abysmal stupidity that they even had the effect of goading me, paradoxically, to a wrathful defence of something I well knew not to be very good. What is one to say of a critic who amazingly compared the book to *The Young Visiters*? What to the conjecture that the novel was strongly influenced by Henry James, a writer I had never even read and whom to this very day I cannot read? Not one single critic, in fact, made an even remotely accurate estimate of who and what were the sources of the book's inspiration; none was perceptive enough to recognise what Garnett had spotted as simply as a swallow spots a fly on the wing: namely that the main and indeed only influence was Conrad, at whose feet, along with those of Tchehov, Tolstoy, Turgenev, Maupassant and Crane,

I had long been religiously worshipping. So strong and obvious was the influence of Conrad that I had in fact, at Garnett's insistent suggestion, toned it down, even then still leaving evidence enough to show even the blindest fool that I had drunk deeply at the well of the author of *Lord Jim.*

What Garnett had also spotted was something that has been supremely well expressed by Alan Hodge in an excellent note to a translation of Maupassant's *A Woman's Life*: 'Often there is a fine bloom about a first novel which its writer never quite achieves again, however more expert he becomes in technique, or more nearly universal in his sympathies.' Not only was this patently true to Garnett, who had intuitively perceived the talent that lay behind the book's many imperfections. He also warned, in his preface to the novel, of the difficulties, struggles and even disasters that for the young author, still only twenty, might well lie ahead. 'The path of art, endlessly difficult,' he warningly wrote and the words so imprinted and seared themselves into my young brain that I have not only never forgotten them; I have never lost sight of the chilling profundity of their truth. Nor, after nearly fifty years of writing, has the path become even minutely less difficult than Garnett's prediction warned it would be. Art knows no easy passage; its course is for ever through troubled, uncharted and all too often perilous waters.

During that troubled spring and early summer of 1926 I saw Garnett many times: sometimes at his favourite restaurant, The Commercio, in Frith Street, where a few years earlier it had been his weekly custom to forgather with other writers, among them W. H. Hudson, greatest of our nature writers but still, at that time, a figure I hadn't really discovered; occasionally at Bedford Square; sometimes at the old 51 Restaurant in St Martin's Lane, heart of the theatre-land I longed, but longed in vain, to conquer; but most often at No. 19 Pond Place, Garnett's flat, at which he puffed, coughed over his herbal cigarettes, spilt ash over his undone fly-buttons as he half-lay, half-sat on a *chaise longue*, like some mischievous, irate, slightly forbidding potentate of letters, verbally bashing the heads of critics and public alike, his constant text being 'They don't *know*, Bates, you see, they don't *know*.' Once, I remember, he took me to a Russian restaurant, where we ate *borscht;* once to meet Desmond MacCarthy, who didn't turn up; once or twice to the theatre. Always he was alternately forbidding or charming; serious or diabolically jocular; soothing or critically keen as a fresh-sharpened sword. Always his god was literature, his temple art, his altar that of good taste.

I met him also at The Cearne, the stone cottage which a disciple of William Morris had built for the Garnetts, in medieval style, on a beautiful pine-clothed slope of the North Downs. My first visit there was on a warm late May afternoon when the air was richly aromatic with the scent of pines and when the entire Weald of Kent, where my own home was eventually to be, lay spread out below the hills to a seemingly infinite distance, like some miraculous landscape by Constable. That so superlative a day should have been, for me, one of apprehension is explained by the fact that, having already met in Edward a puffy, forbidding, asthmatical bear, I greatly feared that I might be about to meet a comparable she-bear in Constance, on whose many translations of Tchehov, Tolstoy, Turgenev and Gogol I had already fed with great avidity and much fervent admiration. I felt not at all unlike a penniless youth trying to screw up courage enough to ask a fearsome father for the hand of a rich, distinguished and clever girl in marriage.

I needn't have worried. Constance Garnett was certainly not rich, except in brains and charm. Anyone less like a she-bear it was impossible to imagine. When I first saw her, frail, white-haired, short-sighted, she was feeding chickens on the edge of the pine-wood, in a little orchard, that lay behind the Garnett house. Instantly she reminded me of my great-grandmother, whose sister, physically, she might well have been. It also struck me that she might well have spent all her life in busy pursuit of homely, country tasks such as that of feeding chickens, gathering eggs, weeding flower-beds, sowing carrots and things of that sort. She looked totally unlike the brilliant woman who, after a girlhood spent in a household darkened by an atmosphere almost Brontë-esque, had won for herself a three-year scholarship at Newnham College, Cambridge, and this at a time when universities, like clubs, were virtually male preserves and when the conventions of female behaviour in public were of such strictness that her father warned her on the day of her departure for college never to be seen in a hansom cab, an act which would instantly have condemned her as being disgracefully fast, if not plain wicked.

At Cambridge she at once showed a brilliant aptitude for languages, in particular Greek. (It was from her, indeed, that I learned much of the correct pronunciation of classical plant names, so that to this day I constantly shudder when I hear gardeners pronounce them in a way that would have filled her own classical brain with horror.) Painfully shy, awkward and becoming progressively more and more short-sighted, she nevertheless won for herself the great distinction of eventually being bracketed top in the Classical Tripos, equivalent in those days to a first class honours degree. This enabled her immediately to earn her own living and presently led to her meeting the young Edward, whose chief virtue at that time appears to have been hanging about bookshops and bookstalls, a pursuit that he may well have thought might do something to compensate for the fact that though his father, Richard Garnett, was Keeper of Printed Books at the British Museum, Edward had had, unlike Constance, little of what could be called conventional education.

Edward was in fact virulently anti-convention, anti-academic, anti-government. His son David has explained this 'repudiation of the respectable academic approach' as being in part a reaction to the atmosphere and ways of the British Museum and it may well be that this same dislike of the conventions had some part in attracting him to the brilliant young girl from Cambridge, who, though she may not have ridden in hansom cabs, had by now become unconventional enough herself to belong to the Fabian Society, attend Socialist meetings and make friendships with Russian revolutionary exiles and such firebrands as Bernard Shaw. Not only did Shaw, in fact, ask her to marry him but it was a favourite story of Constance's that more than once, as she walked home with him after some Fabian gathering, she would forcibly and eloquently propound Socialist theories of her own, only to see them, a few days later, appear as an original article in some weekly periodical, the author of course being Shaw.

Happily the marriage never came off, Shaw explaining in typical fashion that he couldn't afford it and that a marriage of improvidence would have ruined his career as a writer: a remark of such typically Shavian charm that many a woman less nice than Constance would have promptly punched him on the nose. Instead she married the improvident and unconventional Edward, who was by now working as reader for the publishing firm of Fisher Unwin, where his uncanny perception in search of new talent was already earning him both reputation and success. The marriage in due course produced an only son, David, who has recounted how his mother, 'in the enforced idleness of pregnancy' brought her brilliant brain to the study of Russian, which she learnt with such singular speed that she almost immediately began to translate Turgenev, the first of whose novels she published in 1896, four years later. As if this were not feat enough Constance then further proceeded to demonstrate her own disregard of the conventions by announcing her intention of visiting Russia, alone. The fact that her child was only two years old must have seemed, to the conventional eye, to make a crazy proposition crazier still. It must further have been labelled even more lunatic by the fact that she proposed to carry with her, in ten-pound notes, a largish sum of money which had been collected in England for famine relief in Russia, where that year the grain harvest had failed. A further and yet more dangerous hazard in this extraordinary trip by this frail young mother was that she was not only carrying with her a large sum of money in cash but also letters and proposals for the arrangement of channels of communication between Russians exiled in England and secret revolutionary organisations in Russia.

Not only did I know nothing of all this as I had my first meeting with the little woman feeding her chickens on that soft, warm May afternoon; I would never have believed it at that moment if anyone had told me. It would have been rather like being told that Little Lord Fauntleroy had habitually killed lions in the Colosseum in Rome. There was no hint in the frail and gentle woman of sixty-five as she presently led me into her garden gay with scarlet poppies, columbines, pinks, lupins, pansies and aubrietia, of any immense physical courage, revolutionary or otherwise. I had been prepared for a she-bear and in a totally unexpected way I had been, in a sense, confronted with one, though I didn't know it then and the she-bear looked infinitely more like a shepherdess of sheep. That all this was a youthful misconception on my part scarcely matters now; what does matter is that all my fears and apprehensions as to that first week-end were instantly blown away like dandelion seed on a warm May wind. Though there was a difference of no less than forty-four years in our ages I immediately felt that I had known Constance Garnett all my life and that she was, warm, gentle and a passionate lover of flowers and the countryside, my sort of person. A great bond of affection between us was wrought that afternoon and for my part it has never broken.

The two main strands in that bond were flowers and the Russian classics. I had inherited my passion for flowers from both my father and my maternal grandfather and the sudden emergence of my green fingers at the Cearne prompted in Constance much delight and the eventual remark that at last a successor to D. H. Lawrence had arrived, an author with real feeling and love for flowers. Constance had made her garden on a difficult hillside, on intractable sandstone, by sheer hard labour, lugging rocks into place for flower beds and wheeling down from the woodlands above huge quantities of leaf mould. She was never, or scarcely ever, to be seen standing up as she gardened. So wretchedly poor was her eyesight that she was always kneeling, spectacles a mere inch or two from the ground as her hands groped to distinguish gentians from weeds or seedlings from cuttings and so on. My enduring impression of her is one in which she is always in that prayerful position, brown bloomers exposed, thick spectacle lenses glinting, her frail hands fingering the soil half blindly, as if trying, not very successfully, to piece together some extraordinarily complex jig-saw puzzle.

I suppose I went to The Cearne some scores of times after that first visit, almost always taking with me seeds or seedlings or cuttings from my father's garden and always plunging with youthful energy and enthusiasm into helping Constance in her garden tasks, weeding, digging potatoes, gathering peas and raspberries, slaughtering the dying rubbish of autumn flower beds. The abiding impression of all those days is one of constant joy and light. The days when Conrad, Hudson, Stephen Crane, W. H. Davies, Galsworthy and all manner of other celebrities of the turn of the century had been constant visitors there had long passed, and of Edward's new discoveries, Sean O'Faolain, H. A. Manhood, Geraint Goodwin, Liam O'Flaherty, Malachi Whitaker and many others, none ever came as visitors to The Cearne while I was there. But young visitors of some kind there always were and it may well have been a deliberate scheme on Constance's part to invite them, since all of them in recollection seem to have been girls, purely for my companionship. I recall a pleasant niece of Edward's and a Swedish girl of great glamour, a veritable goddess, with whom I confessed to falling in love, though doing nothing more positive about it than worship her from the other side of long rows of raspberry canes.

If the constant impression of those days at The Cearne is one of continual joy and light it must be said that this had little or nothing to do with creature comforts. It was a characteristic of the Garnetts, as David Garnett himself has justly pointed out, that they viewed worldly comfort with much suspicion and worldly success with something approaching scorn. The latter, in my experience, seems to be an almost exclusively English trait, more especially where art and literature are concerned. It really isn't quite nice, in certain English eyes, to make money out of writing and painting; it really isn't done; the right thing is to wait patiently for Parnassus; you really can't have your rewards up there and enjoy them down here on earth too. So it was that Edward, after the initial elation of some new discovery of his had worn off and the discovered one himself had found success – a success that all too often Edward had predicted with the fiercest pessimism the obtuse British public would never have the perception to allow – frequently abandoned the protégés he had so brilliantly spotted and had so unselfishly and tirelessly fought to see established. Of these Galsworthy was, I suppose, the clearest and most notable example. The prodigious success of *The Forsyte Saga* (I speak now of its literary success and not of its still vaster success on television) caused Edward's back to be turned on what was probably the most eminent of his discoveries and drew from him the remark that Galsworthy would 'always see life from the windows of a club'.

So if the atmosphere at The Cearne was not precisely spartan it was certainly not luxurious. There was no electric light; all cooking and lighting was done by oil; the privy was in the yard. (I am supported in this recollection of a certain spartan air at The Cearne by an occurrence that took place some few years later, when Edward paid his first visit to my wife and me after our marriage and, on going to bed, immediately ripped off the sheets and, much to my wife's annoyance, proceeded to sleep in the blankets.) At meals we ate simply but not frugally. If Edward was present for the week-end we invariably had wine, though he could never afford the best. If it was Edward who, in his typical fashion, frequently teased dear Constance about what he called 'her Scots caution' it was he who mixed water with the sherry (making, in fact, a very pleasant drink) and often retired with a hunk of plain bread to eat with a final glass of wine as he read in bed and far into the night.

If Constance and I shared a passionate interest in gardens we shared an equally ardent one in literature. Her range in that direction was vast, her taste never less than impeccable: so that if Constance was sometimes moved to praise a story of mine I was not merely greatly flattered; I always, unhesitatingly, took it as gospel. And though her eyesight, always poor, had pitifully deteriorated, her mind had most certainly not, evidence of which was always there in the long, fertile and perpetually rewarding and amusing discussions we had on books and in the literary parlour games we often played in the lamp-light after supper. In one of these Edward would read out various passages from various authors, leaving us to guess who had written what; and in this, since I had long since made a deliberate study of style for, so to speak, style's sake, I was often fairly good; but when it came to making as many words as possible out of, for example, the word 'conscientiousness' it became, as far as Constance and the rest of us were concerned, a case of a thoroughbred running against a gang of donkeys. In the space of minutes Constance's prodigiously quick brain, so long trained in languages, would produce shoals of words, sometimes well over a hundred, while the dunces about her were struggling with mere dozens.

We also shared views on other matters, notably on what we both deemed to be the decline in poetry. Fervent lover of the Elizabethans as I was and still am, it seemed to me that much modern poetry could be likened to turnip wine; and in this view I had in Constance, a woman nearly fifty years my senior, an ardent supporter. She, in fact, confessed to having given up reading it altogether, in despair, while I, in turn, also in despair, had given up all thought of ever writing verse again. This disillusionment of hers as to the use, or misuse, of language seemed to me to have a parallel with another: that of a certain disenchantment with the socialism she had once so bravely championed and for which she had, for all her frailty, risked so much. I may be wrong in this; but she had, of course, been brought up with, and had made friends with, some of the foremost intellects of her day. Though beautifully human and sweet, she had nevertheless been almost fearsomely well educated, so that she could hold her own in any company and could, as she had demonstrated, take even a man like Shaw for a ride. It was perhaps not surprising therefore that when, in the late twenties, the voice of socialism started to express itself through men like Bevin and J. H. Thomas, she found herself listening to it with some of that same despair with which she listened to the abrasive rattle of modern verse. In this theory of mine – and something in me seems to testify that it isn't wholly a theory – I am supported in a recollection of sitting with her one evening at The Cearne, by the radio, listening to a speech by a leading Socialist. The voice was what I can only call a cloth-cap voice, but to her, who had been brought up politically with the élite and had 'heard great argument' it must have seemed like the voice of some bumbling ignoramus who could neither use nor respect our English tongue. Her few words of total disgust were surpassed only by the pitying scorn that suddenly lightened up her failing eyes.

III

It is scarcely surprising that these new and exciting contacts, through the Garnetts and others, should presently have induced in me a stronger and stronger dissatisfaction with my red-brick, chapel-ridden, factory-ridden, provincial scene. I became increasingly aware, that summer, of a great restlessness.

Back in my Northamptonshire valley there were not, as I have explained, more than half a dozen people with whom I could talk of writers and writing, music and literature. Whenever I came back from The Cearne or from London I was aware of entering some totally negative wasteland. The people of my native Rushden, warm-hearted though so many of them are, will not perhaps thank me for this; and perhaps if I, like Robert Herrick the Elizabethan poet, had visited the town in the early 17th century as a guest of Sir Lewis Pemberton, squire of the Hall in which I later set *Love for Lydia*, I might have been able to express myself differently. But this was 1926, not 1626; and this is how a young man on the exciting but bewildering threshold of a career that was presently to give him rather more pain than joy felt in that otherwise not very golden year: the year that was presently to lead to that other long dark shabby wasteland, the Great Depression.

Of the half dozen people to whom I could talk of literature and companion things two were younger than I; one twenty years older. All came from working class families. Sam Smith, the older man, unlike Constance Garnett, was virtually self-educated, though later, as a shoehand in his forties, he was offered a scholarship to Cambridge, an opportunity he declined. A small, virile, athletic man, not entirely uninterested in the arts of boxing and ladies, as well as pubs and literature, he had been a soldier in the First World War: rifleman, stretcher-bearer, foot-slogging it out in a very different wasteland. We too found common ground in books, countryside, flowers and even boxing. H. N. Ginns and A. G. R. Britten were two other good examples of the truth that not all the best brains come from the richest families. Harry Ginns' father was a blacksmith whose forge stood opposite the church, where in fact it had probably stood since Herrick had turned into Sir Lewis Pemberton's parkland domain only fifty yards away. A brilliant boy, he rose in time to be Deputy Chief Engineer at the Ministry of Transport. Arthur Britten did equally well by becoming headmaster of one of the largest comprehensive schools in the south of England.

These were my closest companions, though hardly ever by day. By day I frequently stuffed a sandwich and a book of

poems into my pocket and did my own foot-slogging far out into the countryside, pausing to stare at pike lying in the shadow of river bridges, lying in woods and gazing in solitude at the broken blue of sky above the branches of oak and hazel, gathering mushrooms, dozing on grassy banks in the sun, sometimes scarcely seeing another soul, just occasionally passing in some remote lane a girl on a horse, she aloof, I too shy even to bid her good-day. On these excursions I grappled with wild thoughts for stories, built for myself great towering steeples of ambition, wrestled with my growing restlessness and was lonely.

I was prompted at last to seek help from Edward Garnett, begging him to do something or other to help me escape from a solitude now made worse by the fact that Madge, for a reason never coherently explained, had suddenly decided that she wanted no more of the impetuous, impatient and sometimes imperious young author who had courted her so passionately along the rich banks and woodlands of the lovely Bedford Ouse. Deeply hurt, even lacerated, I snatched at the chance Edward found for me with his typical kindness and promptitude: that of a job with Bumpus, the Oxford Street booksellers then housed in the old Marylebone Court House and presided over by that king of booksellers, John Wilson, who had already shown his own kindness and help by pushing *The Two Sisters* whenever and wherever he could. Nobody could sell books as John Wilson did and quite what he thought of me, dreamy, unpunctual, impractical, indolent and more or less useless in his busy territory I never really knew at the time. Perhaps it wasn't wholly bad, since we were afterwards good friends for many years.

Presently I found digs at thirty shillings a week with two old ladies somewhere off the Bayswater Road and John Wilson put me into the Children's Department of the celebrated bookshop in Oxford Street. The old ladies fussed over me with drinks of hot lemon at night as cures for the colds that continually assailed me that autumn and in the bookshop I slightly assuaged my conscience by writing for John Wilson a little children's book, *The Seekers*, which he promptly published and which is today something of a collector's rarity. But my loneliness persisted and in an effort to assuage that too I sought out the prettiest girl in the shop, a beautiful, well-built goddess, and asked her out to dinner. To my infinite chagrin she refused and I think we never spoke again. But many years later, such are the inexplicable ways of woman, she wrote and asked me if I remembered the incident, amazingly adding, as if to rub salt into an old wound long forgotten, that she had never read a single book of mine, leaving me to ponder, also amazingly, as to why on earth she had written in the first place.

Before long, however, I made three friends, two young men whose names I have now forgotten and a shyly nervous, sensitive, bespectacled girl some few years older than myself. These three cajoled me into going to Promenade Concerts while I in turn shocked them by expressing a savage hatred of the brassy vulgarities of the Wagner they loved. We forgot our musical differences in a mutual love of Keats and Shelley and the girl gave me Keats' letters to read. We ate cheap lunches at tiny tea-shops and I was hardly ever free of indigestion.

Soon the girl was presenting me with other books and more and more and more we were going out together. Margaret was the daughter of an architect who lived in one of the many pleasant squares of Bloomsbury and sometimes she took me home to dinner. The impermanence of our friendship was solely and entirely my fault and I regret the wounds it caused; but Margaret is nevertheless important in my life for the reason that it was she who held the key to another door beyond her own and which in turn gave access to yet another and in turn to that blossoming world of which I am now writing.

That this friendship was on my part purely and utterly platonic there can be no shadow of doubt whatever; that it was something totally different on her side, though I did not in my selfish stupidity grasp it for some long time, is equally certain. I believe that she loved me deeply and suffered, as a consequence, much and in silence. But I in turn had no love either to declare or to offer and it would have been then, as now, an hypocrisy to pretend that it was otherwise. When a man is friendly with a girl who never makes his heart beat the very minutest fraction faster there can be no question of his having love to give, however great the love may be on the other side. Margaret, shy and sensitive, was too proud, perhaps too genteel, to declare her love and not subtle enough, or gifted enough with what are sometimes called feminine wiles, to express it in other ways. Her continual gifts to me of beautiful and expensive books, typical as they were of her nature, were simply not enough; nor was her deeply enthusiastic praise of my writing. When she did at last bring her femininity to bear on the problem, I suspect in desperation, it was to invite me out into the country for a Sunday picnic. Its effect on my emotions may be likened to applying a match to an iceberg; all afternoon I never once experienced the very remotest desire to kiss her. I would even go further and say, cruel though it may sound, that if she had suddenly stripped off every shred of clothing and offered me her pale naked body I should not only have refused. I believe I should have walked away in silence and embarrassment.

On my part, therefore, I was merely content that we should be, as is often said, just good friends; and this, for me, is how it was. But Margaret's importance to my life lies in the fact that without her brief intervention it might well have taken a totally different and perhaps less fruitful course. One day I received a warm and glowing letter of praise for *The Two Sisters* from a lady whose name then meant nothing to me but was soon to mean a very great deal. Violet Dean, sister-in-law of Basil Dean, the celebrated theatrical producer, was herself a writer and came from the family of Longman, the publishers. She was also Margaret's cousin.

It was from this new friendship that the full pattern of *The Blossoming World* will presently be seen to emerge. Violet Dean was a remarkable woman who was never happier than when solving, or trying to solve, the unhappy problems of others. If a man should have been confronted with the painful problem that his wife was about to commit certain suicide he had only to find Vie, who would undoubtedly have sorted out the whole matter in no time. She was not only ever willing to unravel the problems and tragedies of others; she unselfishly revelled in doing so. Paradoxically, as so often happens with people of her kind, she had problems of her own that she found insoluble. Sometimes, indeed, I shrewdly suspect that she may not have wanted to solve them: that she was in fact one of those people for whom trouble is, if not an actual source of satisfaction, certainly one of excitement. These are the people who, having no trouble on hand, speedily set out to make some. If they fail in making some they swiftly seek to find it in others.

Thus Margaret was the key to Violet Dean, who in turn was the key to another new friend: one of the most beautiful women I have ever met.

She too, with her ravishing beauty and great talent, caused my world to open its petals in a remarkable way.

IV

Violet Dean not only moved much in the world of literature and the theatre but in that of music too; she was a woman of no little influence in spheres still far removed from mine. She, like Margaret, had read and praised *The Two Sisters*. Now she began, in her typical fashion, to impart her enthusiasm to others.

The result of this was that presently I received, on deep grey notepaper and in a handwriting both exciting and excitable, another ecstatic song of praise for a book in which, on its publication, I had virtually lost all faith and affection. The writer in this case wrote that 'your book is, for me, like a dark red rose'. This lovely sentence was flattering enough in itself but when I read on and found that the writer had read the novel at the instigation of Violet Dean I knew that the fates had been once more working hard for me.

I suppose that when she wrote that first letter to me – the first of very many as it turned out – Harriet Cohen was almost at the height of her fame as a pianist. She was certainly at the height of her dark, distinguished, Russian-like beauty. After I had replied to her letter, imparting in it my own delight that so celebrated a musician had found my book to be a thing of beauty, she wrote back immediately, inviting me to lunch. That lunch, like her letter, was the first of many.

When I duly turned up at her flat in Bryanston Square I found her to be a woman of ravishing loveliness. Like many Jewish women she radiated a strong sexual warmth, so that merely to be in her presence was to feel under the influence of someone disturbingly sensual. But the fact that she also had brains together with a great single-minded dedication to her art made her attractive on two planes. I will not go so far as to say that I instantly fell in love with her; it was more truthfully an affair, on my part, of utter adoration. Nor, for all the passion with which she returned my subsequent kisses, was there any question of her being in love with me. It is true to say that she was irresistibly and compulsively attractive, full of a strong sexual feeling that nevertheless always stopped just short of that complete and blind abandonment which must come of true love. The best expression I can find for her is that she was a seductive tease. Even this is in no sense a full description of her. She recurs constantly in memory as rather like the dark red rose to which she had likened my novel. The deep sensual perfume attracted you with the ravishment to the heart of the flower; then, as you prepared to drink of it to the full, the petals either dropped or were snatched away.

It was never possible to resist this strong physical attraction. Indeed from the very first she encouraged it. On only my second visit to lunch she met me at the door of her flat, walked side by side with me upstairs, paused half way up to kiss me and then with slow deliberation took one of my hands and drew it to her exquisite breasts. This appeared surely to be an invitation to love but in fact was not, either then or afterwards. Not that I worshipped from afar – and worship it most certainly was; on the contrary we were constantly in the embrace of rapturous intimacy without ever reaching the ultimate moment of making love. That this was an experience both lovely and enduring is proved by the fact that we remained deeply fond of each other for another forty years, until that very last moment when I stood in the crypt of St Paul's Cathedral, where so many great figures from the arts have been given their last requiem, heard the choir sing with great beauty some of the Bach she loved and found myself unable to suppress the tears of thankfulness that welled up in my heart in sorrowful gratitude for the part of her life she had given me when I was very young.

That part of her life was, in my twenty-first year, another great key in mine. My acquaintance with music and the world of music was really ludicrously slight. She, on the other hand, besides being world-famous, knew almost all the great composers, conductors and artists of the day, and soon she was seeing to it that I met many of them too. She took me to the old Queen's Hall so that I could meet Vaughan Williams, Arnold Bax and Frank Bridge. She took me to Broadcasting House and let me sit by her piano while she did a broadcast, the only other person there being her equally charming sister, who turned the pages of her music for her. Always eager in musical experiment, she played for me, and sometimes gave me records of, composers of whom I had never heard. Thus I first heard de Falla and Sibelius. With rapidity, thanks almost entirely to Harriet (always Tanya to her friends, since she did indeed look strongly and beautifully Russian) my musical horizon widened. In due course it was embracing Mahler, Bruckner, Poulenc, Ravel, Debussy and a host of others, so much so that to this day, though I cannot read a note of music, I still sit down frequently and briefly at the piano and improvise for myself ten minutes or so of some *eine kleine Nachtmusik* after the manner – and very much after the manner I must confess – of one of those composers she first championed and introduced to me.

She was also vastly interested in literature – indeed she was an intelligent writer herself – so that my horizon also widened in that direction. She too, like Constance Garnett, knew Shaw; she knew Arnold Bennett and Somerset Maugham; her mind was keen and it helped to sharpen mine. Some of her many friends were rich and it was one of these who, one afternoon at tea, heard that my Nonesuch Press Bible, one of the many expensive presents Margaret had given me, lacked the volume containing the Apocrypha, and promptly sent me a copy the very next day. To these friends, rich or otherwise, musical or literary, she also imparted her enthusiasm for my work, especially my short stories, so that the little reputation I had already acquired began to be enlarged too. With Violet Dean also industriously singing my praises (it was somewhere about this time that Margaret's mother worriedly inquired of Vie whether or not I was trifling with her daughter's affections?) I began to be better known and more talked about in circles which, only a few months before, I had never remotely dreamed of entering.

If all this creates the impression that I had now become a Literary Personality, a Social Figure, lionised and fêted and sophisticated, let me at once dispel it. I had by now returned to Rushden, to my self-made shell, and was working on the long novel which Edward, much as he too admired the sketches and short stories I was constantly producing, had been for some time strongly urging me to write. 'The outlook,' he had already reminded me, 'is pretty bad for literature and literary men. It's a luxury trade and the printers' strike is going to mess things up for the publishers badly, not to speak of the fact that the public isn't going to buy books in unsettled times.' The production of a long ambitious novel was therefore, he also pointed out, of very great importance to me; and I now prepared myself for the long hard slog on a 150,000 word affair that was to be called *The Voyagers*, a task that was to occupy me for almost a year.

All through that long and exhausting task I still roamed the countryside, much of it half-decaying under the growing shadow of depression, alone; played football and cricket in their seasons; danced a lot; flirted a great deal; had many more lunches with Harriet, revelling always in their passionate and sometimes enchantingly musical aftermaths; and often went to see my grandfather, to help with the threshing on cold gusty autumn days or to play dominoes with him by the fireside on dark winter nights to the sound of the old American clock ticking away on the wall and the fragrance of potatoes baking on the hearth.

The times were indeed far from propitious for literature and literary men and the immediate struggle ahead wasn't merely to be hard; it became a sort of literary penal servitude. I scarcely ever had more than ten pounds in my bank account and once I was so flat broke that I had to borrow exactly that sum from Edward, a debt I repaid in less than a couple of weeks, greatly I think to his astonishment. How indeed I got through that year financially I shall never know. I was too proud to borrow from my parents and still too dedicated to my iron resolution never to be anything but a writer and therefore never to take a job. To these financial hardships there was, however, added something far worse. As the portentous pages of the novel grew and grew (and sometimes I worked eight or ten hours a day on it, ending in utter exhaustion) there also grew in my heart the souring, torturing suspicion that the book was bad. It was in fact to turn out to be something infinitely worse: an utter, absolute disaster.

It is now to this disaster, since it was probably the most precious but important turning point in my entire career, that I must turn; but before I do so it is necessary to say something of another Garnett – namely David, whose place in my writing life was to become as influential, and as much touched with affection, as that of his father and mother.

I had so far been more than fortunate in the friends who had influenced me in literature, the last four of them women, the last three of them leading, as if by some mysterious design, from one to the other. I was now to be further blessed.

I am often told, and I think it correct, that I have a singularly good memory; but every memory has its blanks and lapses and I am not now sure quite when David Garnett first wrote to me from his home, Hilton Hall, in the neighbouring county of Huntingdonshire. Here I must also confess to another lapse, though not one of memory. For some inexplicable reason I had never then heard of David Garnett, though I had been reading his mother's translations and his father's criticism for some considerable time. For all my excursions in literature I had somehow missed David's famed *Lady into Fox*, which had collected both the Hawthornden Prize and the James Tait Black Memorial Prize.

This is now, however, a minor point compared with the gigantic effect on me of the simple word Hall. In Northamptonshire especially, but also in other counties, the word Hall really means something. One instantly thinks of huge houses such as that splendid half-ruin Kirby Hall, or Haddon Hall and great houses of that style and standard. When therefore I was invited to go to spend a week-end at Hilton Hall I was at once put into what is nowadays called no end of a tizz. Two subsequent visits to Windsor Castle failed to scare me half as much.

Many questions vexed me. First what kind of wardrobe should I take? Would my two very ordinary suits be good enough? Should I go out and buy or hire a dinner jacket? I had chilling visions of grand tables adorned with silver; of valets, even butlers. When Edward had first invited me to The Cearne he had been good enough to allay any such fears by pointing out that he and Constance lived very simply and that 'we are quite without fuss'. This David unfortunately neglected to do, thus leaving in my head the discomforting notion that the word Hall couldn't be anything but synonymous with grandeur.

This highly uneasy illusion grew larger and larger as the day of the visit drew nearer and nearer the following Spring. Though I didn't buy myself a dinner jacket for the simple reason that I couldn't afford one I nevertheless spent two days pressing my suits until the trousers were knife-edged and about the same amount of time on my shoes, until they shone like new-fallen chestnuts. The only new thing I did buy was a suit-case, comforting myself in doing so that at least its outward appearance would satisfy Mr Garnett's butler and valet, even if the contents didn't.

When my mother's front door-bell finally rang on a warm May afternoon I had been waiting in readiness for Mr Garnett of Hilton Hall for more than an hour, growing more and more nervous, even half-hoping he wouldn't come. Finally, in deep trepidation, I went to the door to meet him and there had one of the great shocks of my young life.

On the threshold stood a man of large stature, immensely untidy if not even shabby, shod in great heavy shoes and dressed in clothes that might have been handed down from some mid-Victorian navvy or farm labourer. There can be little doubt that David will be much amused if and when he reads these words but I beg to assure him that the occasion, for me, was very far from being funny. For a few wild moments I even thought that Mr Garnett, unable for some reason to come himself, had sent one of his many gardeners to fetch me. But somehow I managed to murmur 'Mr Garnett?' and when he answered 'Yes' asked if he wouldn't come in and perhaps stay for a cup of tea? He declined, murmuring that he had to pick up his wife, who was shopping in the town. I duly went to fetch my brand new shining suit-case, which now looked disconcertingly grand, and we then got into Mr Garnett's very small car, which in its own shabbiness made the suit-case look more ludicrously and painfully aristocratic still.

There then began one of the most extraordinary journeys of my life. After we had picked up Mrs Garnett, a small, shy, dark-haired woman, we started the thirty-five mile drive from Rushden to Hilton, not far from St Ives. In my beloved Higham Ferrers I pointed out the beauty of the little square, with its charming little town hall that is also a court house and which looks today almost exactly as it did then; I also pointed out the magnificent 12th century church; I think I may also have mentioned that the town was at one time to have been a university town, its associate body being All Souls, Oxford; and I added one or two other passing notes on the little borough of which I was devotedly proud and where my grandfather and mother had been born and where I myself had spent some of the happiest, sovereign days of my childhood. I think I most probably also have mentioned that the town, and more especially the church, formed the setting of *The Two Sisters*.

To all this I got no word of reply, no single syllable of comment. At first I put this down to the fact that the car was an open one and that I was sitting in the dicky, which made the passage of conversation a little difficult anyway. But as mile after mile went past with scarcely a word falling from the lips of the Garnetts I grew more and more profoundly wretched. What had I done? Why, if they wouldn't speak to me, had I been invited in the first place? Was I not of their elevated Hilton Hall standard? Not grand enough? Miserably puzzled, I thought of Constance, charming, full of animated and amusing conversation and laughter, and then of Edward, to whom I could and so often did talk, with ease and profit, for hours. I fell to pondering on what among my deficiencies could be the one that had forged this iron forbidding barrier of silence. Perhaps I was after all a pitifully bad writer, not up to the standard of the author of *Lady into Fox?* Perhaps I had merely been invited in a gesture of duty, out of deference, as it were, to Constance and Edward? To all of these questions I got no reply except one from deep inside myself: a ghastly, growing sense of homesickness. I wished profoundly that I had never heard of Mr Garnett and that I were back home, playing cricket or roaming the fields among the darling buds of May.

The explanation of this strange, almost wholly silent journey through the charming little town of Kimbolton, then St Neots and then on into the almost soporific pastoral countryside of Huntingdonshire, where surely grow the most splendid, most royal cowslips in all England, rich and golden as the sun of heaven itself, lay in fact in Mrs Garnett, Ray. This small – and as I discovered later, charming, talented and intelligent woman, was the victim of a shyness so vast and stultifying that it amounted almost – and I think this is by no means an exaggeration – to a disease. And it was eventually Constance, who herself had to suffer the same long, painful disconcerting penalties of silence as I, who at last explained it all to me. It would appear that Ray's father, if not actually tyrannical, had belonged to that race of parents whose household gospel is based on the ruthless text that children should be seen and not heard. Unless my supposedly good memory now serves me very badly Constance even went so far as to say that in that particular household it was actually forbidden the children even to speak, or indeed to make any kind of noise, in the presence of the father. Thus Ray had been cursed, from childhood onwards, with that cruel affliction of enforced dumbness, the terrible, wickedly engendered shyness that so bewildered, mystified and pained me on that May afternoon more than forty years ago.

As a result of all this, since people who marry and live together tend very often to become more and more like each other, David seemed to have contracted the disease of silence and shyness too. Scarcely credible as it may now seem I too presently fell victim to the same infection. I too began to feel that to speak at all was something wrong. This in turn induced in me a gnawing, unnatural shyness that engendered in turn miseries of uneasiness and still further homesickness. I longed for Monday to come, so that I could go back home.

There was, however, one comforting feature of the visit that awaited me. Hilton Hall was not grand. It did not, in fact, measure up at all to the standard that the word Hall denotes in my native Northamptonshire. Instead it turned out to be a pleasant red brick house, a sort of Lord of the Manor farm-house, perhaps of a date slightly earlier than Queen Anne, standing in a garden both pleasant and unpretentious. It was rambling, untidyish and friendly. David, who had for some time been in partnership with Francis Birrell as a bookseller, had acquired for himself in consequence an excellent and hand-some library which he housed in a biggish room, its elm floor bare and uneven, upstairs. And it was that room, friendly with its many books, that first started to dispel the discomforting disease of shyness I had so suddenly and unexpectedly con-tracted. Soon I was torn between liking Hilton Hall and its garden, and then wanting to flee from it. It would be foolish to pretend that I was ever at ease or quite myself that week-end but my miseries slowly dispersed as May suddenly gave all the best of its incomparable self: so that from all the bewilderments and discomforts there still stand out a few indelible lyrical moments, among them the cowslips, then my planting a lime tree in the garden, and then the three of us, Ray, David and myself, standing by a hedge of hawthorn and listening to a band of nightingales singing their hearts out at the height of noon. That at least was a moment when human speech, for once, was unnecessary.

One of the consequences of pain very often comes in elation. And it is perhaps the strangest thing of that strange week-end that I went home elated. The conviction that the Garnetts after all didn't dislike me (David and I have remained firm and affectionate friends ever since) was coupled with a new mood in me that was both uplifting and creative.

It is not too much to say that I felt a new bloom to have spread over my life. Alas, in my stupefying folly, I was to proceed to destroy it.

The long, grinding stint of *The Voyagers* ended in early August or perhaps late July, 1927. Utterly exhausted, I snatched at the chance of a short holiday in Germany, my first trip abroad, like a fainting man snatching at a brandy.

That holiday had really come about as a result of a supper, some time before, at Edward's flat in Pond Place. The only other guest was the Irish writer Liam O'Flaherty, author of the celebrated *The Informer*, and whose wonderful short stories of Irish life both Edward and I so greatly admired. Supper being over, Edward suddenly produced his last Will and Testament and begged that O'Flaherty and I should witness it, as we duly did. Rising at last to go, I was checked by O'Flaherty, who asked if I had come across a bookseller named Law, who kept a bookshop somewhere in the region of Red Lion Square. I replied that I hadn't. 'Remarkable feller,' said O'Flaherty in his rich, winning Irish accent. 'A rare boyo of a character. German. You must drop in on him. I'll write you his address. Tell him I sent you.'

When at last I got time to go along to the bookshop in Red Lion Street I found it to be little more than a cubicle, about 12 feet by 8, its walls lined with books, paintings and drawings from ceiling to floor. Its owner, whom I had thought to be Law, turned out to be Lahr, a German who had run away from his native village near the pleasant little Rhineland spa of Kreuznach, where some of the most expensive hocks in all Germany are produced, before the First World War. Charley Lahr, with his slightly eccentric habits, one of which is going about practically bare-footed at all seasons, has been a familiar figure in London's book world for more than fifty years. Of slightly more than average height he was, when I first met him, possessed of a singular, almost maniacal energy which enabled him to cycle, run or walk about London in a passionate and tireless search for books. His devotion to literature and writers, and indeed to painters, was phenomenal; and his shop, never capable seemingly of holding more than six people, always seemed to be populated by a couple of dozen, with more chatting and lounging away in the passage outside.

They were men and women from all walks of life: poets, novelists, artists, solicitors, schoolmasters, business men, book collectors in search of first editions or autographed copies, journalists and editors. It would take far too long to name even a fraction of the persons of small or considerable eminence who forgathered there; but among artists there was Pearl Binder, now Lady Jones, wife of a recent Attorney-General, and William Roberts; and among writers Rhys Davies, O'Flaherty, T. F. Powys, Nancy Cunard, Rupert Croft Cooke, Malachi Whitaker and a host of others. Together with an uncanny gift for nosing out first editions and rarities in the Farringdon Road, on market stalls and back alleys, Charley always seemed to have on hand, in some garret or other, a tame old printer ever ready to earn a few pounds by printing pamphlets, tracts, odd poems, small magazines and smaller books, including those limited editions which were then the craze of the book world. In pursuit of this side-line he would cajole young and scarcely known writers such as myself to produce stories for slim volumes or magazines, poems for Christmas cards or somebody's wedding and all manner of bits and pieces, often of a rude or revolutionary nature, for pamphlets. For a time he co-operated with an editor in the production of a magazine called *New Coterie*, for which Roberts and others provided pictures and a not at all undistinguished band of writers provided prose and verse. Copies of *New Coterie*, besides being pretty rare today, provide an illuminating guide to what was going on among up-and-coming writers in the late twenties. For such books as I and others did for him Charley offered no contracts; all was haphazard, if not indeed plain mad; and when we were paid, as we always were, it was in cash, in unexpected dribs and drabs, to which Charley would often add some handsome book or two as a bonus. I cannot speak for others; but for myself those dribs and drabs were welcome manna indeed.

Not that I was ever far from being nearly flat broke; and it was solely for this reason that when Charley first suggested I join him and some others to go on holiday in Germany in August 1927 that I had to refuse; I simply hadn't the cash. Charley instantly countered this by saying that he would pay the fares if I could somehow conjure up enough for food and hotels, adding further that if I couldn't do even that I could borrow from him and pay at some unspecified date later. It was all madly and delightfully vague but nevertheless an opportunity too good to miss. The rest of our companions were to be Rhys Davies, William Roberts, his brother and a book collector, a lawyer as I now recall it, whose name I have forgotten. Quite where our final destination was to be God only knew.

Accordingly we set off one warm August night to catch the night ferry from Gravesend to Rotterdam, arriving in Holland early next morning. The subsequent breakfast and a breakneck tour of the city set the pattern of all that was to follow later. I felt as if caught up in some half-real, crazy maelstrom. From Rotterdam we rushed like a gang of dotty refugees fleeing from some unnamed wrath to Amsterdam. There I had a mere hour or so in which to decide that I liked the city very much before we were again on the train, belting it into Germany. Cologne, Mannheim, Mainz, Coblenz, Bingen, the Rhine and the Lorelei passed in a lunatic flash. I had just time to decide that I liked the Spa of Kreuznach very much too when we were off again, this time walking as I remember it, lugging suit-cases and rucksacks, across hot and dusty roads lined with pear and apple trees and sometimes winding through valleys along which could be seen the tents of companies of the British Army of Occupation. Always Charley was fifty yards ahead of the wearisome rest of us and always he concealed from us, with careless laughter, all clues as to where the hell we were heading.

Those roads, weary though they made me, nevertheless remain with me to this day as something marvellously idyllic. Wild yellow snapdragons, scarlet poppies, blue chicory, white yarrow, meadowsweet, reddening apples: it was all like some early glowing pastoral piece by Renoir or Monet. So idyllic did it seem then, as now, that I later wrote a *novella* about it all, calling it *A German Idyll*, its setting being not only the flower-blessed roads but the tiny remote village of Steinbockenheim, Charley's birthplace, now revealed as our destination.

The return of the prodigal son to the bosom of a large farming family living in a large and ancient farmhouse was as mad as the wearying business of getting there had been. We were instantly regaled with vast quantities of hock, the excellence of which I was too inexperienced to appreciate, and then equally vast quantities of scrambled eggs, potatoes, bread, fruit and cheese. There was also, as I vividly recall, redcurrant wine,

which for my uneducated taste seemed far nicer than the hock. For ever I shall remember the great beauty of its colour, a distilled crystalline crimson-scarlet. It too symbolizes, across forty years, all that was lovely in a Germany which, though outwardly so beautiful to the eye, was in fact at the bottom of the darkest pit. Those were the days of a mad despair that made our own crazy journeys by train and foot seem of not more account than a child's street game: the days when a German farmer or peasant could take a cart-load of potatoes to market in the morning and come back with a load of Deutschmarks in the afternoon, only to find them totally worthless next day. Never have I seen such quantities of money, so many millions of marks, as I saw in chests and chests of drawers in that tiny village, all of it paper, all of it worthless, all of it being hoarded by farmers and peasants in the pitiful, touching belief that one day God would produce in the financial world of a Germany bludgeoned and bled to death a miracle that would at last raise them all to the standard of millionaires. Small wonder that in one farmhouse the farmer had installed for himself a tap connected by pipe to the cellar below, so that if and when despair or thirst moved him in the middle of the night he could refresh and perhaps restore his faith with a draught or two of wine.

There is in one of Tchehov's letters, written about 1896, a passage in which he describes his being at a Russian wedding and in consequence being drunk for four days. I won't go so far as to say that my five companions and I were, for our four days in Steinbockenheim, quite in that same parlous state; let me simply say that there were times, drowned as we were by the hospitality of those simple and generous Germans, it sometimes seemed like that. For all the singing and rejoicing and dancing I finally reached a point where I never wanted to see, let alone drink, a glass of hock again.

At last, having paid such few bills as we had been allowed to incur (we lived for about three shillings a day) we set off for another crazy railway journey through pine forests illuminated all along the boundaries by wild yellow evening primroses, to Leipzig and then Berlin. Suddenly, in Berlin, my heart sank, covered in the pale cast of homesickness. The reason for this was all too painfully simple. Some time before this Madge had decided that, after all, she wanted to see more of the impossible young writer she had lately rejected, so that we were once again together, more in love than before. The fact that I found Berlin a city of depressing coldness may have had something to do with my sudden longing to go back to her and England. But back I knew that I had to go and presently Charley put me on the Warsaw-Ostend express, and I was back home the next afternoon.

A few days later I heard what Edward Garnett had to say about my novel. It was a moment I had long dreaded.

Nor was my dread misplaced. On the morning of September 5th, 1927, Edward put on a sort of Jack Dempsey literary punching act, using me as the punchbag. He wrote not merely that my novel was terrible, impossibly terrible, but that it simply could not be published. It was written in a 'facile, flowing, over expressive, half-faked style'; it was cursed with 'generalities, vague cynicism, washy repetitions'; it was 'Hardy and water. Hardy at his worst romantic side'; it was 'hollow-sounding, repetitive, semi-poetic, semi-journalistic'; it was 'unreal, long-winded, romantic and cynical'; and so on and so on and so on, each sentence of criticism more ferocious than the last. In fact Edward, that morning, hit me with everything he'd got.

Two things are worth noting, I think, about this long and blistering letter. The first is that there was in it a brief sentence which said simply: 'Don't despair. You have a facile demon in you, who gets hold of the reins, as well as the real artist in you who retreats into the background.' I interpreted this as meaning, quite correctly, that Edward hadn't lost faith in me. This in turn was responsible for the second thing of note: my astonishing and quick recovery from that morning of disaster. I hadn't, in other words, lost faith in myself; and this is how, in *Edward Garnett, a Memoir* (now out of print) I expressed my feelings:

'It is something to my credit, I think, that I recovered from that letter in a day. It blasted me; it skinned my soul; it seemed momentarily to sever every hope I had. But the very fierceness of its chastisement, which I knew to be just, was purifying in its complete chastening. It induced in me a great sense of isolation and above that a great stubbornness of determination not to be diverted from the things I wanted to do. It touched, deep down, the fibres of that part of me that slept, ate, dreamed and thought of nothing but writing all day and every day without lessening of tensity or rest. In fact, in the finest sense, it woke me.'

It has often been said that behind every successful man there is a woman, whether she be wife or mother. I think it may also be true to say that behind every good novel there is a bad one. *The Voyagers* was my bad one, though not by any means the last of mine to be written and rejected. But with a natural buoyancy of character and an infinite determination not to be deviated from my set course I put it behind me like a bad dream. And it is now only just to say that, for all the severity of his judgements, there was in Edward a singular streak of sweetness and generosity. In only a few days after that catastrophic mauling I had received at his hands he was sending me comments on two stories, thus: 'I am delighted to know that you returned home relieved and soothed in spirit. Both *The Dove* and *The Voyage* I think are admirable. Both are spiritually true and delicately expressed. I don't see anything to criticize in either.' So was I finally restored.

It may well be, as George Moore has said, that 'youth goes forth singing'. It is equally true that it goes forth making a damn fool of itself. And now, as if I hadn't made enough of a damn fool of myself by wasting an entire year spawning 150,000 spurious, stupid words, I was about to make a damn fool of myself again.

But this time in quite another direction.

V

I have already explained, in *The Vanished World*, how strictly I was brought up at the Methodist altar. I have also described how the good corn my father so diligently sowed Sunday after Sunday finally came up, to his intense disappointment, as tares. In these matters of church and chapel there was much in me of my paternal grandfather, who scorned in no uncertain terms 'popery and humbug and sciencing about in nightshirts'. His true God, like mine, was really Nature.

My own scorn for all organised religion took the form of angry revulsion somewhere about the age of seventeen. It was not merely piety I suddenly found myself despising and rejecting; more truly it was those who dispensed it. I conceived for the Methodist clergy, most of them ill-paid, it is true, some of them fools, a few humbugs and certain of them spongers, a very icy contempt. Not long later I turned my back on the polished pine pews, the phoney stained glass windows, the pained preachings and the all too often baleful singing for ever.

As a result of all this, when my mother's front door-bell rang one summer afternoon and I went to answer it only to find a parson standing there, I was ready with my sword of scorn, spitefully sharpened and dipped in acid. My moment of asinine truth was about to be unveiled. The man I saw there was tall, fair, bespectacled, pleasant-looking, indeed handsome. Politely he introduced himself as the new incumbent, at which I declared with a smart, rude lack of tact and manners that I didn't care a damn for him, his church, his cloth or his faith and that if he wanted to know why there were no doubt plenty of his flock who would be ready, even eager, to tell him.

He took all this very mildly, raised his hat with courtesy, said he was sorry about it all and bade me 'Good afternoon'. That this grossly stupid display of rudeness on my part might have made me an enemy for life is all too patently true; instead it turned out to be a remarkable example of the Christian turning the other cheek and unexpectedly made for me a wise, amusing, witty and generous friend for many years.

Bernard Harris in no way fitted into the Methodist parsonic mould as I then knew it; in fact I had chosen entirely the wrong man as victim of my scorn. Bernard was broad-minded, unfond of ostentation and show, whether of church or otherwise, gifted with a great sense of humour and an even greater love of literature. He was also fortunate enough to have a wife who, besides being charming and broad-minded too, was very well blessed, in her own right, financially. There was therefore never any thought or necessity for Bernard Harris to go through the nauseating act, as so many ministers did, of sucking up to rich boot manufacturers who paid handsome premiums for their back pews, paid pitifully low wages in their harsh red brick factories, believed on Sundays that the Lord was their shepherd and spent the rest of the week worshipping the theory that business is, after all, business. Intelligent, educated, unbiased of mind and eye, Bernard saw through them with a clarity of mind that matched my own.

His quick discovery that I had written and published books with the highly reputable firm of Cape immediately caused him to invite me to the Manse to tea, all as if he had utterly forgotten every moment of my asinine sword-attack. We instantly got on well. His wife was gracious and intelligent too; his two children, Dennis and Catharine, were delightful. Dennis was later to be killed in action in the Second World War, a young officer worshipped by all his men, and Catharine, by then a brilliant linguist, was to write a deeply touching memoir of him that proved that she had a splendid mastery of her own language as well as of others.

Bernard also had a brother, Frank. Not a strong man, he had given up ministerial practice in order to collect and sell first editions, manuscripts and rare books, a business in which he proved to have a judgement both rare and shrewd. On his not infrequent visits to Rushden we invariably met and Frank would often bring with him some new and uncommon discovery to show me or tell stories of others he had found. Among these was an early pamphlet by Norman Douglas on, I think, the exploitation of children in the Lipari island quarries, that had been published by the Stationery Office: price, one ha'penny. Having discovered the great rarity of this early item Frank shrewdly wrote to the Stationery Office and inquired had they any left? They had. He promptly bought up the whole stock, some fifty or sixty, I think, at a ha'penny a time, and made himself a modest fortune.

Another book he brought to show me was some voluminous work by his notorious namesake, Frank Harris, who had presented the copy to Joseph Conrad. Conrad's reply, in letter form, declining the book, was pinned to the title page and constituted one of the most blistering items in literary history ever written. It has always reminded me of Conrad's long and devastating criticism of Edward Garnett's play *The Breaking Point*, which it must have required formidable courage to write and even more formidable courage to read. That Edward was courageous there is no doubt; that he had also little experience of things theatrical is proved by David's description of the play's first night, when all that Conrad had feared and predicted came horribly true, with the result that 'the agony was prolonged and the effect was nightmarish'. In turn Conrad tore into Harris as an infuriated tiger might tear into a bloated rat, the result being that the book, as a collector's item, was of much historical literary interest.

Another result of Bernard's brother's excursion into the book-collecting world was that Bernard and his wife, most likely at Frank's instigation, were now kind enough to begin buying MSS of some of my short stories. The few modest guineas they paid were like manna added to my frugal and uncertain income and soon, happily, they were followed by others. Hugh Walpole, at Rupert Hart-Davis' instigation, bought the MS of a novel. A lady in Suffolk, another collector in California,

Charley Lahr and some of his customers in London: all from time to time now bought MSS, thus adding a little more to the Bates' till. The most important of these collectors was without doubt Sir Louis Sterling, the wealthy head of the Gramophone Company. Louis Sterling is the classic example in reverse of the poor Jewish boy going West to get rich; instead he came East to London, from New York, to make his fortune. With only a few dollars in his pocket he came across the Atlantic in 1903, on a cargo boat, bringing a few modest books in his baggage, and got work as a commercial traveller. Soon he was collecting books and then manuscripts both old and modern, finally acquiring a library embracing almost all that is notable in our literature, the whole of it now being housed in the library of London University.

Louis Sterling was a friend of both Harriet Cohen and Charley Lahr and once again, in these friendships, I cannot help seeing the hand of 'the divinity that shapes our ends', since it may well have been at the instigation of Harriet, as it certainly was of Lahr, that Sir Louis now bought an early MS draft of *The Two Sisters*, 218 sheets long, to which I added the note 'This is the earliest draft, much shorter than the final but contains almost all the story, if not all the scenes, from that from which the work was set up. The pages are numbered awkwardly and the style is awkward too, but was a product of only a month or two before the other.' For this first MS Sterling paid me £150, a sum so vast that I suddenly felt like the millionaire he himself was. Soon he also bought *Catherine Foster*, 357 sheets, *Alexander*, 97 sheets, *Charlotte's Row*, 380 sheets, *The House with the Apricot*, 70 sheets, together with other shorter items, all of them proving by the copious and complicated nature of their deletions and corrections that I was at this time taking Edward's preachings and injunctions greatly to heart and was working like a diligent beaver to rid myself of silly and extraneous influences and take firmer step after step towards becoming a wholly conscious writer.

It may seem slightly fantastic to say now that if I had only trusted to the instinctive artist in me instead of looking so much to others for influence, Edward's lambastings of me might not have been necessary. As early as 1925 I had written *The Flame*, an economical little sketch of a tired waitress of whose technique and feeling even Edward could find no adverse word to say; a little later I was beginning a story, *Fear*, with the words 'on the horizon three thunderstorms talked darkly to each other', thus getting more atmosphere into ten words than Hardy ('one of George Eliot's many miscarriages', as George Moore has well said) and his kind could often get into a page. Not that I was out of the wood by a long way yet. Much evidence exists, in fact, to show that I was still stupid, recalcitrant and slow to learn.

Among other stupidities I did a blindly silly plagiarisation of Tolstoy which Edward rightly pointed out had neither sense nor virtue and who was then very angry, also rightly, when I accused him of 'throwing mud at me'. To this Edward retaliated with words so wise that it amazes me how I could possibly have missed the penetrative point of them. 'Don't you understand that both my being upset and the necessity (after reading your cool and airy letter) of making you realize the position – is the very best proof of my interest in you . . . You don't imagine, I suppose, that it is a pleasure for me to strike you with a hammer to reach the sensitive spot in your perceptions.'

It is not in order to draw continual attention to my shortcomings and dunce-headedness that I reiterate these things – I could go on to the point of utter tedium in that direction. It is rather to draw attention to the extraordinary nature of Garnett's devotion to literature, and of his rare combination of critical insight, profound sympathy and infinite enthusiasm, all so great that it is perhaps not surprising that few of his kind, if any, exist to succeed him today. He was no mere ordinary publishers' 'reader'. I am truly convinced that he believed his sole mission in life to be literature; his vocation was to bring the bud to flower. How many reputations he discovered, made and nurtured it is quite impossible to say, but it is David's firm contention that in all his life Edward never missed a single talent, and I believe it to be true. He saw reputations soar with dazzling brilliance and rapidity only to expire, after a book or two, like damp fireworks; he saw writers ruined by success; he saw the temporary extinction of writers such as Conrad in the inevitable period of reaction immediately after death; he must have seen scores of cases where legend overshadowed talent; he saw the furore cast up by that silliest of books, *Lady Chatterley's Lover* and passed on it the final, blistering, crushing verdict – 'it's the last pressing of the grapes, Bates, it's the last pressing of the grapes'. Indeed it was.

So I went from crisis to crisis, now producing something good, now something bad. In those moments of dark misgiving and depression which beset every artist, leaving him with the lacerating conviction that either he will never paint or write again or if he does so that it will be either atrociously or without success, I took my problems out for long, solitary walks, incapable always of sharing the often insoluble equations with another person. Nature, sometimes in the form of primrose woods, hayfields and harvest, skating or merely gathering mushrooms, and often and often in visits to the gardens at The Cearne, was always my healer.

That I was all too frequently in need of a healer there is no doubt. The hard continuous slog to master my craft presently began to affect my health. For weeks on end I would suffer acute abdominal pains which in turn induced bouts of depression accompanied by tensions both mental and nervous. This condition I had increasingly to endure for another twenty years until at last an operation removed it. I suspect that the Garnetts sometimes discussed this harrowed condition of mine and there was an occasion when a chance remark of Constance's, only slightly veiling her concern, seemed to indicate that she thought I was suffering from the disease which finally killed D. H. Lawrence. Happily this was not so. I shall tell later, I hope in not unamusing terms, how what was wrong with me was at last diagnosed and in an extremely unusual manner.

Perhaps I can best explain my feelings about my condition, back in the 1920's, by saying that I continually felt that I was looking at the world not through the rose-coloured spectacles of youth but with the slate-coloured ones of a premature middle age. There is a portrait of me done by William Roberts, when I was perhaps 22 or 23, which shows a young man gazing out at the world with a clenched, harrowed intensity. It is not only a remarkable likeness of the person I then was; it brilliantly reveals the inner struggle and even torture that was going on behind what have been called my vivid and hauntingly blue eyes. It may give some further indication of my state in those days when I say that, as I write these words more than forty

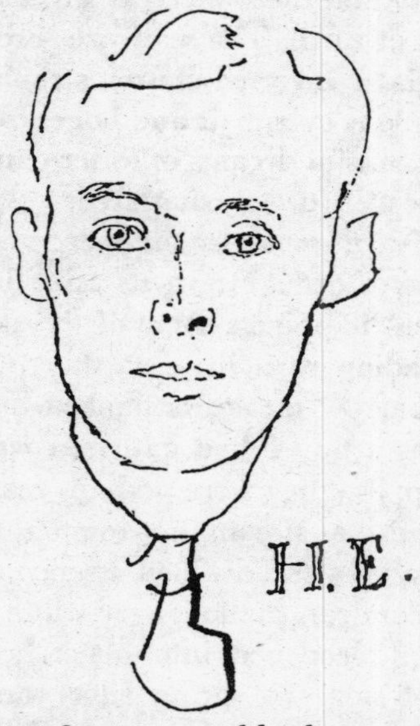

years later, I feel not forty years older but a good forty younger. Furthermore, without at all wishing to lay all the blame on ill-health, I will confess that I was more than a little difficult to live with, so much so that I wasn't merely an angry young man; I sometimes acted with an almost savage intensity and impossible selfishness against those who either didn't agree with me, wouldn't or couldn't understand me or who drove me to anger or irritation by what I thought were their own stupidities. One result at least of this was that my American publisher lamented to Edward Garnett that 'Bates behaves like a prima donna'.

No man, in fact, ever felt less like one. Finally, early in 1929, driven almost to despair by the gnawing ache of ill-health, I fled from Rushden, where the winters always seemed to be of an equally gnawing, chilling bitterness, and took a brief holiday in Bournemouth, where there were a few good bookshops and a resident orchestra, and which also had, reputedly, a soft winter climate. It was early February; on the day I arrived the first crocuses were brilliant and wide open in the warming sun. The next day there began, with a huge blizzard, a winter of such prolonged intensity that there was scarcely a sign of leaf on any tree until the end of April. The sea froze. From the cliffs hung vast icicles, like glassy inverted church steeples. The wind was wicked, solid ice. Your eyes, hair and bones froze as you walked the sea front. My blissful dreams of softer climates than that of Northamptonshire were utterly shattered.

There followed a miraculous summer: very hot, very dry, with long months of drought. In its scintillating brilliance I retraced with great happiness some of the steps of childhood, some of them leading to a little earthly paradise consisting merely of three narrow meadows flanked by a stream where often and often as a boy I had gathered watercress with my grandfather. I suppose they were perhaps really very ordinary, those meadows and that stream, but to me they were then, and still remain today, like the distilled essence of paradise. Here and there the stream ran shallow over white and sepia stones; in a few places it deepened into black holes shadowed by ancient bushes of sloe. In spring silver and yellow sallows positively seemed to dance with bees. Little fish darted, silver and gold too, in and out of shadow and sunlight. In August forests of pink willow-herb, of the sort known as codlins-and-cream, softly filled long stretches of the banks, together with purple loosestrife and tall cane-like reeds, feathery brown at the tips. On hot days cows sought shade under vast old hawthorns, rubbing their backs against them until the trunks shone like polished mahogany. The air, bereft of bird song, whirred with that concentrated chorus of grasshoppers that seems in the strangest way to deepen silence, so that the air was hotly and hauntingly hushed. Even the yellowhammers, on those intensely hot days of late summer, were silent, as if thirstily asleep, and on many an afternoon I lay, sweating in some pool of dark parched tree-shadow, and slept too. And thus I would find myself healed again.

Perhaps some day someone will write a treatise on imagination, both of what it is and of how it can affect, through periods of concentrated use, the centres of nerves and emotions. It is a subject of which, I feel, we know very little. Is imagination, either in part or whole, a sort of sixth sense? The theory fascinates, and in the holding of it I am supported by certain strange things that have, from time to time, happened to me as a writer. On not one but many occasions I have written stories, inventing their characters purely and wholly from imagination, only to meet the same characters, in almost precisely the same situations, in real life, some months later. In a *novella* of mine called *Summer in Salandar*, where every incident and character is drawn exclusively by the power of imagination, a woman both rich and selfish sets out, having left her own husband, to destroy, rather after the manner of a spider with a fly, a young man she meets while on holiday on an island. Her name being Vane, I fitted her out, in the story, with an expensive set of matching luggage, each piece stamped with a V. Two years later, travelling by ship to the same island on which the story is set, I saw the set of matching luggage, each piece with its V, going aboard ahead of me and then watched, for the next three or four days, the woman of whom I had written, rich and selfish, proceed to her spider act of destruction. Is this an example of the workings of a sixth sense? or what? Oscar Wilde tells us that life imitates Art. Is it perhaps not also possible that imagination creates life, as it were by some process of magical foresight, before life itself does? The temptation to say that all human life exists as a preordained pattern is one which has, for many people, a strong appeal. Are some of my stories, in some strange way, preordained? I wish I knew.

Some time before this a curious event seemed to have occurred in my fortunes. One evening Liam O'Flaherty had rushed into the office of Jonathan Cape in Bedford Square, excitedly urging 'Get *The Two Sisters* reprinted. Bates has won *The Hawthornden Prize.*'

Bates had not in fact won *The Hawthornden Prize*, but that there may have been some slight substance behind the rumour is shown by the fact that for a good many years afterwards it was not at all uncommon for me to meet people who, on hearing who I was, would instantly declare 'Oh! yes, you're the man who won *The Hawthornden Prize.*' The prize was worth £100, a pretty fair sum in my youth, and it is not impossible that if I had won it Madge and I might well have made our decision to get married earlier than we did.

When we did in fact make it at last we were both sure of two things: that we would, if possible, go to live far away from our native Rushden, in the south country of W. H. Hudson and Edward Thomas if possible, and that we would ask my former schoolmate, Harry Byrom, to be best man. On visits to London I saw Harry pretty frequently, one of our joint pursuits at that time being the theatre, in which he had recently made an exciting discovery, as he wrote to me, of a brilliant new young actor. We accordingly began to follow this young man all over London, whenever he appeared in some new production. Charles Laughton was not then famous as the ebullient King Henry VIII throwing chicken bones over his shoulder; he was merely a small part actor of much intelligence, content to be playing small parts for the sake of experience. One of these parts was that of a slouching, slippered layabout in Molnar's *Liliom*, with its repeated refrain of *Wake up, wake up, you vagabonds, the damn police are after you!* a part that Laughton played with such comic realism that we were convinced, and correctly, that here was one of the great actors of our time. Many years later I dined with Laughton, then world famous but sick of the theatre, as in fact I myself was too, and found him to be a man of charm and an intelligence far above the average of the acting profession. I told him how much and how often he had enriched my youth and he was, I think, touched to feel that he had done so.

At all events many other affairs and persons – Violet Dean, Harriet, Louis Sterling, Charley Lahr, Bernard Harris, the selling of more MSS and stories and the increasing if relatively slight success of the novels I was now managing to write – were all adding up to the same course: marriage. The event itself was still some time ahead but meanwhile I had prudently introduced Madge to the Garnetts and on a number of occasions we went to The Cearne together, often making it a centre from which to look for the cottage we eventually wanted. Though we met with no success it was good to know that Constance, and indeed also Edward, of whom Madge was at first terrified, approved of the girl I had chosen, a girl whom they had rather feared, I fancy, might turn out to be a flashy and useless piece of goods, though for the life of me I could never think why. These visits also had the effect of endearing Madge to the south country, so that presently there was no atom of doubt in our hearts as to where eventually we would make our home.

With all this in mind my wanderings about the Northamptonshire countryside now had a new purpose. I cycled from one country house sale to another, picking up for a few shillings odd chairs, corner cupboards, chests, china, glass and bits and pieces of all kinds. Together we searched antique shops and junk shops and pretty soon I developed a fair nose for a bargain, though there were many (a set of six genuine Georgian mahogany dining chairs was beyond our financial range at £6!) which we had to forgo. I had also been given an excellent tip, which I still think holds good, by Margaret's architect father: namely that one should always ask oneself if one could get a piece of antique furniture made today for the price being asked for it. If the answer is no then you have a bargain.

This is now the moment, I feel, in which to reintroduce Margaret into my life, though I fear rather painfully. There had evidently been some growing crisis behind the scenes and certainly there had been some talk of 'that young man trifling with my daughter's affections', as Violet Dean was later to tell me. The resulting tensions were soon to become unbearable, so that presently I was to receive a letter from Margaret in which she bared her heart, and indeed her soul, as far at least as feminine pride would allow, and asked what, if anything, was I going to do about her and the great affection, if not indeed love, that she felt for me? I was stunned. Since there had been neither inconstancy nor duplicity on my part I found it hard to bring myself to believe that she could think I had misled, deceived or cheated her. But this, though she didn't say it in terms quite so explicit, was clearly what she did think and it was all too desperately clear also that she was on the verge of being broken-hearted. Sad as I was about this, it seemed to me that

there was no point in being otherwise than honest about it, telling her that I did not and indeed never had loved her and that if in my purblind stupidity I had wounded her I was deeply sorry. With as much tenderness and understanding as I could summon I told her about Madge and where indeed my real love lay.

Precisely what all this did to her it is impossible to know. The ecstasies of first love, even when returned, engender a pain peculiarly their own; when they are rejected God only knows what torture and torment follow. I deeply blame myself for all this, and long ago though it now all is I can only wish that I had had the wit and perception to see that it would surely happen.

Alas, I was too obtuse to have done so and the heart of a charming, generous, intelligent girl was surely broken. It says much for her character that I think she forgave me and, bitterly painful though it must have been to say so, that she understood.

It is now a good moment also to bring Violet Dean back to the scene. Our search for a cottage having been unsuccessful (it was now 1930 and the nearest we had come to buying a cottage was in my grandmother's little Bedfordshire village, Souldrop, a sketch of which may be seen in *The Vanished World*, the cottage in left foreground, the little church steeple behind) I now sought the aid of Vie, the tireless helper in time of trouble. Indefatigable and willing as ever, she responded by inviting us down to Kent, to her manor house at Little Chart: a lovely but strange house, with dark episodes of history, standing on the edge of a large rolling park from which the Great Depression had just evicted its owners, leaving behind a trail of shattered tree tops where formerly had stood a noble splendour of ancient oaks, elms, sweet chestnuts and beeches. There was an air of sadness about that littered wreckage, a lovely pastoral piece of England shattered as if by war, that lives with me still.

It was February, 1931, when we took the train to Kent. Spring seemed to be coming; the air was damp and fresh and you could almost smell the not too distant sea in it; thrushes were singing and along the dykes a few varnished celandines were waking and here and there even a primrose or two. Rain fell all through Saturday night and on into Sunday morning, cheerlessly.

The village of Little Chart, though very small, is divided, like Gaul, into three parts. The centre contains a few dozen houses, a church, a pub, a shop and two small lakes on the edge of which stands a paper mill where, three quarters of a century ago, was made a good deal of paper, by hand, on which books of the Kelmscott, Ashendene and Doves Press were printed. Alas, hand-made paper is now also part of a vanished world. Another piece of the village, containing what is reputedly the oldest hop-garden in England, stands a mile or more away, and here too was once a church, unique in that it contained a Roman Catholic chapel under its Protestant roof, and now blasted to a ruin by a Hitler doodle-bug. The third part lies another mile from the centre in another direction and consists of a village green of great charm, called the Forstal, surrounded by a dozen houses of stone, half-timber and that soft bronzy red brick seen at its loveliest in villages such as Goudhurst, away towards Sussex, westwards.

The Forstal
Little Chart

It was on this elm-fringed green, the Forstal, that Vie, after her miraculous fashion, had discovered a cottage that she thought might suit us. The rain stopped at lunch-time and after lunch we walked out to see the house. It was a horror. Much depressed, we were about to walk back when its owner declared that he might have one further possibility to offer. This was a building for conversion, a granary. We walked across the sodden grass, then only a rough area of pasture with a shaggy brown horse grazing on it, today mown smooth as a bowling green for cricket, to look at it. It stood in a half-flooded farmyard: an oblong building of stone, weatherboard and tile, open to the winds on the ground floor, still littered with straw and grain upstairs.

We looked, poked about a little, went upstairs and pondered. We went outside, looked and pondered again. We stood for a few minutes by the thick, yellow-lichened old stone walls and suddenly the sun came out. Its rays were the very faintest degree warm and we saw now that we were facing due southwards. Madge looked at me and I at her. We said nothing; but in that moment of sunlight we suddenly knew that this was it.

Once again the mysterious divinity, this time in the person of the unfailing Vie, had shaped our ends and performed its miracle.

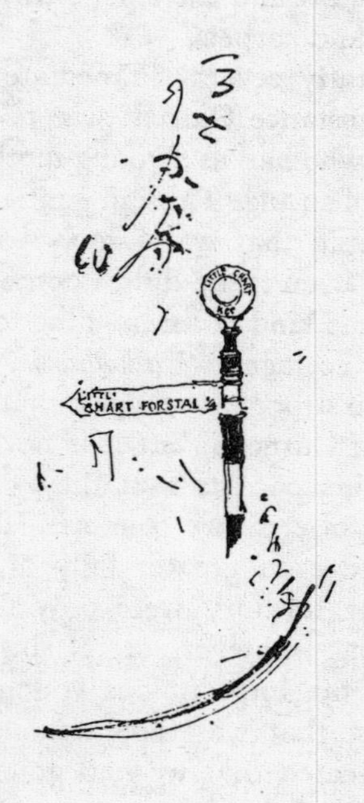

VI

Within hours we had decided to buy the granary. Within a couple of weeks the plans for its conversion were ready.

For the stupendous sum of £600 we were to get a large living-room, four bedrooms, a study, a bathroom, a kitchen and nearly an acre of land. Between us we had something over £400, some of it due to much hard work by Madge, the larger part of it thanks to Louis Sterling, and I decided to borrow the rest of the £600 on mortgage. We had almost enough furniture to make a tolerable start and the chief of the things we needed were curtains, cups and carpets.

There were instantly several immediate reactions to this decision of ours. Constance Garnett was profoundly alarmed, even horrified. She, who had as a young mother travelled alone or in the company of strange Russian gentlemen by sleigh and *droshky* across a Russia that was largely without railways at that time, indicated even if she didn't actually say so, that we were committing some kind of sin in going to the extravagance of buying a country cottage *with a bathroom.* I think perhaps it may be putting it too strongly to suggest that there was a streak of masochism in the Garnetts, but it is nevertheless true that David has said of his parents that they viewed with severe suspicion the world of creature comforts. That Madge and I were to commit the even greater folly of installing electric light and an indoor lavatory were only further reasons for Constance wondering whatever sort of sins against the Holy Ghost of prudence the impecunious young were coming to. She did not suggest that we were actually mad; her Scots caution merely indicated that we had gone far beyond mere imprudence into the regions of the unwise.

It soon became clear, however, that both our families and our circle of friends and acquaintances also thought we were stark, raving barmy. Of course you never knew with these

writer fellows – they clearly hadn't got their heads screwed on the right way. They were not as other men. But whatever was *Madge* thinking of? – a sensible, hard-working girl from a respectable working-class home – going to live in a *barn?* The very thought was outrageous. The scheme was a lunatic one that could only have been invented by a young man slightly if not utterly deranged. A *barn?* It conjured instant visions of straw and hay, bare brick floors, bare earth and even perhaps of Madge and me sleeping, like the good infant Lord himself, in a manger.

Most amazed and disbelieving of all our friends was, I think, Bernard Harris. Bernard had only the very vaguest idea of what in fact the countryside consisted of. For him, I think, it was a kind of uncharted wilderness in which unidentifiable trees and plants existed to form a general pattern of greenery in spring and summer and a forbidding, naked nothingness in winter. He marvelled at my knowledge and passion for it, confessing that he himself (perhaps a little with his tongue in his cheek) didn't know a cabbage from a potato in growth, and confessing still further that in his botanical ignorance he was quite unable to identify an ash from an oak. He too found himself quite unable to swallow the idea of our living in a barn. It was clearly one of an astonishing craziness. Many years later, when he came to stay at the Granary, when we had *two* bathrooms, I truly believe he thought we had in fact committed a further sin of actually telling a lie about the barn in the first place. He really couldn't quite grasp that the cow-barn of his first conception had turned out to be, after all, a very comfortable, elegant house.

£600 down the drain too: further madness. It must of course be remembered here that in the early depressed 1930's the idea of converting this, that and any other kind of building into houses was utterly unthinkable. Today we live in a world where people thirst for, and even pay heavily for the privilege of, being able to convert pig-sties, cow byres, old windmills, malting houses, oast houses, hen houses, warehouses, old railway stations, old signal boxes, disused forts, ancient barges and almost anything else into places in which to live: these are the new, the modern status symbols. But in 1931, when you could have bought such places for a song we were, among the people we knew, the only people to dream of such a thing – the one exception being H. A. Manhood, also a short story writer and a protégé of Edward's, who lived in a converted railway carriage which he had bought, I think, for £25.

That summer was wet and cool. On some evenings, even in July, you needed to wear an overcoat. The previous summer had been better and in the August of it I had persuaded Madge to come away with me and share some of the joys of foreign travel that I had known in Germany and that are of such enduring enchantment still. We accordingly went to Brittany. We travelled to St Malo by night boat, slept on deck and were very sick. From St Malo we went on to the old and beautiful town of Morlaix and thence to the little coastal village of St Jean de Doight, once the home of the late-impressionist painter Gustave L'Oiseau. It was all very like going back into the world of Maupassant or of Gauguin and his friends who had painted at Pont Aven, living there, as we now did, for a few modest francs a day. The country restaurants full of peasants and farmers all eating at one big central table, the insular suspicions of the Bretons towards strangers, the flowing native cider, the fishing boats with their pink and blue seine nets that later Christopher Wood depicted so well, the street markets where live ducks and hens sat with their legs tied to wheelbarrows or cart-wheels, the little train that ran from the main street in Morlaix across the pink-purple moors of heather to the coast where the tide ran out for miles, leaving great black castles of rock exposed on deserts of pure white sand, the strange angelic white headgear of ancient Breton peasant women sitting asleep in the sun: I remember it all as an idyll, perfect in every degree, as if it were yesterday.

From St Jean de Doight we went south to Rouen, where the Seine, the waterfront and the old city too were Maupassant-like and we once paid the staggering sum of fifty francs, less than ten shillings, for a dinner, instead of our customary ten

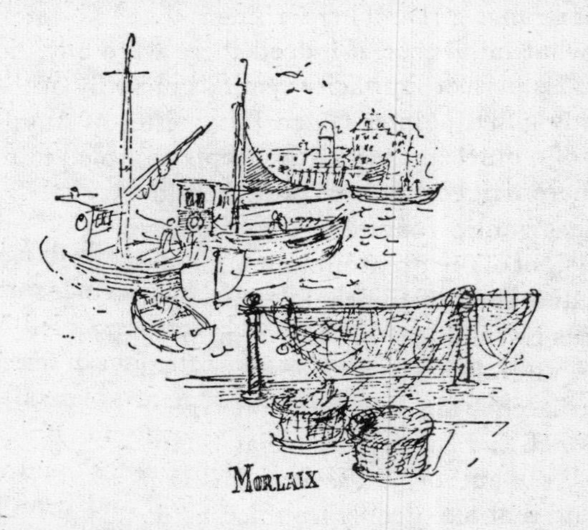

MORLAIX

francs, an event that caused me to come out in a long hot-cold sweat. From Rouen we went on to Paris, where we met Margaret, who was staying with American friends. One of the characteristics that least endeared me to Margaret was that she was an impossible chatterbox and I seem to hear her still, prattling away like some light pianola as we toured about a tiring, torrid Paris in an open taxi. Paris has never, except on one or two occasions, seemed so lovely since. Nor will it ever be so cheap again.

It was also during that summer, if memory serves me correctly, that I paid another visit to David Garnett at Hilton, a visit that is worth recording for several reasons. I recall that David and I bashed a cricket ball about the lawn with his two young sons, Richard and William, David showing that colossal physical strength which had so staggered D. H. Lawrence and which made him such a powerful swimmer. Shortly afterwards there arrived a young Welsh writer, a strange, taut-looking girl, fair and blue-eyed, dressed in a black velvet cloak. Dorothy Edwards was an ardent socialist who wrote only two books, *Rhapsody*, a volume of short stories, and *Winter Sonata*, a novel. In *Rhapsody* there is a short story, *The Country House*, which I deem to be one of the best in the language. The strange thing about this strange girl and her writing is that I find it impossible to trace what influences, if indeed there were any, lay behind her work. Its perfect simplicity reminds me only of the work of that greatly gifted painter Gwen John, sister of Augustus. It is the work of a quiet but evidently deeply troubled mind.

Soon there arrived another visitor, heralded by the gigantic roar of a huge motorbike. The sight of this great Brough Superior machine and then of the slight, blue-eyed figure of its rider, dressed in the uniform of an R.A.F. aircraftman, was enough to tell me immediately who he was: none other than Colonel T. E. Lawrence, alias Shaw, alias Ross, the author of *The Seven Pillars of Wisdom* and that also deeply troubled book, *The Mint*. He was introduced to us as Mr Shaw. The fact that he had breakfasted with Mrs Thomas Hardy far away in Dorset and had roared his way across half England in a matter of a couple of hours or so had no sort of effect on Dorothy Edwards, who merely remained utterly ignorant as to who he was.

We finally went into the house for sherry and lunch, during which Lawrence began a discussion on Greek poetry, a subject on which he was no small authority. This sudden excursion into the realms of classical verse had the immediate effect of putting Dorothy Edwards' back up. Her instant conclusion was that this aircraftman, this Erk in his ill-fitting blue uniform, was showing off; could there be any other explanation for a mere serviceman holding forth on Greek poetry? The air grew tense. By this time it had also dawned on both David and his wife, as well as on myself, that the ardent Welsh writer-socialist hadn't the slightest notion that she was talking to a man who had become so much a legend in his life-time that he had sought to flee from it into the monastic anonymity of the R.A.F. The air grew tenser still, the argument more aggressive, not to say belligerent.

To David, Ray and me all this had about it a certain air of comedy. Not so to Dorothy Edwards, for whom the situation merely worsened. It may be that Lawrence, sensing that his identity hadn't been disclosed to her, worsened it deliberately and that he too was secretly enjoying the fun. The entire situation had about it something not a little Thurberesque or perhaps rather in the vein of those shorter farcical plays of Tchehov.

But, as so often in Tchehov, the epilogue to the story is not comic, but tragic. Not long after that meeting both T. E. Lawrence and Dorothy Edwards killed themselves: he accidentally, on his motor-bike, she deliberately, by throwing herself under a train.

Soon, with the prospect of the Granary lying before us, Madge began to undergo a slight period of madness of her own. There was good reason for this. From that sunlit moment in February when we had stood by the lichened walls in Kent to the moment when she walked into the house on her wedding day in July she never once set eyes on the place where, in our supposed craziness, we were going to live. From time to time I really believe she wondered if it actually existed. It is true that I myself made one or two visits to it, once I believe from The Cearne, and went through such mundane essential business as measuring the windows for curtains and discussing paint and drains.

It was in fact the curtains that were the cause of Madge's

temporary aberration. For economy's sake she had decided to make them herself, a reasonably simple enough task except for the fact that she could never be sure that I, never very good at practical matters anyway, had got the measurements of the windows exactly right. This worried her to such an extent, even to preying on her mind, that the poor girl actually began walking in her sleep, hanging the curtains in the middle of the night at her mother's bedroom windows. It finally turned out that I had miraculously got the measurements right and all was well after all.

I have the impression that I wrote little or nothing at all that summer. The chief task that now occupied me was to raise vast numbers of plants, both from seed and cuttings, for the garden I was determined to create in Kent. Inspired by The Cearne, I raised primroses, polyanthus, pansies, poppies, alpines and heaven knows what else; I begged from other gardens, including The Cearne itself, from which numbers of things still survive in a garden that is now nearly forty years mature.

The story of how this garden was created out of the wilderness of an old farm-yard is not unfascinating; but before I tell it I ought to speak of another friend whose importance to me has been considerable. Somewhere about this time there had come to Jonathan Cape a new editorial assistant: Rupert Hart-Davis, now Sir Rupert. Handsome, tall, friendly, a great bibliophile, Rupert eventually became perhaps the best publisher's editor in London, as his masterly editing of Oscar Wilde's letters goes to show. We at once got on supremely well together. Rupert was very much my sort of person and of my generation, which the two partners of Jonathan Cape were not. Rupert therefore became a liaison officer between the heads of the firm and myself, so that I found myself able to take to him problems, financial and otherwise, which I found it difficult to take to them.

Rupert had also been to Oxford at a particularly fruitful period and numbered among his fellow students Peter Fleming, Osbert Lancaster, John Betjeman, Louis MacNeice, Quintin Hogg, Harman Grisewood, Alan Pryce-Jones and John Sparrow as well as others of talent and influence. One of these was the then literary editor of *The Spectator*, Derek Verschoyle, who at Rupert's instigation now began to give me books to review and to ask for other articles. *The Spectator's* list of writers in the early thirties makes rich reading: Graham Greene, Peter Fleming, Alastair Cooke, Dilys Powell, Stephen Spender, C. E. M. Joad, Kate O'Brien, L. A. G. Strong, William Plomer, Rupert himself and many other talents of brilliance. A year or two later Rupert was responsible for further kindness, so that I was given *The Spectator*'s weekly *Country Life* column to do, an opportunity that gave me the very first regular income, a magnificent 6 guineas a week, that I had had since first beginning to write; but of this I shall say more later.

What chiefly strikes me now about the dawn of the 1930's is the great richness, literary-wise, of the times, not merely on our side of the Atlantic, but on both; we have nothing comparable, on either side, today. The consequence of this was that the period was one of the most stimulating and exciting for a writer, especially a young writer, to be living and working in. As in a great period of painting – i.e. Impressionism – or music, the sudden birth and fusion of great numbers of talents at the same time has an immensely dramatic influence on the rise in the general artistic temperature. This in itself creates a climate which is not only right but perhaps, above all, infectious. Men and women of true artistic talent find themselves frustrated by a climate that is either sour or sterile, as happened in the 1950's, or that of the 1960's, which have seen literature descend, as that excellent actor Richard Hearne recently pointed out, to the depths of the snob-pit. It would be tempting to pursue this theme but perhaps it is better simply to say that when art sinks so low it is its own destroyer.

In the 1930's there was nothing of this. There actually existed, amazingly, a large body of writers, not merely young but drawn in fact from three generations, who actually cared, and cared greatly, as Milton and Donne and Shakespeare and Dickens and Tennyson and hundreds of others had done before them, what English should look like on the printed page.

The word charm had not become derisory; there were still writers who fashioned their words lovingly, not regarding them as lumps of offal to be cast down for dogs to eat. Of the generation before the First World War, a very considerable number of big figures were still highly active; though Conrad was dead, Hardy, Galsworthy, Shaw, Wells, Maugham, E. M. Forster, Belloc, Masefield, Bennett, Housman, D. H. Lawrence, Huxley, W. H. Hudson, W. H. Davies were still very much on the stage; of the writers who had survived that war Sassoon, Graves, Linklater, Compton Mackenzie, Richard Church, A. E. Coppard are only a small part of a lineage that was also rich; finally when we come to the generation that had been too young to bear arms in the war we are confronted with a truly astonishing array of talent: Evelyn Waugh, Graham Greene, Peter Fleming, V. S. Pritchett, William Plomer, John Moore, W. H. Auden, Stephen Spender, C. Day Lewis, Sean O'Faolain, Frank O'Connor, James Stern, William Sansom are only a few of the host of talents making up that exciting company. Nor was this all. Across the Atlantic another army of writers, headed by figures such as Hemingway, Faulkner, Erskine Caldwell, Katherine Anne Porter and Sherwood Anderson were helping to lead yet another generation of younger talents away from the sterile folly of merely imitating second-rate English talents and to discover for themselves the rich indigenous veins that were awaiting exploration over there, so that an entirely new, fresh, living flow of ore was about to be tapped.

It could not have been otherwise than immensely exciting to be part of this new generation, a generation which, in my view, has remained unmatched ever since. It was surely closely comparable with being a young painter at the time when Pissarro, Sisley, Signac, Seurat, Bonnard, Van Gogh, Picasso and Matisse and many others were so enriching French painting towards the end of the nineteenth century. Like Sisley and Pissarro I was poor, but cash or the lack of it was of all things at that early period of literary flight of the least importance. 'The path of art, endlessly difficult', I had been told and had not only found it so but was still so to find it, for many years, time and time again. To this eternal truth I was now conscious of adding another. I was now more than ever dedicated to a situation 'where the artist's power of compelling imaginative persuasion transforms them (i.e. his stories or novels) into a living truth'.

The apparent folly of marrying on nothing, and in a converted barn at that, did not therefore seem to me to be folly at all. It was rather a compulsive challenge; and it is of this long and severe challenge and how I met it but often didn't conquer it that I must now proceed to tell.

VII

In August 1930 Madge and I had tramped over a good part of Kent, rucksacks on our backs, looking for possible houses in which to live. One day we walked little short of twenty miles from Canterbury to the village of Pluckley, which stands on the very edge of that ridge that lies, like a long step, between the North Downs that the Pilgrims to Canterbury once trod and the vast Weald that stretches away in its wide magnificence to the South Downs of Sussex. At Pluckley there is a small forest, perhaps a surviving part of the great ancient forest of Anderida that once covered so huge a part of southern England. As we toiled up the last mile or two to reach the ridge we passed a small church standing on a grassy hillock above a stream. Sheep were grazing under the old stone walls and Madge paused to take a photograph. We didn't know until later that that church, with its safely grazing sheep, was to become a closer part of our lives.

This then was Little Chart; and to it we finally came, newly married, unable to afford a honeymoon, on a July afternoon in 1931. It must now be recorded that there was a certain slight element of irony about our wedding day. I, the parson-hater, the rebellious chapel-goer, rejector of the Methodist faith in which my father had so strictly brought me up, had at last been married in the realms of strict nonconformity, in chapel, and furthermore not by one parson but by two, Bernard Harris, jocular and kind as ever, being one, Harry Byrom, my erstwhile school-mate (the *only* member of the upper sixth at Kettering Grammar School) being an admirable best man. The affair was a simple one; and what I think perhaps lingers sharpest in my memory of the after ceremonies, simple as they too were, is the face of my grandfather, reflectively sad that we were leaving our native heath and were going to live, as I think it must have seemed to him, a thousand miles away. For him, I think, it was really a farewell. Exaggerated though it may be to say that our going broke his heart, it is true to say that I saw him only once or twice again and then in decline. Just after the publication of *The Vanished World* there occurred, in Higham Ferrers, in the little ancient square we both loved, one of those episodes that from time to time occur unexpectedly in life, forming a sort of late epitaph to someone or something long lost. On a beautiful October morning I met there a man who introduced himself as the person who had taken over the little farm my grandfather had once worked, where horse after horse of his had dropped down dead, where I had bird's-nested, tried in vain to lift the great sheaves of bearded wheat and had looked for skylarks' nests among the yellow coltsfoot flowers in the spring ploughed land.

We talked briefly of his, and my, vanished world: of the days of labour on land intractable and unyielding, long ago. Suddenly he asked me if I knew what that field of my grandfather's, back at the beginning of the century, when horse and man were almost the only means of traction on a farm and where he had tried with all his strength to wrench a living from soil almost as unyielding as rock, had always been called. I confessed that I didn't know.

'The Sorrowful Field,' he said and on that soft October morning, warm with sunlight, there were sudden tears in my eyes.

But in Kent, on that afternoon in mid-July, when the air was smothering with the odour of sweet chestnut bloom, the field was not sorrowful. It suddenly seemed miraculous, happy and fertile, full of promise and of an infinite beauty. Not that there really was a field, as such; our granary stood in what seemed to be a wasteland of giant dock and thistle and old grass grown yellow with summer. Nowhere was there to be seen the remotest sign of the garden I dreamed of. All this, and much else, had still to be created and fought for.

In what was to be the garden stood a decaying haystack. Beside it stood a decaying willow and beside that another. There was still another, huge and old. Piles of rock and rubble lay strewn about in this forest of dock, grass and thistles. Beyond a raw, new, ugly snake-fence lay a meadow and this at least had features of splendour, surrounded as it was by a rectangle of great Turkey oaks, perhaps two hundred and fifty, perhaps three hundred years old, cylindrical, majestic and almost black in full summer leaf.

Ludicrous though it may now seem there is an incident both small and trivial that marks the start of the garden that I now see from my window, the giant golden Turkey oaks backing it on a rainy autumn morning in the field beyond. It is the sowing of a packet of radish seeds. Is it sometimes the very smallness of things that makes them linger so long in the memory? Not a packet of gentians, of rare campanulas, of fabulous lilies, of Himalayan blue poppies, of alpines; but radishes. This tiny ridiculous piece of creation was the first I ever achieved on my own piece of English earth. Since then I have sown thousands of seeds and planted thousands of plants, bulbs and shrubs, but still those radishes remain in the memory like a string of white and scarlet pearls.

Every penny we had, with the exception of some twenty pounds, had been sunk into the house, and the problem now was how to survive while Madge attacked the house and its domestic affairs and I the garden. The result was that we lived on two pounds a week. Fortunately food was very cheap but at the same time there was nothing to eat as yet from the garden. Once or twice a week a travelling greengrocer called in on us, his produce in an old-fashioned covered cart, not unlike a small replica of those prairie wagons you see in Western films. After nearly forty years I have utterly forgotten what the man himself looked like. It is the face of the young daughter who was always with him that haunts me still as it also haunted me all that long time ago. It seemed to me a face moulded out of yellow clay: a face born to tragedy. I believe it is true that Hardy saw his Tess only once and also in a cart, in a country lane, and from that fleeting experience, haunted also by a face, created his celebrated novel. Soon I was to create mine shaping it into a story called *The Mill*, a story that was not only

far and away the best thing I had written up to that time but the story that firmly and beyond doubt established my reputation as a writer of stories and revealed me at long last as a fully conscious writer, wholly aware of what I was doing, a master of the craft I had worked at so relentlessly and intensely.

It is said that Tchehov, like me a great lover of flowers, wanted to turn the whole world into a garden. So too did I: but with the difference that I wanted to do it, if possible, overnight. As a young man I cannot flatter myself that I was exactly patient, but the fact that I have still not finished the garden after forty years of toil and thought on it perhaps goes some way to proving that the impatience of youth has been replaced by something less volatile in middle age. At all events I began the grand attack on my piece of earth: uprooting vast quantities of gigantic docks, mowing down nettles and thistles, seeing to the removal of the haystack and the burning of the more useless of the willows. I worked like a slave, from early morning to night, writing nothing and therefore earning nothing, my bank balance dwindling with frightening rapidity.

Too proud to borrow in case it should prove to the disbelieving that after all we *were* mad to have got married on nothing and madder still to have chosen a barn in which to live, I was saved from utter penury by the arrival of a few late wedding presents in the form of cheques, each of them a god-send.

Sometimes, however, it was necessary, if only for sanity's sake, to escape; and so sometimes we did, occasionally to the sea, most often to the great beechwoods which lie so majestically along the North Downs, three or four miles from the house. Seen from a distance these woods look like thick, gigantic bearskins; when you enter them they become like vast cathedrals, pillared by thousands of immense beeches whose elephantine trunks show up like bleached grey bone against the black frames of numbers of scattered yews. In spring these cathedrals are strewn all over the upper edges with millions of bluebells, a festival and miracle of purple. In autumn, shining in the sunlight of October and November, they look like golden temples. We visited them over and over again, always in a state of perennial wonder. From the primroses and bluebells of spring to the wild strawberries and golden yellow rock-roses and even wild columbines of high summer we felt, I think, that this was the shrine at which we had come so far to worship. Beside it our native Northamptonshire seemed bare and cold and desolate. From these hills you can see, on very clear days, the sea. A black whip of smoke, in the days before oil replaced coal, marked the passage of ships up and down the channel; and there were days of crystal sea-whitened light and running breeze where you felt that below you lay half the world, pasture separating woodland in the same repeated pastoral pattern for miles and miles. This, you told yourself, was ageless, an affair of eternal greenness, sea-washed light and snow-pure cloud. This, you told yourself also, must have been what the climbing pilgrims saw; and perhaps Caesar and his legions too.

It wasn't long before we were faced with a new problem. To the labour of the garden was suddenly added the prospect of another kind of labour. Madge had begun to feel distinctly ill in the mornings. It was to Violet Dean that we at once turned and she, in her typical fashion, ever eager to help in time of crisis, took Madge off to her doctor, who confirmed what we really knew already. Our first child was on the way.

Whether we were part fearful, part excited it is now difficult to say. I only know now that I believe every act of creation to be re-creative. I am strongly of the opinion that the way to negation, even unhappiness, even disaster, lies in fighting against the current of the creative stream. In other words I knew, now, that I had to work like hell.

And work like hell I did. Often, again like Tchehov, I wrote a story between breakfast and lunch; an article between lunch and tea; a review between tea and supper. I wrote until my hands trembled and I could scarcely see straight; until I was appetiteless, half-sick and cursed again with a greyness of vision and the gnawing ache of abdominal pains.

Any artist who works after this fashion, at such blind pressure, will tell you that sometimes there comes a moment when he is not quite of this world. I do not mean by this that he becomes wholly or partly insane; he simply ceases for a time to know what day it is. Such an experience overtook me one day when, after a long penal spell of especially hard work I went to London to meet and have lunch with Violet Dean, who was ever good to us. After wandering round the bookshops of Charing Cross Road during the morning I suddenly found myself standing on an island in the middle of the street, my mind black and blank, unaware of who or where I was, why I had come to London, who I was going to see or what time it was. I suppose the experience lasted for less than a minute, but when I presently came to myself and looked at the nearest street clock it was to discover that I was already an hour late for my lunch with Vie, who was waiting for me somewhere far down in the City, beyond St Paul's.

It is not an experience I care to repeat; and I mention it now only as an answer to that all too common remark that readers often make to writers: 'aren't you lucky?' I do not rebuke them, however, for that. Perhaps it is difficult for them to understand that there are times when the gift of imagination can also be a curse.

That first autumn in Kent was long and mild. Many leaves stayed green on the oaks until Christmas. By December hazel catkins were in flower. By January primroses were blooming in the woods and I remember how, once, we gathered them by moonlight.

A letter to Edward Garnett in the mid-winter of that year tells me that I was now working on a novel, *The Fallow Land.* The successful completion of this book was of the very greatest importance to me. If it could be successfully brought off I knew that I would be able to draw an advance on it in the spring: a desperate financial necessity, since the baby was expected in May.

It would seem that the book was going well and that I hadn't committed another folly; for this is what I wrote to Edward:

I feel immensely pleased with it . . . I have done roughly 250 *pages, which is roughly half way, and I can't hold myself. This is the book I have always wanted to write – the struggle against the soil, the whole exactly a woman struggling to live on the land. I have made her a shrewd, quiet, level-headed creature with a sort of fatalistic streak in her; she has a will like a mule and a head for money; her husband is exactly her opposite – spoilt and a fool about money. She saves the money and he wastes it. Her children, of whom she is passionately fond grow up and grow like their father.*

It would also appear that I had taken Edward's excellently sensible advice and was getting the first chapters of the novel typed so that he could take a critical glance at them instead of leaving the entire affair until it was fully completed, thus putting myself into the painful position of *The Voyagers* all over again. That this was a most wise course is clearly indicated by another letter to him, written in the middle of January:

Your letter was like a gallon of wine – I went rollicking off to the novel drunk with delight. I can't tell you how glad I am that you like it.

Drunk with delight: that indeed is how I must have felt after all the caustic castigations of the past. At last, perhaps, my world was beginning to blossom.

The setting of *The Fallow Land* was precisely that part of the Nene Valley where I had grown up with my grandfather as a boy; and in a sense it was his story, his struggle, that I had transposed to the woman, and her struggle, in the novel. It now occurs to me that, if I only had known of it at the time, *The Sorrowful Field* would have been the apter title. However that may be, it is certain that there was a hint of the paradoxical in the fact that although the great beauty and variation of the Kent countryside had already inspired me to rhapsodic love for it, it had also succeeded in making me see with a clearer, far more objective vision the native Midland land I had left. Perhaps it was a case of standing back and letting the dog see the rabbit; but it remains a certain fact that I was to write another half dozen novels of that native Midland soil before at last war, with its many revolutions, not the least of which was in the countryside, together with other causes, decided me to leave it and turn in other directions. Novels such as *The Fallow Land*, *The Poacher* and *A House of Women* are not written today; nor could they be. They are, in a sense, historical novels, portions of a world that has vanished as surely as the world of my boyhood street games has vanished. War, the senseless destroyer, kills not only men; the Second World War revolutionised the countryside as nothing, not even railways, had done before, killing all hope, in the process, of a writer of my kind ever being able to write again of man or woman battling their guts out in order to tame by means of horse and hand fields that were sterile or sorrowful.

However, the completion of *The Fallow Land* was a happy and important event; and was presently to be followed by another equally so. In May, at the time of the blossoming of that 'loveliest of trees, the cherry', our first daughter was born; and I was presently able to write to Constance Garnett that the child had 'intense blue eyes, and a lusty voice with which she cries all night.' Her first name was Ann, her second Catharine – the spelling of the second being the result of a promise to Bernard

Harris, who had insisted, as he had done for his own daughter, on the classical middle 'a'. Ann, in fact, was cast in the classical mould herself: the classical, blue-eyed, flaxen-haired Anglo-Saxon mould of the Midland valleys, the world that had produced her mother and grandmother and still produces some of the loveliest girls in all England. It was fitting, I always thought, that my beautiful first daughter should have been born when, in A. E. Housman's immortal words, the cherry was 'hung with bloom along the bough'.

A disturbing thought now occurs. In Tchehov's *The Cherry Orchard* it is the sound of the axe striking at the trunks of cherry trees, in pre-Soviet Russia, that symbolizes the prophecy of doom for the old régime. Today, in Kent, the home of the cherry in England, precisely the same thing is happening. Everywhere cherry trees, so black of branch and so white of blossom, are falling under the axe. A symbol of doom, the end of an era, of the further tightening of the strait-jacket of the State, or what? I find the parallel of absorbing, sad, disturbing, even tragic implication.

But in the summer of 1932 neither war nor the axe that falls on cherry trees had begun to cast either their sinister shadow or echo. Madge was now a mother, I a father; the garden was growing; my world was, as it seemed, blossoming: perhaps not so splendidly as that of the cherry trees, but let us say modestly.

And perhaps this, it would seem, is a good place in which to say something of my own mother.

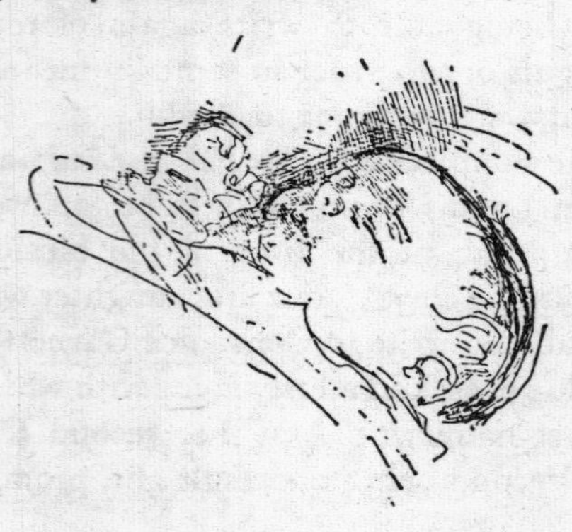

VIII

It may have seemed to certain people an odd fact, even a deficiency, that I had little or nothing to say, in the first volume of my autobiography, *The Vanished World*, of my mother. It may well have been thought that, for some unexposed and unexplained reason, I had largely left her out of it. This is not so.

The two great influences on my earliest years were my father and my grandfather. To the first I owe my literacy and love of music; to the second my love of Nature and the countryside; to both, perhaps, an ability that has sometimes been called the faculty of 'thinking through the pores of my skin'. My mother, excellent mother though she was, exerted no such influence on me.

Born Lucy Elizabeth Lucas, in 1878, elder daughter of my shoemaker grandfather, my mother is now in her ninety-second year, her life thus spanning almost all of what is indisputably the most revolutionary century of all time. It says much for her that she is not merely alive but lively; possessed of all her faculties both physical and mental; keenly interested in domestic and world affairs – an ability and interest she undoubtedly gets from her father; avid reader of newspapers and watcher of the television box; living alone in the largish house built by my paternal grandfather at the turn of the century; still able to stitch and sew beautifully, to do her own cooking, housework and shopping; devoted to visiting, coach outings, church-going, and what my father and grandfather would have called 'shop-window fuddling'; highly critical of what she deems to be the deplorable decline of manners and language and especially of the sponging indolence rife under the contemporary umbrella of the Welfare State; forthright in opinion, reserving the higher of her scorn for political tricksters typified largely by so-called socialists.

One of the Old School: that, I suppose, is the readiest and

commonest description of her and her kind. When I read of men tottering into fumbling retirement at the age of 60, so often to moulder away through what should be the riper years of male maturity, afflicted with the grey blight of pensionitis, I like to think of my mother, thirty years their senior, entirely unpensioned because she happens to be a victim, by reason of her age group, by that iniquitous and infamous gap in the cradle-to-the-grave graph of the Welfare State, staunchly holding to her nonagenarian independence and still extracting interest and pleasure and amusement from living. Perhaps her

generation is still better exemplified by a friend of hers, even further advanced into her nineties, who when solicitously asked by my mother if there was anything she needed by way of extra comfort in life replied after singularly brief thought:

'Yes: three things. A new pair of specs, a new set of teeth and – a man.'

My mother was born, like my grandfather and my wife, in the pleasant little stone Northamptonshire shoe-making borough of Higham Ferrers, where she began work at the age of 10, thus doing a little better than her father, who had begun at 6, scaring crows. Her starting wage was two shillings a week. This doesn't sound so bad when you remember that it was for half time only. My father was similarly a half-timer: school in the morning, work in the afternoons, or *vice versa*, I am never sure which. For this splendid sum, anyway, my mother tied knots in a shoe factory, later rising to a position, like her father the shoemaker, where she worked only on special orders demanding exceptional skill.

Northamptonshire, like its neighbouring counties, has long been a stronghold of Nonconformity and at the earliest possible age she was dedicated, as I was later to be, to the cold and unremitting altar of Methodism, my grandfather, as I have explained in *The Vanished World*, being contemptuously of the opinion that the Church of England was composed of nothing but a psalm-chanting gang of Papists. Methodism, she was telling me only recently, claimed her at half-past six every Sunday morning before breakfast; she had a good mile to walk to Sunday School. The disciples of Wesley, in those days, had no use for idle hands. Prayer and parsons and all the rest of the frigid paraphernalia of Wesleyanism kept her, as Chaucer says, 'narwe in cage', until the last session of Sunday School began at 5.30.

Not only Nonconformity but liberalism greatly helped to shape her. On each side of the fireplace in my grandfather's front parlour hung portraits of John Bright and William Ewart Gladstone: the revered twin gods of Victorian liberals. And a liberal she has remained all her life: scorning the soppy humbug that surrounds so much of socialism and the flabbiness of character among modern youth that, in her view, so largely stems from it. She is not one to show emotion easily, though this by no means indicates that she is incapable of feeling it. Her capacity for self-reliance has given her a quite extraordinary aptitude for sitting still; she can embalm herself for hours in an aura of peace but at the same time is ever ready to put on her best hat and gad out for a while, either on some shopping expedition or 'just for the ride'. One of her characteristics that has perhaps diminished least with age is her derision of humbug in all its forms. She scorns falsity, arrogance, fuss, self-pity, ostentation, palaver, showing off, high-falutin speech and above all snobbery, whether of rich or poor. She can detect it all from a mile off and this, I am glad to say, forms a good part of my inheritance from her.

Physically she is also cast in that pure Anglo-Saxon mould which, as I have said, has made and still makes the people of the English Midland valleys the best-looking in England, perhaps in Europe. The girls here are renowned for their good looks and my mother, in the days when girls really dressed like girls and looked like flowers, was one of them. I see all the special features of that fine Anglo-Saxon type not only in her but repeated also in my wife, my daughters and my grand-daughters: the delicate bones, the fine soft skin, the blue eyes, the fair, light-textured hair. Age may wither, but time cannot alter the bone structure of a face; and at ninety my mother displays a profile beautifully clean in line, handsome and almost unwrinkled, so that she really looks some twenty years younger than she really is.

Does she carry a cross about with her because she once worked for two shillings a week or that she was once so poor, in her early married life, that she was left, one Friday morning, with only sixpence in her purse? Not, as they say nowadays, on your nelly. Today the statisticians would put her last remaining sixpence fifty fathoms deep below the poverty line. But statisticians have no code index for pride and it so happens that the word poverty is not, and never was, in her language. Perhaps she remembered that her own mother had once sat up half the night, by candle-light or even a farden rush-light, and made shirts at sixpence a time; and perhaps it comforted her.

In turn I confess it rather comforts me to be told that as I grow older I tend to become, in looks, not more like my father, whom earlier I was said so much to resemble, but much more like my mother. It would, in fact, not at all surprise me if I too didn't one day inherit her astonishing capacity for sitting still, in prolonged meditative contemplation, a capacity that is, perhaps, the secret of her great age and the smooth, almost unwrinkled shell-like quality of her face. I have an early photograph of her, probably taken about 1883, in which she is wearing an extraordinarily elaborate coat for one so young, a sort of furbelow affair, and in which she is staring at the camera not merely with uncommon gravity, but with a glare positively pugnacious: as if to say 'Life, I'm going to lick you'. It reminds me a good deal of the portrait William Roberts did of me in my early twenties. There is something pugnacious about that too.

In speaking of influences it now occurs to me that the business of contracting early influences in writing and painting may perhaps best be likened to that of contracting common infectious diseases in childhood. The victim comes out in clearly defined but rather nasty spots, all over. Thus an artist such as Christopher Wood contracted nearly all the possible influences, chiefly French, available at the time, before unhappily putting an end to himself at the very moment when he might be said to have gained a clean certificate of health. So it was with the author of *The Two Sisters*, except that gradually, painfully and certainly he shed the contagious influences of his early youth as he had also shed the peeled skin of an early attack of scarlet fever.

The near-fatal lesson of Hardy having by this time been well-learned, I now determined that any new influences on me should not by any chance lay that particular curse on me again. I now in fact fell under the spell of no less than four new masters, two English, W. H. Hudson and Edward Thomas, and two American, Hemingway and Sherwood Anderson, but this time not fatally or even dangerously, but with singular profit. I contend that these two widely separated pairs of writers have a good deal in common. That Edward Thomas was influenced by W. H. Hudson is pretty certain; that Hemingway was influenced by Sherwood Anderson is undoubted. It has also always seemed to me possible that Hudson, being a great friend of Edward Garnett, must have read Turgenev in Constance's translations, as Hemingway most certainly did. Indeed Hemingway actually called one of his shorter novels *The Torrents of Spring*, which of course is one of Turgenev's own titles. This book, intended as a parody of Anderson's *Dark Laughter*, itself a book that clearly reveals a certain lack of self-criticism in Anderson, ironically ended up as an even greater parody of Hemingway himself, with the result that the two books are equally bad. This, however, does not detract at all from the great and revolutionary influence both Hemingway and Anderson conferred on the modern short story. Anderson's own contribution on that score was to break with what he himself called 'the cold, hard stony culture of New England', where the established and cultured writers saw everything as 'a preparation for life after death'; and then to turn away to find the indigenous material of the Middle West, where he began to record, with no touch of false romance, the lives of poor whites, remote farmers, negroes and boys who hang about race tracks, obscure dreamers in the back streets of Chicago, country school-teachers and lawyers of frustrated ambition living in the desolate dust of forgotten townships and unloved women who walked 'out of nowhere into nothing'. If I were called on to pick one story that is the very essence of Anderson it would be, I think, *The Triumph of the Egg*, an essay in the tragedies of frustration that must surely rank as Anderson's masterpiece.

Anderson, like Hemingway, showed us life not in woolly, grand or 'literary' prose, but in pictures. E. J. O'Brien put this succinctly and well by saying that 'almost for the first time an American artist attempted in his fiction to present a picture rather than to write an ephemeral play', though 'the pictorial values of Sherwood Anderson were not at first apparent because his pictures lacked colour'. Hemingway performed in much the same way, going for that same direct pictorial contact between eye and object, between object and reader. To achieve this he cut out a whole forest of unnecessary verbosity. He trimmed off explanation, discussion, even comment; he hacked off all metaphorical floweriness; he pruned off the dead, sacred clichés; until finally, through the sparse trained words, there was a view:

'The road of the pass was hard and smooth and not yet dusty in the early morning. Below were the hills with oak and chestnut trees, and far away below was the sea. On the other side were snowy mountains.'

So simple, so un-literary and yet so powerful in pictorial

effect were such pieces of Hemingway that they had a great effect on me; and in consequence I learned much from them.

To Hudson I had come rather late, although his book of South American stories *El Ombú* (he had in fact been born in the Southern American continent, in a house called *The Twenty Five Ombú Trees*, the *ombú* being a tree of great size) had been the very first book that Edward Garnett had ever given me. But now, living as I was in that part of England, so rich in wood and downland, so splendid in its great variation of scene and wild life, I turned to him and discovered not only a new master but one with whom I instantly felt the closest kinship. It is largely to Hudson, though also to Edward Thomas, that I owe the enrichment of my ability to put the English countryside down on paper. Galsworthy, who had also been influenced by Constance's translations of Turgenev (that melancholy idyllic little scene of old Jolyon dozing away in the garden in *The Forsyte Saga* is, unless I am much mistaken, almost pure Turgenev) called Hudson 'the rarest spirit, and has the clearest gift of conveying that gift . . . Without apparent effort he takes you with him into a rare, free, natural world, and always you are refreshed, stimulated, enlarged by going there.' Conrad perhaps put it even better by declaring that 'this man writes as the grass grows', which indeed he does. It is evident too that Hemingway also knew Hudson's work, since he refers on one occasion to *The Purple Land*, one of Hudson's two South American romances, peopled as it is with the most gorgeous and seductive of dark-haired beauties, as 'a highly dangerous book to put into the hands of a middle-aged man'.

So Hudson not only enlarged my vision of the natural world, and in particular those parts of it that were now topographically so close to me, but also my ability to write of it. I think that, in the thirties, I must have read almost every word of Hudson and came away, as Galsworthy says, refreshed, stimulated, enlarged. The step from Hudson to Edward Thomas was an inevitable one and though there is unhappily far less of Thomas than of Hudson to be read, I nevertheless rate Thomas' *The South Country* as indisputably the finest piece of prose ever written about the countryside of southern England. Not only is it incomparably beautiful as prose and equally so in its pure quality of evocation, but it serves to reaffirm a truth I have long held to be indisputable: namely that you do not necessarily have to express yourself in hexameters in order to write poetry. *The South Country* is of the purest poetry and Thomas, with Hudson, our greatest nature writer.

Are these two prose-poets read by the generation of today? I cannot say; if not, more's the pity. I will only say that when the snob-pit and the sewers of the 1960's are lost in the limbo to which they are clearly doomed to be sunk, Hudson's truth, expressed in *The Purple Land* will still be valid: 'Ah, yes, we are all vainly seeking happiness in the wrong way'; just as his prose, like that of Thomas, will still be poetry:

'The blue sky, the brown soil beneath, the grass, the trees, the animals, the wind, the rain, and stars are never strange to me; for I am in, and of, and am one, with them; and my flesh and the soil are one, and the heat in my blood and in the sunshine are one, and the winds and the tempests and my passions are one.'

Is it possible that in this almost Biblical passage there can be found the finger-post pointing to the happiness that so many in our subtopian, permissive, soured society are seeking but in vain? Perhaps. But there arises from it a thought I find worth pondering on. Perhaps it would do us no harm to try, for a change, living as Conrad rightly maintained Hudson wrote: 'as the grass grows'.

IX

Soon, just as grass grows in the somnolent heat of June, my garden began to grow. The labour of hacking it out of a ruined farmyard, on virgin soil, was inevitably tough; and it soon became clear to me that my own hands, extremely small as they are (it is said of my mother that when I was born she took one look at my hands and made the instant declaration that '*he'll* never get his living by hard work') were not going to be adequate for the job. Ill though I could afford it I knew that I had necessarily to get in, as help, some good strong labour.

I was fortunate enough to find two good men. Alfred was a hefty, cheerful Romney Marsh man of eighteen, his theme song when at work being that then popular ditty *Oi'm 'appy when oi'm 'oikin'*, which he belted out lustily almost all day long. The second man was not eighteen but eighty, and not from Kent but from Cornwall. Very soft spoken, very courteous, very strong for a man of his years, Mr Haley possessed a horse and cart, or could borrow them: I cannot now quite remember which; but immensely useful they turned out to be.

I should now explain that *The Granary*, in its beautifully squared rag stone, was in the shape of an , the shaded part only of which belonged to us; the rest was a disused stable. I knew that I could, God one day being my helper, buy the stable portion for £100. But God not being a bank and I having about as much chance of finding £100 as I had of striking a pot of gold under the willow tree, I had spoken to Edward Garnett about the possibility of borrowing the money from him, promising to pay him back in five or six instalments. Edward was very willing to help but it was I, not he, who at the last moment got cold feet, fearing that I would never be able to repay him.

It was here that 'the divinity that shapes our ends' took yet another hand in our affairs. One of the first things that Alfred had persuaded me to do on coming to work for me was to buy a ticket in the Irish Derby Sweepstake, which I did, though rather reluctantly. Shortly afterwards the telephone rang one evening and a telegram informed me that the ticket (pseudonym 'Lucky Ann') had won £100. Since the owner of the stable (one of the often repeated maxims in his puritanical creed was 'the greatest good for the greatest number', on which I used acidly to comment 'Yes: Number One') had already issued thinly veiled threats of turning the stable into two bungalows, thus ruining The Granary, I now felt that I could either have said a thousand prayers or wept for joy. In no time the entire building was ours.

After this blessed stroke of fortune I felt freer to pursue the most important of my horticultural passions: namely the building of a rock garden. But rock being expensive to buy and deliver, this possibility began to seem almost as remote as the £100 until suddenly the hand of Violet Dean again generously stretched itself out to us. In the parkland on which stood her house there also stood a disused rock quarry, and from there, Vie was good enough to tell me, I could take all the rock I wanted.

So began a period of great and exciting toil, in which the man from Romney Marsh, the man from Cornwall, myself and the horse and cart all took strenuous part. Alfred had never heard of a rock garden being built before and now entered into the spirit and sweat of the thing with an ardour that seemed a compound of a fiendish enthusiasm and a kind of disbelieving joy. We might have been building the Pyramids. With equal but quieter strength Mr Haley joined in. Armed with picks, shovels, crowbars, spades and levers we went almost daily to quarry rock: great cheese-green lumps of it, beautifully mossed, often weighing several hundredweight. These Mr Haley, the man of eighty, used to lift bodily into the cart as if they were mere new-born babes.

My role was largely that of instructor; I was the architect. I had swotted everything up; I had soaked myself in the Gospel According to Reginald Farrer. In consequence I knew that a rock-garden should not resemble a cake with stone almonds on top or the grave of a dead elephant stuck about with naked tombstones. As a result we were soon moving the huge lumps of our lovely Kentish rag-stone, which somehow in its mossy-green-cream-yellow appearance reflects all the beauty of this southern countryside, into natural order and place. I was excited and happy in doing it all and Alfred sang *Oi'm 'appy when oi'm 'oikin'* with even more joyous gusto.

Alfred, in his youthful strength and ardour, was soon also engaged in another activity. He was digging my first herbaceous border. At some time in his still young life a man had taught him the technique and advantages of what is known as 'double-

digging'. With almost an air of guilt Alfred informed me that this would cost me 'half-tidy bit o' money' – wages at 10d an hour! – but would pay 'half-tidy middlin' dividends' in the long run. 'Double-digging' in fact takes at least three or four times as long to execute as plain digging but the dividends are indeed truly rich. After thirty-eight years Alfred's border is still as fertile as when it was first made and yet has never had a spoonful of manure or sprinkle of fertiliser on it since the day it was first planted.

From the first the soil was unbelievably rich. It had the substance and appearance of dark brown sugar. The top layer of it went down for a distance of three feet and everything in consequence grew with miraculous rapidity. Roses climbed as if they were Jack's beanstalk. Great pools of the richest gold appeared where Siberian wallflowers grew to a width of a yard per plant; Canterbury bells were like great towers decorated with ballooning old-fashioned bloomers in purple, pink and white. Splendid steeples of delphinium rose. We had a row of peas which grew to a height of eight feet. That no true alpine could survive for long on this over-rich diet of brandy and Christmas pudding was not to be revealed to me until much later. All that mattered now was that my soil, my little plot of England, was heaven-blessed in its fertility. I had inherited the earth and to my joy it was neither fallow nor sorrowful.

After the hard graft of *The Fallow Land* all these excursions into physical activity were also a blessing. My health improved; I felt rampageous as a puppy set free in a forty acre field. It was all both restorative and exhilarating, deeply satisfying and exciting. It is said in fact – and it is not impossible that it is true, since Kent is virtually an island, two-thirds of its boundaries being water – that this particular piece of England, more especially this village and its environs, enjoys an air that is more than usually rich in iodine. But whether true or not you certainly feel that as you breathe it you are breathing something compound of champagne and the sea; and sometimes in those days, when smoke still blackened London and the homeward trains, you felt as you stepped back into the country that you were breathing an air that was not merely pure, but paradisaical, distilled.

The following year, in November, we were still further blessed: this time by the arrival of Ann's sister, Judith. Petite, with the most perfect of heads and lightest, thistledown hair, she too came to us in the pure Anglo-Saxon mould.

At the foot of the narrow little lane that runs by the house flows the young River Stour: shallow, softer than Thames flowing softly, its course taking it through meadows lying under the fringes of woods of hazel, sweet chestnut, alder, poplar and birch, all of them home of a million bluebells in spring, the scent a total embalmment of the air. In spring too the alders

bear russet-brown-gold catkins that dip down to the surface of the stream and in summer the banks are lined with meadow-sweet, purple loose-strife, willowherb and wild yellow mimulus. In summer too long emerald water weeds skein out into the currents, sinuously, and water ranunculus sprinkles the surface of the pools with white flowers. Today the stream is stocked with trout, but in those days you saw only a few shoals of roach and perch, an occasional pike lying in wait under the little stone bridge that spans the stream by the lane, and there were crayfish under the stones.

Just as I had once spent golden days with my grandfather gathering watercress on the little tributary of my native Nene, so I now began to spend days just as golden, indeed even richer, by the young Stour gently flowing. There is something of endless fascination in these smaller streams; they evoke an affection that I find all too often that larger rivers fail to inspire. You couldn't row a boat on the Stour at this point; but you could sit and watch and dream an afternoon by, see a heron poised like a predatory grey statue among the tall bottle green reeds and watch snipe and kingfisher swoop swiftly, royally past you.

In the lane itself bracken grew higher than a man, thick green in summer, gold-brown as the turkey oaks become in November, when at this moment, as I write, they are like purified gold against the thin blue of winter sky, above the first light fall of snow. And here in the brown-gold bracken, as winter began to turn to spring, I remember once how we disturbed a half-waking dormouse from his long hibernation and how he crept half-sleepily out and gently, like some soft brown miniature squirrel, crept up Ann's arm and sat there unafraid, bright little eyes just open, turning hesitantly this way and that, as if wondering how he had come to wake, after winter, in the spring-like hand of a child.

Such tiny incidents not only remain long in the memory. They grow in memory, their power of illuminating the past growing also as time itself goes past. I remember also other tiny things: white wild violets fat as snowdrop buds on spring banks, drifts of white wood-sorrel in the woods themselves; the silent swim of water voles on summer afternoons and of grass snakes idly swimming too. And often and often simply the mere silence of it, especially in high summer, when the grand spring opera choruses of birds have died away. There are still times, when I come home from London or from some noisy journey by road or train or air, when that silence says more than a thousand orchestrated chords, so marvellously evocative that it too achieves a state of embalmment so deep that it often takes me a day or two to get used to it.

It is sometimes said of me that I evoke only the golden days. Indeed I once remember a female reviewer rather testily inquiring 'Where *does* Mr Bates get his weather from?' as if the Almighty had provided some special dispensation for me in that direction. But certain it is, as I note from a letter to Constance Garnett, that the year 1933 was a golden one. In the August of 1933 I was writing to her 'What a summer. What a parched desolation for gardens . . . like you I feel inclined to throw it all up until crocus time.' About this time too I was writing to

Edward that I was wrestling with the 'udders of imagination, hoping that milk will come'; and also about the same time to Constance of 'acute worry about money and stories and so on'; and then again that 'in the interest of trying to knock debts on the head I am planning a novel – to be robust, long, rich, full of country stuff, with a poacher-vagabond in it'.

So though the days in memory may be golden, just as I am certain they were golden in reality, the bank balance was not. No sooner had I begun *The Poacher*, in the winter of 1934, than I had to give it up in order, as I wrote to Edward:

'To try to get some ready cash. Things are for the moment a bit desperate and I have been wondering if you could lend me £20 until, say, the end of February? I have money owing me by various editors, but I can't get a cent of it and *The London Mercury* has failed and left me a creditor for £15. The doctor's bills for my wife have drained me a lot and I've insurance to meet this week too. I hate asking this – but if you could manage it I should be more than grateful. I can safely pay you back in a week or two. I am doing some country essays and stories until I find my feet again.'

'Finding my feet again' took, in fact, another year, that being the time it took to see *The Poacher* through to publication Happily it got the best press of all my early novels; but by the time it was out I was under the enforced necessity of starting another novel, this time *A House of Women*, a book again set in my native Nene Valley. And so the pattern went: novel, expired bank balance, stories, reviews and articles in order to restore it, dunning editors for money, begging the Garnetts for their opinions on MSS., which they always freely and kindly gave; and always the struggle to pay bills, the struggle against gnawing abdominal pains, always the dread of making another botch-up with a novel and thus wasting half a year or even a year; and always the uncertainty, the irregularity of income, the constant nagging of insecurity, the fear of drying up, of greater debts, of failures and rejections.

But then, who was I to complain? This, surely, was the life I had chosen to lead, this the profession I had sworn to pursue, come hell or high water. If fate appeared sometimes to be a bit tough on me I had to be honest and tell myself that there had also been times when it had looked on me with good grace and no doubt would do so again.

It was no use weeping against the wall. Indeed it was just as well that I had in me that touch of pugnacity.

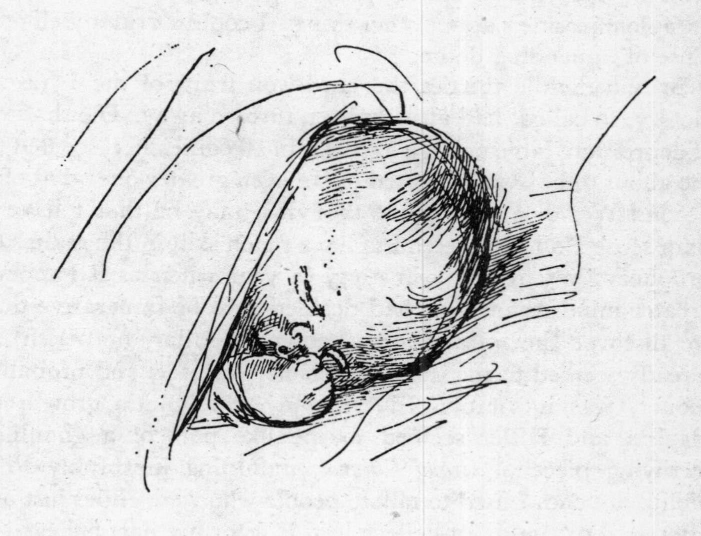

X

As the golden days increased, like my family, and as the garden grew in beauty and maturity, there also grew in me a comparable uneasiness about other things. I couldn't rid myself of a sense of impending doom.

By the middle thirties the hard-won fruits of the 1914–18 victory, so-called, had already been thrown away. The shadow of depression, large enough as it was in all conscience, seemed to me about to be overshadowed by an even greater one: that of a Second World War. Possible though it may be that I have a sixth sense I do not pretend to have much skill in the realms of prophecy; yet by the year 1935 (a year when as it happens greater minds than mine had decided it to be imperative that we discover the miracle now known as radar, or perish) it already seemed to me that war, sooner or later, and probably sooner, was inevitable. In Germany the lunatic growth of Nazism and Hitler seemed to me like part of a ghoulish, terrifying piece of *Grand Guignol*, unfolding inexorably to a nightmare end. I used to talk to people who were either just not interested or could not believe in this. I for my part believed it so passionately, though with an embittered reluctance, that I used to have open fits of anger about it and sometimes inner fits of frenzy. Man had been insane enough in 1914; I found it a matter of excruciating and impossible difficulty to believe that he could be as wildly insane again and yet in my heart I was utterly convinced, though against my will, that soon he was going to be.

I was fortified – the word is ironical if you care to read it that way – by the dispatches then being sent to London by *The Times* Berlin correspondent, Douglas Reed, who was presently to expand these dispatches into a book called *Insanity Fair*, which Jonathan Cape published. My most awful fear having been confirmed by *Insanity Fair* I begged that Cape should send a free copy to every member of Parliament, a suggestion that Rupert Hart-Davis received with the wearily ironical sentence 'My dear boy, what's the use? They can't read anyway.'

The most terrifying thing about Reed's book was the accuracy of its prophecy. He had watched, listened and had been horrified by what he had seen and heard in Germany. On several visits to Germany Madge and I too had watched and heard the reflections and echoes, in reality, of those of which Reed had written: the confiscation of certain English newspapers in trains at the frontier, the nightly tramp of the feet of Hitler youth in school playgrounds, the swastikas, the swaggering jack-boots, the furtive voice of a doctor whispering to us on a Rhine steamer 'You say you have a daughter named Judith. That is a Jewish name. Are you Jewish?' It was of little avail or comfort to him to tell him, jocularly, that I had named my daughter Judith because Shakespeare had also had a daughter named Judith and that I had vowed to have at least one thing in common with him. He, the doctor, was a Jew. Nor was it of any comfort to us to be told by a young Nazi on the same boat:

'In the war you made us eat pig-swill. Soon, now, we will make *you* eat pig-swill.'

Reading *Insanity Fair* was, in fact, rather like eating pig-swill. It made you sick: not bodily sick, but sick in mind, spirit and soul. Here, as in some hideous glass ball, the future was set out with terrifying accuracy for all to see: the Saar, the Sudetenland, Czechoslovakia, Dantzig, Austria, Belgium, France and lastly, of course, England. Every ghoulish prophecy, and a thousand more that we didn't yet know about were eventually to come true with uncanny, bitter, sickening accuracy. And it seemed to me that Reed set out his arguments with such power and cogency that no one of right mind could deny them. I certainly could not; everything intelligent and civilised in me told me that we had looked into a glass darkly and had seen the black, diseased doomed face of Europe's future.

I used to go about trying to convince all kinds of people of the reason and realism of my fears about these things; few listened. Once I even got up and delivered an impassioned homily to a parish meeting (I was now, incredibly, chairman of the Parish Council); I might have been talking to an assembly of moles. Not that this greatly surprised me. One of the first things that had struck Madge and me on our first coming to live in Kent was the depth of rural insularity we found there; people existed, rather than lived, in a rural vacuum. There were cottagers who never went into the nearest market town more than once a year. The level of political consciousness, compared with that of the Nene Valley, where it is conspicuously high, was pitifully low. I do not much care for the word yokel, but this, more or less, was what we found: a withdrawn, dark, ungiving people, insular, defensive, highly suspicious of strangers, distrustful of all intruders, hard to make friends with. That they didn't want to listen to my impassioned prophecies of war therefore didn't surprise me; what I found ironical to note was that soon, if and when war came, as I was positive it would, it would be they who would be in the front line of battle.

Insular as they were, they inevitably had insular customs and traditions. In winter it was customary, every ten years or so, to cut down the sweet chestnut trees which almost always grow, very closely together, in small copses called *cants*. Men, as they still in fact do, would set up little huts among the thinning dark grey trunks and blue smoke from their fires of bark shavings drifted and hung about the air. Soon too, wherever the light came in, the very earliest primroses began to bloom, then crowds of white anemones, then bluebells, then petticoat-pink campions. The poles were invariably cut and split for snake-fencing or used whole as hop-poles. The Romans, it is said, first brought over the sweet chestnuts, since the nuts were part of the staple diet of the soldiery. In other copses, largely of hornbeam, charcoal burners still worked, since charcoal, so much used in the old bakehouses of London, is apparently best made from hornbeam.

And then while the chestnut was still being felled and split, the first actual work in the hop-gardens began: that beautifully fascinating business of stringing the poles so that the whole garden takes on the look of some gigantic white-gold spider-

web. Then soon came the white of pear and apple blossom, the even whiter bloom of cherry, and then last the pinks and reds of apple. In mid-summer hay turners, still horse-drawn, rattled about the meadows and in August binders, horse-drawn too, clacked about the fields of oats and wheat and barley. By the time plums had grown purple-fat on trees and had been gathered the real festival of the year, the English *vendange*, the hop-picking, began, bringing the centuries old fusion of Cockneys from London and the people of Kent, in almost precisely the way peasants forgather for grape-harvests in autumn in European vineyards.

I always felt that this festival, for which surely every working family turned out, was not only gay, as indeed it was with all the chaff and joking old-buck backchat and teasing and beery fighting and wenching that went on in and around it, was something more than just the mere business of picking hops for brewers; it always struck me as being a sort of pagan rite. And thus, I always felt, the people of Kent perhaps also saw it, though not of course consciously; it was a rite that had to be attended, a festival that had to be worshipped at. Nobody, except toffs and squires, ever missed hop-picking. Every mother took every child with her to the hop-gardens and every child, except those still being suckled at the breast, picked hops, from the first dewy misty light of September mornings until the soft descent of dusk and its shouted evening benediction that rang out down the pale green lines of fallen or half fallen hop-skeins: 'Pull no more bine!'

They pull the bine by machine today and every year the Cockneys come in smaller and smaller numbers. There are things called quotas and you see somewhere every year the saddest of sights that can surely blight a fertile country: whole gardens of hops being burnt as they stand. Now too they pile fertilisers with desperate prodigality on to cereal land, so that the corn grows dark and rich and much of it falls flat, still green, at the first moderately heavy rain. In turn combine-harvesters suck at the ripened grain rather like huge scarlet pigs rootling at the earth for food and in turn again the stubbles are burned, leaving scorched earth in black zebra stripes, depressing as if a burning, invading army had just passed through.

If the villagers in September escaped to their festival of hops, we in August escaped to the sea. We loved most, I think, to go by way of that strange, flat, wide-skied kingdom that is Romney Marsh, where grey-mauve marsh-mallows line the dykes and herons stand poised above the still waters and the sea seems to be for ever reflected with a pure salty brilliance in the air. I always felt a sense of flight as I crossed this marsh and its dykes, an uplifting as if I were a bird. Soon you came to stretches of shingle that lie between marsh and shore and breasted sand-dunes often as white as salt too. Wild yellow horned poppies grew about shore and shingle, together with big floppy trumpets of pink convolvulus. Long stretches of seakale in white flower stretched out, in places, almost to the edge of the sea, and sea-thistle rose everywhere as blue and sharp as steel.

In places strange little black huts lined the shore, like abandoned sentinel boxes, and in dazzling contrast blue and copper kingfishers flashed along the dykes. Black fishing boats drawn up on sand and shingle were exactly like pictures out of Boudin, and fishermen sat mending or drying nets beside them, gossiping and smoking, waiting for the turn of tide. Farther east we made for Folkestone, the harbour, the blue fishing boats and the little stalls selling whelks and cockles and mussels and soles and mackerel and plaice. I didn't know in those days that Manet's *Les Bateaux de Folkestone* marks the very beginning of Impressionism, though so it evidently does; but the scene cannot have looked vastly different to the young and despised Manet, back in the nineteenth century, than it did to Madge and me and the young Bates sisters on salty, fishy August afternoons thirty odd years ago. You could buy a good fat Dover sole then for 9d, a big plaice for 6d, a little one for a penny, a herring for a penny and enough sprats for a family for 6d.

For some curious reason – perhaps because they went to sea

in ships and knew great waters – there was always something far less insular, far less defensive, about those Folkestone fishermen and their nearly always fat, jolly wives than about their dark, resentful-looking brethren farther inland. The men of Kent are sharp and shrewd; and even the sharpest, shrewdest Cockney, so they will tell you, can be gypped there. But for my part I always got a feeling of openness, a sort of sea-free carelessness, perhaps deriving from a sea-to-shore, hand-to-mouth existence, down in that rather shabby, often muddy harbour, with its fish stalls, fish auctions, wet fish being sliced and beheaded and pale gold nets hanging out to dry.

They, like our inland primrose woods, helped to prevent my brooding too long and too hard on the thunder-clouds of war. But soon two other events of more importance took place in my life: one sad, one a further extension of its blossoming.

XI

Those were the days, the mid-thirties, as were those of William Morris, when select Private Presses flourished and there was in the air a certain slight madness about first editions. One result of this was that the Golden Cockerel Press had, in 1935, commissioned me to write a book for them. They had in fact already published two books of mine, *The House with the Apricot* and *A German Idyll*, the latter the long story I had conjured out of that half-crazy visit to Germany with Rhys Davies, William Roberts, Charley Lahr and other friends.

My memory, normally good, now serves me rather hazily; but unless I am greatly mistaken it was in June 1935 that Christopher Sandford and his fellow directors at The Golden Cockerel kindly arranged to give the book, *Flowers and Faces*, an afternoon party in Kensington, the party being in the afternoon so that guests could also see the King and Queen go past on their Jubilee Procession. I felt very flattered at all this and the affair was naturally, on a pleasant June afternoon, very gay.

During the course of it I was asked to meet a young publisher. Michael Joseph, dark, charming, intelligent, goodlooking, proceeded to tell me that he had just hung out his sign, *The Mermaid*, in Bloomsbury, thus setting up in his own right as publisher. We took to each other instantly and found we had much in common. We liked, among other things, football (Michael had once been selected to play for the British Army, having been chosen in the belief that he was an international of the same name), fishing, the countryside, books and especially fiction.

M. J. proceeded presently to ask me if I was entirely satisfied with my present publishers. I replied that I had seen no reason so far to be otherwise, at which he said:

'Then we'll forget the matter. But if ever you should change your mind will you remember that, of all our young authors, it is you that I would like to publish most?'

There and then, genuinely and not with that mere politeness

that parties so often generate, I said that if ever at any time I was forced to consider a change, I would go to him. M. J., in fact, had already outlined several ideas about publishing that much appealed to me. He thought, quite rightly, that in those days far too many books were being published, a great many of them indiscriminately, with the result that each book got far too little individual attention and in consequence authors were poorly served. This struck me as sound sense. What I also liked was that his new publishing house was largely to be based on fiction, of which M. J. had considerable knowledge, and this of course was my field.

I do not believe, on the whole, in authors changing publishers. The impression created, as I see it, can be an exceedingly bad one. But when the time came for a reasoned and logical dissatisfaction with Jonathan Cape there was only one other publisher to whom I wished to go.

It was to Michael Joseph. But that event was still nearly ten years ahead and war, my damned inevitable war, was still to separate that gay afternoon in Kensington, with its celebratory party, its fluttering colours of bunting and pennants and flags and the King and Queen driving past in a world of what seemed happy peace, from the day I joined M. J. and his Mermaid in Bloomsbury Street.

It was another two years before the other event of importance occurred and when it did it was one of the deepest melancholy.

Edward Garnett, rising to dress himself one February morning in 1937, suddenly complained of a violent pain in his head and collapsed, fatally stricken by cerebral haemorrhage. In that moment I lost a friend, guide, counsellor, confidant, comforter and critic.

I say critic: yet I think it right to say that I never really thought of Edward as a critic and that it is probably just as true to say that he probably never thought of himself as one either. He had a singular contempt for the academic critic, who 'he thought boiled the old bones of the great departed but could not recognise a living genius'. No doubt he cherished an equal contempt for many others of the species, most of whom

MICHAEL JOSEPH Ltd
26 Bloomsbury Street

are still with us: the literary club armchair critic, the critic egotistical, determined to show how far finer fellow he is than he who is under criticism, the smart-alec critic, the pontificator critic, the wind-bag critic, the critic who dresses it all up in jargon that only he himself can understand, the elephant critic, who never forgets old wounds, the pay-off-old-scores critic, the critic who deludes himself that success is inevitably synonymous with badness and that the seclusion of ivory towers is likewise synonymous with a rare and exclusive greatness.

In all these senses Edward was not a critic. He provided, instead, the light by which literature is discovered, the diagnosis which reveals what is only suspected. The critic, as Mr William Gerhardi (now Gerhardie) has pointed out in an admirably perceptive assessment of the novel in a preface to his own novel *Futility*, rarely teaches. He has little or nothing to offer that will assist the creative mind. He is tasting wine, sampling it with approval or disapproval, for the public appetite; the torturing mysteries of creation are utterly hidden from him. Garnett, on the other hand, being unfettered by academic training in literature, was left free to be able to penetrate the creative mind with the rarest insight and having penetrated it was capable of recognizing, shaping, nursing, and bringing to fruition its infinite possibilities. That is true criticism: the criticism that is also creative; the criticism that brings the bud to flower.

In that field Edward Garnett had, and has had since, except perhaps in a few minor instances, no rival. His type is so rare, his combination of insight, profound sympathy and infinite enthusiasm (an enthusiasm that flowed till the end of his life) so great that it is not at all surprising that no one succeeds him today. The very term 'publishers' reader' is one of horror; it conjures up a picture of the wretchedest sort of underpaid hack poring over impossible beerstained, tea-stained manuscripts in a dingy back office, anonymous, bronchial, long-suffering, eaten away by cynicism. Nothing could be further from the truth as far as Edward Garnett was concerned. A certain playful sort of cynicism, revealed by a diabolical glint or two of the eyes, the natural product of a temperament exposed to the treachery and disillusionment of modern society and modern literary and publishing society in particular ('We are not in it for our health, Mr Garnett, we are not in it for our health') undoubtedly revealed itself in him from time to time, but it was almost always accompanied by laughter; but as to the task to which he undoubtedly felt himself solemnly called, just as other men may feel themselves called to the church or medicine or teaching he brought no kind of cynicism at all – a truly astonishing fact when one considers that he was engaged in one of the most profitless and thankless of literary tasks for over forty years.

He was never a prey to deceptions. He never believed that because the surface of a work of art is light its heart is therefore frivolous; he had undoubtedly heard the precise opposite in Mozart, whom he adored, and must have seen it in his parallel in painting, Watteau. The sketchy vernacular surface of Henry Lawson's stories of the Australian outback didn't prevent his instant detection of the sadness, even tragedy, lying underneath. Nor was he deluded into thinking that because a subject is 'lofty' the sentiments extracted from it are automatically 'lofty' too. It is a sad mistake to assume, as Mr Gerhardie points out, that 'a place of honour is assigned to 'serious' subjects expressing lofty, solemn and sonorous sentiments, betraying an unhealthy preoccupation with the other world to the exclusion of common everyday sense. The truth is, in fact, the reverse. The more deeply rooted in life, the more steeped in humorous tragedy . . . the more serious in the real sense will be the heavenly forces released in implication. And the more highfalutin the subject, the more grandiloquent the manner and dead-earnest the aim, the more nebulous, windy, dogmatic, flat, inaccurate, woolly, lifeless, trivial, shallow and worthless will be the result because the writer has seen fit to use his own foolish tongue to state that which a wiser man would have left implied. No *intellectual* belief is required from the pure poet.'

Exactly. The word to note here is 'implication', since it takes me directly back to Garnett's preface to *The Two Sisters*, in which he had noted that events were implied rather than chronicled, a truth that, when after long and painful struggle I had recognised it, finally provided me with the living key to all my work as a writer of stories. Nor was it the only truth towards which Garnett had directed me. In a preface to a volume of Turgenev's stories he had pointed out that the novel, far from being dead, as is often declared, 'can become anything according to the hands that use it'; and in an even more memorable passage had said: 'if you love your art, if you would exalt it, treat it absolutely seriously'. And this, whether the subject has been tragic or comic, light or apparently casual, I have ever since tried to do.

On a February day with the first touch of warmth in it Edward was cremated at Golders Green. Yellow crocuses were blooming about the grass and I thought of Constance and the garden at The Cearne. I could not help reflecting too that Edward, like me, had begun his literary career as a very young man. Almost all his first discoveries, Conrad, Galsworthy Hudson, Doughty and so on, had been men much older than himself. Now, by the nineteen-thirties, all of them were dead and he had reached a period, his rare enthusiasm diminished only by death, when all his stars were much younger than himself. So it was a following of very young men who stood that day to pay homage to him – H. A. Manhood, Geraint Goodwin, Hamish Miles, Arthur Calder-Marshall, Rupert Hart-Davis and myself.

All of us, but I think myself most of all, owed him much; and all of us had delighted in him.

XII

By this time Madge and I were expecting a third baby and it will give some idea of the high state of my finances if I say that one day I accepted with alacrity an invitation from Graham Greene to lunch with him at a restaurant he had just discovered: 'You can eat for one-and-ninepence.' The place was in fact that splendidly Edwardian pub in the heart of London's theatre-land, all brass and red plush and mirrors and beer-engines and snug corners, *The Salisbury* in St Martin's Lane. Graham, as impecunious as I was, had discovered with delight that for one-and-ninepence you could get soup, a large plate of boiled or roast beef, roast lamb or pork, some sort of pudding or cheese with perfectly magnificent celery. It was all excellent.

Neither of us had enjoyed, up to that time, anything more than a *succès d'estime*, to which on my behalf Graham had contributed a generous appraisal of *Cut and Come Again*, the volume of stories containing *The Mill*. In it he had compared me fairly and squarely with Tchehov, saying that he didn't think me the lesser artist. In consequence my literary stock now stood pretty high and I therefore felt that the time had come when I should attempt to build something of ambition and solid worth on these foundations.

One of the things that had long fascinated me about the English landscape was the Great House, of which Northamptonshire is particularly rich in beautiful examples, both in glory and in decay. What had further fascinated me was the subject of the growth of the selfmade man, often virtually uneducated, often rough and crude, who through sheer force of native energy and character had bulldozed his way to the top: yet another example of the fact that character not only assails bastions where education fears to tread but is capable of engendering a warmth and attraction that figures academic and over-civilised all too often lack. What was in my mind was

THE SALISBURY

to write a novel in which these two forces come together: on the one hand the grandeur of the Great House that seemed unassailable and unpossessable except to those privileged by right of birth and inheritance, and on the other by a character born in poverty, ignorance and even squalor, deprived equally of material care and opportunity, who in spite of it all forges his way through like some blundering ambitious ox until at last he is the possessor of the Great House from which, in the bitterest of winters, he once stole coal in order to keep his dying mother warm.

The theme seemed to me to call for bold and powerful treatment; it was no pastoral sketch. I saw in it not only a personal struggle but a piece of social history, a segment of the late Industrial Revolution that had marked my native landscape with so many soulless, hideous red-brick scars. In this landscape the remnants of the pastoral would serve to heighten the deadly nature of the new world of the machine, and *vice versa*. Its life would be robust but also lyrical, the progress of its main character ruthless but also sympathetic and sensual. Set in a mould of extreme ugliness, he was to have in fact a compelling and fatal attraction for women, for each of which, in his progress to the top, he was to feel a variety of passionate attachments.

I forged ahead with the Chronicle of Bruno Shadbolt with a conscious strength and confidence I had not experienced before. I felt, from the first, that the theme itself was right and that the foundation on which I was building was also right. I wasn't building on clay; underneath me I could feel, perhaps truthfully for the first time as a novelist, impermeable layers of rock. In the ill-fated *The Voyagers* all my instincts had seemed to warn me that its foundations and workmanship were jerry-built and Garnett had proved me right. Now there was no Garnett, either as boss or foreman, to guide my literary trowel and plumb-line, but now all my instincts, tempered hard by another ten years of experience, told me that I was building true and straight. When on the last page of the book Bruno Shadbolt at last stands by the Great House he has battled for and won there is a moment when the reader must feel, if I have done my work correctly, that material gain and wealth do not necessarily build an altar of happiness. He is caught up in 'the sudden concentration of years of loneliness. He was a man without friends.' Alone, all ambition, all passion spent, he simply becomes 'one with the stones of the house'.

I had called the novel, which spans the years 1873–1931, *Spella Ho*. I had taken the title from a chance map-reference of the county of Northamptonshire. The reference, *Spella Ho*, clearly indicated *Spella House*, but there seemed to be something far more arresting and dramatic in the brevity of *Spella Ho* and so it became. It also became, after a dozen years of toil in which there had been disappointments which anything but sheer youth could have considered heartbreak, my first commercial success. Not that it even remotely approached the contemporary commercial success that young writers, even with their first books, are apt to achieve today, when radio, television, films and the flares of publicity of all kinds shoot a writer to stardom almost before the ink on his paper is dry. But the book was reprinted three times in the first year of its publication: for me little short of a miracle.

That the miracle had arrived at the most opportune of moments is indisputable. In the July of the previous year our first son, Richard Lucas, named after his maternal great-grandfather the farmer-shoemaker, had been born: a July that miraculously lives in the memory not only for the exquisite nature of the summer itself but for the masses of giant tiger-lilies that regaled the garden and which I have never since grown so well. A lusty and elegant young man, Richard was early so adept at conducting the garden bird-chorus from his pram, with hands of waving enthusiasm, that I wrote to my father to tell him that assuredly, at last, we had a solid musical exponent in the family. Alas, though music is high on the list of Richard Lucas Bates' passions, he too is yet another in the long line of Bates who, in the musical medium, cannot transmute worship into creative activity.

My memory is here a little vague as to immediate subsequent

events, though by no means as to those which were to happen a little later. I have perhaps belaboured the theme of 'the divinity that shapes our ends' but certainly it was at work again in the early part of 1938, when I fancy it must have been Rupert Hart-Davis who sent proofs of *Spella Ho* over to the Little Brown Co. of Boston U.S.A. I may be wrong in this and it is possible that the passage of the proofs took place at the instigation of the Americans, since I well remember that Ellery Sedgewick, then editor of *The Atlantic Monthly*, had asked Sylvia Townsend Warner, on a visit to England, who were the young English writers he ought most to be looking out for and had received the reply 'H. E. Bates'. At any rate the proofs of *Spello Ho* duly arrived in Boston and one spring evening I was astonished to receive a cable from there not only offering me good terms for the book itself but a sum of no less than 5000 dollars for the serialization of the book in *The Atlantic Monthly*.

I went about for days in a startling state of crazy disbelief. Apart from the immense prestige of appearing in *The Atlantic*, a magazine held perhaps in higher esteem at that time in America than any other, the money itself was the equivalent of the discovery of a gold mine at the bottom of the garden. I had never heard of such money. A subsequent letter from *The Atlantic* indicated that the novel as it stood was slightly long and that it would necessarily have to be cut for serialization purposes. Would I object to the editor of *The Atlantic* cutting it according to their way of thinking? or would I care to cut it myself? With alacrity I not only declared I would cut it myself but that I was prepared to go to America to do so.

Accordingly I set off for America somewhere about the middle of May. I travelled by that old ladylike Cunarder *The Aquitania* and I suppose that in a way, compared with our contemporary flights of a few hours, it was rather like having an extremely leisurely meal in the mahogany panelled, palm-fringed restaurant at St Pancras station, where I had sometimes eaten with my father as a boy. The prodigious breakfasts, the heavy lunches and dinners, the lavish afternoon teas with a palm court orchestra playing *Tea for Two* or *Tip-toe Through the Tulips* seemed to belong not merely to an already distant Edwardian era but now, in memory, to something even further away.

I arrived in a New York hot, steamy and objectionable as only New York can be when the first heat of summer strikes it like a mounting fever. There can be few great cities in the world whose greeting to the passenger by sea is more depressing and revolting. The gates of the land of the free, in the grey purlieus of the downtown waterfront, are more like the portals of a prison than the gateway to freedom and prosperity. I was, however, not depressed on that first torrid sweating day as I set

foot on America's sordid soil. I was borne forward on a great wave of exhilaration: a wave I was never to experience on any subsequent visit, when my impression that New York is a cardboard and concrete theatrical set liable to disintegrate and disappear overnight increased until I could no longer bear the overwhelming conviction that this is a city as uncivilised as Sodom and Gomorrah.

I spent a day and a half looking, rubber-necked fashion, at the sights New York's visitors are supposed to look at, and then entrained for Boston. It says much for my abysmal ignorance of America that it was firmly fixed in my mind that Boston was a small parochial town something of the size and nature of

Cambridge, England. I can only suppose that the legend of the stony nature of New England's literary culture had created so false an impression. I was anyway astonished to discover that Boston was a vast port – and a highly entertaining one – and a city of some millions of people, including, it would seem, its own population of gangsters. In one thing, however, my preconceived notions of Boston were not ill-conceived. *The Atlantic Monthly Press* had kindly put me up at one of Boston's many clubs, an establishment that it seemed to me was far more English, far more exclusive, far more Victorian than the Athenaeum, Brooks's, White's or the Bengal Club in Calcutta rolled into one. An abiding memory of this masculine, mahogany museum is of my rising to go to breakfast on the first morning of my arrival and of meeting, on stairs and in corridors, a number of completely naked Bostonian gentlemen, all looking like uncooked kippers, on their way to take their morning baths. White-moustached, military, dehydrated, more English-colonel than any English officer who ever ordered a *chota-peg* in Poona, they gave the impression that they were daily awaiting orders from General Grant to pour the whisky and advance with infuriated dignity on the despicable rebels of the South. I have never forgotten those naked kippers.

In due course, that first morning, I went along to the offices of *The Atlantic Monthly* to meet various directors and other people, most of whose names I have now forgotten. Boston too was hot and sticky. Afterwards we went along to Beacon Hill to meet directors of the parent company Little Brown & Co. and then to lunch. It is the saddest of facts that of the people I met at lunch that day the greater part, though comparatively young, were to be dead within a year or two, it being Little Brown's misfortune at that time that its executives tended to fall by the wayside like stricken flies in the heat of Boston's summer.

I liked Boston, long-scorned for its stuffiness – that is by America's own brash, half-civilised standards – though it was. It is true that its famed magnolias, of which its streets are as gay in springtime as a Kentish orchard is with cherry-blossom, were already over but its park-like centre had charm and its central heart at least wore a recognisable badge of something civilised. It had also lots of restaurants, Swedish, Norwegian, German, French, Danish and so on at which it was cheap and fun to eat and at which I subsequently did. You could eat dinner, as I recall it, for less than a dollar a head (sometimes they even threw in a free dry martini for that figure) just as in London, at the same time, you could eat a marvellously good five-course lunch at the *Café Royal* for 3/6, or a seven-course dinner for 5/- – a dinner so exceptional in quality and quantity that the dramatic critic James Agate was once moved to write a whole article devoted to its gastronomical triumphs.

After lunch, on that first day in Boston, it had been arranged that I should be taken on a tour of the city – this to include all buildings old and historical, the town of Cambridge and naturally the Harvard University itself. The English visitor had to be suitably guided and impressed by those parts of the city whose history was not unconnected with that of his own country. Accordingly I was put into the charge of a young man, Archibald Ogden of *The Atlantic*, who had been provided with a motor car. My impression then was, and still is, that Mr Ogden did not wholly relish the task to which he had been assigned. I rather fancy that he reasoned – and even perhaps feared – that his guest would be an English stuffed-shirt, superior, insular, aloof, inclined if not actually dedicated to the proposition that all Americans are savages, uncouth and of dubious upbringing, who speak a language apparently taught them by semi-literate nasal apes. I rather think that he in turn thought I should speak in a near unintelligible Oxford drawl, my conversation interspersed with witless repetition such as 'I mean to say', 'What-ho', 'Frightfully decent' and 'Ifya know what I mean, old sport, what?'

Anyway we duly motored off, Mr Ogden taking me in the course of duty to see the older parts of Boston and thence to Cambridge and Harvard. We duly looked at Harvard. We duly looked at Harvard Yard. Then we duly looked at Harvard again; and dutifully yet again. Then Mr Ogden said:

'I guess you've seen plenty of universities before?'

I said I guessed I had.

'Oxford and Cambridge I guess?'

I said yes, both.

'You go to either?'

No, I assured him, I hadn't been to either. Nor, in fact, did I regret the omission.

This confession seemed not only to warm Mr Ogden; it seemed almost to cause him to begin to revise his uneasy conception of his young English companion, replacing it with the possible thought that I might even be human. At any rate he was now moved to inquire if I had seen enough of Harvard?

I thanked him and said yes, I thought I had.

'Well, in that case, what would you like to see now?'

My reply was one which Archibald Ogden, my friend now for more than thirty years, will never forget.

'I'd like to see the Red Sox.'

As if emotionally pole-axed Archie stood for some moments speechless outside the near-sacred portals of Harvard and then broke out into the wildest of grins. It was rather as if an American, asked as he stood at the gates of Buckingham Palace if he would like to meet the King had replied No, he'd rather go to Newmarket. The joy and relief on Archie's face were a miracle to behold.

'When,' he said, 'would you like to go?'

'Now.'

We went. I was entranced; and a strange thing happened. Our seats enjoined us to an old Bostonian sweat, wrinkled as a deflated pig's bladder, alcoholic of eye, oyster-like of gaze, tough and toothless of mouth. His mother's breasts had clearly been carved from base-balls. His vocabulary included no word by the minutest degree distant from the language of the game. His bible was the game's book of rules, both authorised and unauthorised. A certain arid cynicism, long born of the truth that all opponents are crooks and all umpires paid servants of the devil, hung about him like a grey shroud. This shroud had obviously covered him in his cradle and would no doubt cover him, embroidered with those cynical words *Three Blind Mice*, in his grave.

As the game progressed this shroud became slowly lifted. It began to be borne upon the old Bostonian sweat that he was sitting next to a grown man – none other than myself – to whom the very rudiments of a game he had sucked in with his mother's milk were having to be explained, as to a child, syllable by syllable, word by word. It was utterly beyond belief; it simply couldn't be; it just was not possible that there could exist on earth a man, a grown man, who had no fundamental

understanding of things as fundamental as pitcher, striker, home-run and all that. As the game grew and the excitement grew the great wonder of his disbelief also grew, until the oyster alcoholic eyes had me fixed in a stare that told me that never again would he believe that Englishmen were anything but pitifully, primevally mad.

But by the end of the ball game one thing was certain, incontrovertibly and incontestably certain: Archie Ogden and I were not only friends but friends for life. Even Archie's dry-martinis, of ill-fame and unrecorded strength, produced for my edification two evenings later and causing me to be carried home – on, I think, a bier – failed to destroy a friendship so happily begun. We discovered, among other things, that we shared a not dissimilar sense of humour, a total contempt for the pompous, a love of life and a passion for literature. Archie in turn has wisely discovered a love of England, where he now lives, and is, if I am not mistaken, now profoundly devoted to Dr Johnson's proposition that 'he who is tired of London is tired of life'.

Archie was only one of several young people then in the editorial service of *The Atlantic Monthly* and as I proceeded morning by morning to the excision and revision of *Spella Ho* for the magazine we made good friends with each other. The process of cutting the cloth of my novel according to the required American pattern was both odd and revealing. My impression that English was English wherever she was writ or spoke was one which was about to be rudely shattered. On those hot June mornings I came face to face, for the first time, with the pitiful, infantile nature of American insularity. In reading American novels or watching American films it is axiomatic for the Englishman to employ his native wit in order to translate, understand and absorb words and phrases hitherto foreign to him. Faced with the word *speak-easy* he doesn't demand that it be translated as a 'place where illegal strong drink may be obtained'; he accepts with joy its vivid vernacular and the word passes into the language, thus enriching it. Given the words *baloney* and *phoney*, only one of whose derivations he may be aware of, he accepts them too, taking only the very shortest possible space of time to acquaint himself with the fact that the one means crazy rubbish and the other a falsity. *Stool pigeon?* – before the talkies of the gangster era not one Englishman in a million would have guessed its meaning, together with that of words like *moll* and the many scores of apt, sharp, highly descriptive bits of American vernacular most perfectly exhibited by such writers as Damon Runyon.

By contrast the simple English of *Spella Ho*, some of it in the

Midland vernacular but even so never obscure or complicated, had to be questioned on every page. 'You see, our readers would never understand what it meant': the strangest comment, it seemed to me, on the readership of what was certainly one of the most literate magazines in America. So morning by morning I had some simple, nearly always unobscure English phrase to delete or adapt for the American ear and not once did it occur to the editorship that it might have been the reader and not the writer who should gird himself towards the effort for change.

Of the then editorial board of *The Atlantic* at that time there was one man for whom I had the very greatest respect and affection and of whom I will speak in more detail presently, and another for whom I had none. Talentless, phoney, pompous, the worst kind of literary snob, an even worse kind of American snob, he had carved for himself a useless *niche* in which he posed, oblivious of his vapid deficiencies, as a suave, good-looking god of cultured countenance. Cambridge, England, had nurtured without educating him: and no man was allowed to forget it. In England he consorted with those who caught the right trout in the right streams and in Scotland with those who netted the right salmon in the right lochs; he shot the right pheasants, the right partridges, the right grouse, all in the right places; he stalked the right stags and distributed the right haunches of venison. Nature had endowed him with an enormous opinion of himself but had neglected, unfortunately, to teach him manners. Some years later, when my novels *The Purple Plain* and *The Jacaranda Tree* were enjoying the sunshine of Book Guild choices and an infinite number of translations all over the world, our American-English snob invited me to lunch in London, enjoining me to turn up early at his hotel for an *aperitif*, 'so that we can have a good talk before lunch-time'. When I duly arrived I was greeted with the most mannerless of stony eyes from the god of cultured countenance and coolly informed 'our lunch is off, I'm afraid. I am lunching with the French Ambassador.'

Ellery Sedgwick, the then editor of *The Atlantic Monthly*, was a person of entirely different and superior calibre. In many ways Ellery was not at all unlike an American Edward Garnett; in many others the two men could not have been more different. Both had the same undoubted flair for spotting literary talent where, very often, others failed to do so. Ellery, for example, had been the only editor in America to have detected in Hemingway's celebrated story *Fifty Grand* an entirely new voice: a voice that was to become not only famous and much imitated but in the end legendary. Yet every editor of importance in America had seen *Fifty Grand* and had rejected it. It remained for Ellery to see not only its inherent virtues but the vast talent of the man behind it.

This was merely one example of Ellery discovering genius. At the further end of the scale he proved himself just as adept at discovering the popular. Walking one day into the offices of the little-known periodical *The British Weekly* and asking if the editor had by any chance any MSS. worth taking away to read Ellery was told 'Oh! there's that little thing over there. We're thinking of running it as a Christmas feature.' Ellery took away the MS. of 'that little thing over there' and read it. It was *Good-Bye Mr Chips*, a sentimental piece about an ageing English schoolmaster which, the average judge might have thought, stood about as much chance in the rough market place of American letters as a slim volume of verse about love-in-the-mist by an old maid. Ellery's shrewd instinct told him otherwise. He recognised at once that brand of sentimentalism, just short of sheer mush, for which the American public is as ready to fall as a child for clouds of candy floss. Ellery took *Good-Bye, Mr Chips* home to America, with results that all the world knows. He was in fact a great editor and under him *The Atlantic* became the kind of great periodical which today, alas, neither England nor America knows.

Ellery's contrast with Edward Garnett was largely based on material things. The Garnetts, especially Edward, had a distaste for, even a contempt for, social or worldly success. They even went so far as positively to avoid it. If not the hair-shirt, then the rough blanket of comfort, was theirs. Not so

Ellery Sedgewick. Ellery, impelled by a need and desire to enjoy the worldly comforts and pleasures of life, had also recognised that he lacked the necessary financial and business aptitude to put his finances, modest though they may have been in his younger days, to the best lucrative use. He therefore had the wisdom to find someone who could do it for him. This trustworthy and expert aide had consequently invested shrewdly for Ellery, with the result that he had reached a point, when I first met him in Boston in 1938, of some considerable affluence.

His first act on meeting me was not only to praise with warmth and judgement *Spella Ho* and such short stories of mine that he had read in consequence of admiring the novel, but to invite me for a week-end to his house outside Boston. We drove there, I remember, in a mighty black Cadillac. The house itself had an interesting history and was yet further proof of the fact that the keenness of Ellery's eye was accustomed to see riches where others either saw dross or simply nothing at all. Travelling somewhere in the Southern States, I rather think Georgia, Ellery had spotted one of those gracious white colonial mansions, of the type one instantly associates with *Gone With The Wind*, falling into utter and sad decay. Unwanted and apparently irreparable, it was going for a song. Ellery at once bought it, had it dismantled and put on a schooner and sailed it up to Boston, probably from the port of Charleston or somewhere near.

On its selected site some miles out of Boston it now stood in all its refurbished elegance, white, gracious, spacious and a joy to behold. All about it Ellery and his wife had planted dog-woods, lilacs, syringas and big-flowered shrub roses which were, on my visit, in the prime of their pink, cream and white bloom. Into this setting, in his light shantung suiting, with greyish drooping moustache and hair, Ellery fitted to perfection, looking for all the world like some benign and benevolent gentleman cotton-planter from colonial days when slaves were a dollar a dozen. His adored garden was itself adorable and the fact that I in turn adored it too led to a friendship which, for all our difference in years, warmed and ripened even as we walked from rose to rose in the humid twilight of the May evening. Inside the house Ellery had introduced furniture of the appropriate colonial period, so that all was elegance. He had even papered some rooms with an antique blue-flowered Chinese wall-paper that, on some of his travels, and with his customary acumen, he had deemed to be of the right scale of adornment for his beautiful piece of Palladian colonial. I admired him greatly for it all and not least because for all its elegance and the expense it had clearly entailed, it was warm, friendly, civilised and a home.

Others, it would seem, did not admire Ellery. The Spanish Civil War was still in progress, a hateful piece of civil blood-letting that had aroused the bitterest of passions among the left-wing young, notably intellectuals and poets, on both sides of the Atlantic. It was unfortunate for Ellery that he had strong ties of friendship with the Spanish nobility and the result was a sneer campaign that seemed to label him, in some eyes, as black as Franco himself. I confess I could not follow the reasoning in this and proceeded to take Ellery as I found him: a rare judge of literature, a man civilised, liberal, urbane, highly intelligent, kindly, and for ever eager and willing to help the young in the world of literature. He was, in fact, of a kind which America notably lacks: a gentleman.

We did not, as I remember it, discuss the Spanish Civil War. Instead I rode my hobby horse, as I was also to ride it for the benefit of the younger members of *The Atlantic*, about the certainty of the coming war in Europe. It was immensely to his credit that Ellery listened with gravity to what to others appeared to be the mere prophetic ravings of a young fanatic who was somehow making nonsensical mountains out of the most trivial of mole-hills. Ellery, whose experiences had taken him further afield than Harvard Yard and games with the Red Sox, seemed to think I spoke with reason. That there was little he could do about it hardly mattered. The ear was sympathetic; and it was yet one more reason for the deepening friendship between us. We also spoke much of literature and he asked me, as he had asked Sylvia Townsend Warner, what names among the younger generation, particularly those engaged in the short story, he should watch out for. Like Edward Garnett, he was a man passionately interested in the most difficult of forms and had done much for it in the course of his editorship of *The Atlantic.* I gave him several names of my contemporaries, among them that of Pauline Smith, a South African protégée of Arnold Bennett's, who in a story called *The Pain* had written what I believed, and still believe, to be one of the most touching and beautiful things in the language. Much impressed by it too Ellery at once included it in an anthology he was in process of compiling, including in it stories by Thurber (the famous *Macbeth Murder Mystery*), Arnold Bennett, Katherine Mansfield, Erskine Caldwell, Lord Dunsany, and my own story *The Ox,* to all of which he contributed a penetrative and highly unacademic preface that would have delighted Edward himself. His famous injunction to remember that 'a story is like a horse race' is a classic not to be forgotten. 'It is the start and finish that count most' – a truth to which I was later tempted to add another of my own – 'and of the two I am not sure that the start is not the most important', a truth with which Ellery in fact agreed: 'I am not sure but it is the most difficult accomplishment in fiction'. Subsequent experience has taught me that it is.

My stay in Boston presently afforded me the opportunity of going northward for a few days into Vermont and New Hampshire. It has sometimes been said that the first settlers from Europe could hardly have chosen a worse refuge for their promised land, their new world, than the hinterland of what is now New England. Rocky, barren, inhospitable, it must have seemed to them a sad exchange for England's green and pleasant land. But perhaps they found compensations in the flowering of Vermont and New Hampshire in late spring. There really is of course no late spring in North America and as I drove up into New England, in early June, the heat of summer had already descended, sucking forth sap from grass, flowers and a million trees. The countryside of woods and small mountains very much recalled the Vosges or the Juras. There were many flowers, their names, alas, now forgotten by me, with one exception. I still see, with the wonder I saw it then, the great cherry-and-gold lady's slipper orchid growing unmolested along the roadsides, common as dandelions in an English spring.

All this prompted me to recall Sarah Orne Jewett's *The Country of the Pointed Firs*. This country of hers is, of course, not Vermont or New Hampshire, but the more northerly Maine. I already knew her book well, having been schooled to it by Edward Garnett, and it was now good to be on the fringe of her country of the pointed firs and that of her sister book *The Only Rose*.

Sarah Orne Jewett was descended from a Yorkshire emigrant who went to America in the mid seventeenth century, but she also inherited French blood on her mother's side. There would seem to be little doubt that her fastidious and perceptive sensitivity and what has been called by one critic 'the purity of her transplanted and strictly preserved culture' owed much to her knowledge and feeling for French literature, through which she was much influenced by Flaubert, who may be considered her master. She was an insistent admirer of *Madame Bovary* at a time when certain English critics were being decidedly sniffy, if not worse, about that novel and as a result her work, at its best, is faithful to Flaubert's own dictum – '*écrire la vie ordinaire comme on écrit l'histoire*'. She was a woman of delicate health; and no man, except her father, ever seems to have interested her. Her work therefore contains no clash of passions, no blighting disharmony; but it has everywhere in it the candour, the clarity and the truth whose expression she must have learned largely from the author of *Madame Bovary*. Her work therefore, for all its apparent modesty and surface delicacy and in spite of its faults, including occasional lapses into near sentimentality, touches chords that lie deeper than they would appear to do. It is consequently deceptive. It is not superficial and remains yet one more example of the eternal truth that violence is not necessarily synonymous with strength and that delicacy can express, in the right hands, profundities that sound and fury so often cannot.

As far back as 1904, in an extremely perceptive article in *The Atlantic Monthly*, a writer praised and explained Sarah Orne Jewett's work in these words: 'I always think of her as one who, hearing New England accused of being a bleak land without beauty, passes confidently over the snow, and by the grey rock and past the dark fir tree, to a southern bank, and there, brushing away the decaying leaves, triumphantly shows to the fault-finder a spray of the trailing arbutus. And I should like, for my part, to add this: that the fragrant, retiring exquisite flower, which I think she would say is the symbol of the New England virtue, is the symbol of her own modest and delightful art.'

That is splendidly put; but in an equally perceptive and generous preface to *The Country of the Pointed Firs* Willa Cather goes even further. (I have incidentally never understood the exclusion of Willa Cather's name from the roll of Nobel prize winners). 'If I were asked to name,' Willa Cather says, 'three books which have the possibility of a long, long life, I would say at once *The Scarlet Letter*, *Huckleberry Finn* and *The Country of the Pointed Firs*. I can think of no others that confront time and change so serenely.' That Sarah Orne Jewett's art was modest and limited, as was Jane Austen's, does not detract, as I have already indicated, from its perfections. 'To note an artist's limitations is but to define his genius.' Sarah Orne Jewett took her material as she found it and made no attempt to adorn it. She wrote cf 'fisher folk and sea-side villages; with juniper pastures and lonely farms, neat grey country houses and delightful, well seasoned old men and women. That, when one thinks of it in a flash, is New England . . . She learned early to love her country for what it was. She happened to have the right nature, the right temperament, to see it so – and to understand by intuition the deeper meaning of what she saw.' Small wonder that Edward Garnett had seen her in precisely this same light, recognising in her, as he had recognised in the

Australian Henry Lawson, a talent that had been able to extract from apparently unpromising, even ugly, material, things of a touching beauty. Parts of Lawson are comparable with O'Henry; part has even been compared with Tolstoy. I cannot easily conjure up any figure with whom to compare Sarah Orne Jewett. But like Lawson she points to Garnett's eternal truth: that the novel, (in her case the short story) 'can be anything according to the hands which use it'. To create beauty out of ugliness, to make the rock flower and the stern New England fir tree blossom was indeed, as Willa Cather pointed out, 'a gift from the heart'.

If you would savour something of this 'gift from the heart', taste the following sample of it:

'I stopped to pick some blackberries that twinkled at me like beads among their dry vines, and two or three yellow birds that fluttered up from the leaves of a thistle, and then came back again, as if they had complacently discovered that I was only an overgrown yellow bird, in a strange disguise but perfectly harmless. They made me feel as if I were an intruder, though they did not offer to peck at me, and we parted company very soon. It was good to stand at last on the great shoulder of the hill. The wind was coming in from the sea, there was a fine fragrance from the pines, and the air grew sweeter every moment.'

How wonderfully evocative, how beautifully descriptive and how full of scent and atmosphere that deceptively simple language is, so supremely typical of her art.

I returned from New England and Sarah Orne Jewett's country to a Boston growing steamier and steamier and more and more unpleasant every day. I had now finished my task of pruning and shaping *Spella Ho* nearer to the American's heart's desire, though whether it was of any remote assistance to the insular American reader I never knew. I had dollars in my pocket and the experience of taking the pruning knife to a large and substantial piece of prose had served to impress on me a truth all would-be short story writers should remember: 'there is no such thing as the sacred word.' The pruning of a story is exactly like that of pruning an apple tree: in comes light and the branches bring forth fruit in greater abundance.

I was now anxious to get home, to see my England, my garden, my family, my year old son. I think, before I departed, that I preached yet again from the gospel of Europe, warning of the wrath that was at hand, and I knew that even the young among my American friends had neither ear nor desire to listen. We went once, I remember, down to Boston's water-front, to the great meat market there and ate a positive acreage of steak for dinner. You sat on roughish chairs and at roughish tables and ordered steaks of whatever size you thought you could defeat from the vast carcasses that hung around. The whole atmosphere was somehow a saloon cum sailing clipper affair that might have come out of Herman Melville. The waiters were wild men gifted with salty humour. You expected fights to break out, as in Wild Western saloons, and through the low windows of the restaurant you could see the spars and smoke stacks of shipping lying at anchor in Boston's harbour, beside a water-front that didn't seem to have changed much since the legendary Tea Party. It was all as far removed from the white moustached kippers in a Boston club as a Covent Garden pub is removed from a Paris fashion salon. I loved it, remember it with pleasure and shall never forget its salty, beefy, maritime, Wild West air.

Financially secure for the first time in my life, I set sail for England in July, well knowing, in my heart, ironically, that she was standing on the edge of doom.

XIII

I was wrong; my immediate overwhelming impression was of arriving in paradise. I went about for some days in a state of semi-drugged, ethereal wonder. I simply couldn't believe that the garden I had only lately made from the wreckage of an abandoned farm-yard was real and moreover that it was actually mine. It stood rich with lilies golden and white, delphiniums, salvias, petunias, geraniums, roses, verbenas and a hundred other things dear to my heart. There was a fragrance and an air about it that couldn't have been matched, as it seemed to me, by any garden of Eden.

Outside, in the meadows, hay was still being gathered in and the fragrance of it was heavy, as only the fragrance of hay can be, on the July air. Meadowsweet, I think my favourite among all England's wild midsummer flowers, clotted the dykes with cream. The hedgerows themselves were rich with wild rose and honeysuckle. The iron rocks of New England and Miss Jewett's pointed firs faded away against the picture of our dark Turkey oaks' brooding shadow over resting sheep in the meadows or the splendour of upland beechwoods on the hills above us. There might be no noble lady's slipper orchids, cherry-and-gold, on the open roadside, but purple loosestrife already illuminated the tranquil waters of the little river at the foot of the lane, the sweet chestnuts were in flower and the wheat had on it that miracle of bloom, half blue, half green, that clothes it just before ripeness. If there was any place where my heart justly belonged this was it.

The hills lured us to picnics. Armed with kettle, tea and food, as Madge and I had long before armed ourselves on excursions to the Bedford Ouse, we used to go on hot, breezy afternoons to a spot that lay wide open to westward, southward and the distant sea. Here had once been a copse, now chopped down. The destruction of its trees had left a certain desolation but had let in light, with the result that nature had responded with a new paradise of flowers born from seed that had long slept in shadow. It is to my regret that I never took a count of the myriads of wild flowers that you could find within the compass of that small destroyed piece of woodland; but in July it put on its supreme floral feast of marjoram and willow herb and rock-rose and burnet and honeysuckle and camomile and a host of other things, including occasional orchids and some stray rarity such as a solitary maroon columbine. Among all this grew a vast crop of wild strawberries with, if I remember correctly, a few wild raspberries too.

We used to gather wild strawberries by the basket: brilliant little crimson-scarlet jewels with that rare sweet-sharp flavour of their own. Their own special fragrance lingers too with the fragrance of those days of high summer, when even on the hottest days the air, coming in from the sea, had in it that certain oceanic tang that saved it from sultriness. Often, tired of gathering the infinitude of strawberries and tired even of the sound and echo of children's voices, I merely found myself a spot among the fallen pine cones and lay back, sun-washed and half-asleep, drenched in a kind of herbal cloud of flower-scent, sun-baked earth and odours illimitable, little dreaming that presently, above these incomparably enriched hills, in parts hardly changed since Jane Austen stayed in one of the great houses in a great park just below, the flower of a new generation would be killing itself in the first great air battle, and perhaps the last, of all time. Without knowing it I was picnicking on the new front line. But there was a taste of wild strawberries on my lips and for a time I no longer cared what the author of *Mein Kampf* was up to.

But one cannot, as I think one of the poets of the Romantic Movement pointed out, live for ever on quince jelly. The summer began to pass into autumn; or as is the way when political evils are being hatched, August came in like an uneasy hen aware of predatory rats hiding and ready to strike in her run. All my fears about Europe began to come back, grey, dark and finally black. I had been too young to express to any really

The Granary

explicit extent my bitterness at the First World War; and all I had done, in a short-lasting aftermath, was to write a few acid verses, now lost, for a periodical called *The New Clarion*. But now I felt it was time for me to get up and say something more.

I think I can best explain what was in my mind at that time by going back once more to the Garnetts, this time to quote David: 'War is the worst of the epidemic diseases which afflict mankind and the great genetrix of many others. While it lasts it impairs the powers of rational judgement; millions are crippled and die and the accumulated riches of empires are destroyed by fanaticism and fear; cruelty and callousness are infectious and these toxins of the spirit make the unconscionable claim that all personal life, happiness, art and human expression must be subordinated to war, or serve it. That exorbitant demand is constantly proclaimed and has to be violently contradicted. Life, love and happiness go on under almost any conditions. Indeed they are quickened by war as the beauty of a face may be quickened by fever.'

These words had not been written in the late summer of

1938, but they would, if written, have expressed almost to perfection what I felt about Europe's hopeless malaise. That it was hopeless was, it seemed to me, beyond doubt; that it might have been avoided if physicians of intelligence had been brought in soon enough, arriving at the right diagnosis, seemed to me to be also beyond dispute. Instead we had had as Prime Minister a man who looked something like a benign hop-sack with a pipe stuck in his mouth, followed by one who looked half like a Baptist church deacon and half like a provincial commercial traveller trying to sell sewing machines. While the voice of Churchill cried in the wilderness Chamberlain watched birds and prayed, I have no doubt, as H. G. Wells' mother had done, for guidance from 'the right quarter'. But when wild boars are ravaging and savaging the countryside it is of small use to chase them with Pekinese lap-dogs. The author of *Mein Kampf* had a pet rude name for Chamberlain; and though even in our so-called permissive society I will refrain from writing it down, apt though it was, I will nevertheless note that it is one with which Chaucer would have been familiar.

Munich was therefore inevitable. I will refrain from going over its lamentable time-table of missed trains and wrong connections and arrivals at wrong destinations. For me it merely represented the culmination of almost a decade of foreboding, fear and finally fright. I was at a football match when I heard its cruel, sanctimonious, funereal knell and I wasn't far away from an impulse to shoot, if not myself, at least the guardians of 'peace in our time'. I thought greatly, then, of my children: my two beautiful daughters and my young son, impeccable as always in his cream shantung jacket. My world, which had at last seemed about to blossom to the full, was instead about to be blighted, together with that of unlimited millions of others. I conceived and shared no illusion whatever about this. War's inevitability had been as predictable as an eclipse of the sun. This was the eclipse and I was mightily, bitterly angry.

I at once, perhaps mistakenly, perhaps without thought

enough, determined to put this mood of embittered outrage into a novel. What was perhaps an even greater mistake was that I was going to attempt to see the sequence of events through the eyes of a woman, always an attitude fraught with extreme dangers for a man. Perhaps I reasoned that when it comes to war the female vision, driven by intuitions, sees things with sharper, clearer, more penetrative power. At all events it was not to be a happy book; nor was it to be born of the Northamptonshire backgrounds that had nurtured *The Poacher*, *The Fallow Land* and *Spella Ho*. My landscape must now, I felt, be widened. I was to chronicle the story of a woman bitterly bereaved by the loss of a brother in the First World War and her attempt to find, through a series of associations with men, some her lovers, the fraternal love of which she had been robbed. Not an easy theme. Nevertheless I felt that I now possessed the technical accomplishment with which to tackle it, as well as the force of moral outrage as to war and its futilities to provide the emotional and spiritual motor power. I was also convinced, and indeed still am, that it is a bad thing for a writer to stand still; it is a poor exercise that never takes him beyond well-charted ground; it is excellent, in my view, when a writer bites off a little more than he can chew. The comfort of merely satisfying a well-tried formula offers no adventure. If adventure in turn offers risk and in turn begets failure, then the writer must set out to learn what failure teaches.

The early conception of a novel or story greatly depends, it often seems to me, on setting it in the right key. Great geniuses in music often seem to make such choices in their art by some divine instinct. It is by no means so easy in literature, where there are no rules and no fixed set of keys, either minor or major, from which the writer can make his immediate or final choice. The composer knows more or less what something will sound like in C sharp minor or in F major. The writer has no way of knowing any such thing. He must invent his own key. If the key he selects is right then it is likely that his music and its themes will flow from it naturally. If the key he selects is wrong then he is likely to find himself in frustrations and troubles of every kind.

It is now my considered opinion that I somehow chose the wrong key for this novel. As to what key I ought to have chosen I have never since been able to determine. It was a book of almost unrelieved melancholy: of a woman searching for a kind of happiness that was not to be found and who could not break the fraternal stranglehold that everywhere frustrated her and for which she blamed the undying stupidity and waste of war. To the very end it had what is called a down-beat and it also went on and on, as Stephen Crane had complained of Tolstoy's *War and Peace*, like Texas.

Some time before this David Garnett had joined the firm of Jonathan Cape in his father's old capacity as reader. As Rupert Hart-Davis was still occupying an editorial chair at No. 30 Bedford Square I knew that I had at that address two allies greatly sympathetic to my work. I therefore had great hopes of the novel, more especially as Madge and I were expecting a fourth child by the latter part of 1939. The dollars earned by *Spella Ho* had now largely been used up during the long arduous months of writing something like 150,000 words and it was now highly essential that my novel should succeed and so raise in some slight degree the temperature of my bank balance.

To my infinite chagrin and pain my two allies turned out to be critics of the most remorseless nature. Having read my MS, they took me out to lunch and proceeded to hurl at me a critical bombardment whose plan they might well have borrowed from Edward. I had spawned another monster; I was the begetter of a two-headed, crooked Mongolian monstrosity whose body would have to be put somewhere darkly away. There is no record on paper, as there was with the letters from Edward, as to what was said on that dismal day, but the words are no less incisively ingrained on the memory for all that. It made it all the worse for me that I had the highest regard for both David's and Rupert's judgement. That they had a few soothing words to offer about a passage here and a passage there did nothing to assuage or disillusion me. Unwarily and stupidly I had fallen again into a great trap, having apparently learned nothing from having fallen into it before. The result was that I wasn't merely angry with myself; I was angry that the anger I felt for war and its stupidities hadn't produced the resounding bang for which I had hoped but merely a flabby moan. 'The path of art, endlessly difficult' indeed.

And where on earth, I could only ask myself, was the path going now? In this new and embittering disappointment, entirely of my own making, I could only ask myself if I really knew, after all, what I was doing as a writer? Was there in me some leaden vein of obtuseness that would never be taught, would never learn? With utter melancholy I could only tell myself that there must be. Moreover I found myself in such a state of depression that I saw no way of possibly putting it right. I had somewhere taken a wrong turning and had wandered off into a morass, a pitiless swamp forest of tragically fatuous entanglements from which I could see no way out.

By this time sand-bags were being piled about the streets of London; gas-masks were being issued; the full stretched wires that had been growing tauter and tauter and nearer and nearer to breaking point ever since Munich were at last at explosive point; and within a week or two war had at last begun.

A pretty picture: war; another novel ill-conceived, a failure; a general chaos of mistrust and uncertainty in the publishing world; a total assured income of about thirteen pounds a week; a fourth child soon expected. Above all, perhaps, a shattering, embittering loss of confidence.

I do not suppose that in the entire history of art, whether of writing, literature, painting, sculpture or even the art of inventing things scientific or mechanical, there has ever been anyone who did not, at some time or other, suffer this erosion of confidence in himself and his art: the shrivelling notion that he has been drained dry, that imagination has withered or died completely, above all that creative impulse will never be reborn. It has been well said that a writer may ask his reader to believe anything he can *make* him believe: to which one can only add that first of all the writer must himself believe in what he wishes the reader to believe. When such capacity for convincing himself of belief is missing, dormant or dead then the writer is lost in a desert, moribund, spiritless, forlorn.

I have said before, and it will perhaps do no harm to say it again, that the general public sees only what it is allowed to see: the picture successfully achieved, the book conclusively wrought, a pleasing whole, perhaps a success. It cannot and does not see the fragmentary, unfinished, blighted, abandoned bits of jig-saw that lie behind the façade, mouldering in the studio, gathering dust in the study drawer. It probably remains wholly unaware that such things ever happen to writers, still less to those who have attained a name and even a degree of success, and it probably labours under the further delusion that once reputation and acclaim have been achieved everything the writer touches automatically turns to gold. I assure them it is not so. Furthermore it is just as probable that the public never has the remotest notion that many writers dislike, or even loathe, their finished products, and never, after the final pain of proof-reading, ever read a word of them again. If this be true of the work that is finished and appears to satisfy its creator's self-critical demand, what of the ugly duckling, the two-headed Mongolian disaster, the thing that should never have left the womb?

In the early autumn of 1939 my own answer, from the pit of despair, was a simple one: I would never, never attempt another novel.

But some time before this catastrophe left its savage mark on me something far more pleasant had occurred. It seemed to me that if the lights in Europe were going out, as in fact they were, it might be a good thing to take a last look at them before Nazism and war cast their final obliterating shadow. In the early spring of that year, therefore, some six months or so before war actually broke out, Madge and I decided to try to find spring on the Dalmatian coast, taking in Venice on the way. We had little money, travelled third class, by slow train, ate our own food and slept on the compartment seats. When after a not very comfortable night we had crossed the Simplon and arrived at Domodossola, the snow was six or eight feet deep. It faded as we entrained along Lake Maggiore, curiously glassy in its winter suspense, and then in the warm afternoon sunshine across a Lombardy Plain without life, every dyke and water stretch rimmed with a crust of white ice.

'I have never in my life seen a town more marvellous than Venice. It is perfectly enchanting, brilliance, joy, life. Instead of streets and roads there are canals; instead of cabs, gondolas . . . And the evenings. My God! one might almost die at the strangeness of it . . . warmth, stillness, stars. A gondola goes by, hung with lanterns. In it are a double bass, violins, a guitar, a mandolin, a cornet, two or three ladies, several men, and one hears singing and music. They sing from operas. What voices! . . . For us poor and oppressed Russians it is easy to go out of our minds here in a world of beauty, wealth and freedom. One longs to remain here for ever.'

The words are not mine; it is nearly eighty years since Tchehov ecstatically wrote them on his first visit to Venice and the astonishing thing is, as I can testify, that they might have been written yesterday. I think perhaps I have been to Venice nearly a score of times since that first visit of ours in February 1939 but the ecstasy Tchehov felt and that I experienced likewise has never faded. 'Of all the places I have visited Venice has left me the loveliest memories', Tchehov went on to say and one can only echo him a thousand times. The February air may have been colder, sharper than iced champagne, but champagne it was. The streets were almost empty but that merely gave a better view of palaces, bridges, dark alleyways, dark still waters. The enchantment was made all the more complete in that the Hotel Bauer Grunwald, clearly thinking we were a honeymoon couple, did us the honour of giving us a bridal suite instead of the tiny box we had paid for.

Whether, in spite of the fact that we had three children, we looked extremely young and naïve I never knew; but the honeymoon myth was repeated on the pleasant little Italian steamer on which we presently sailed down the Adriatic. A party of Germans, gross, thick headed, dutifully marshalled and led by 'our führer', a little courier of peremptory voice and manner who would have done credit to the author of *Mein Kampf* himself, eyed us with covert, curious and calculating glances that finally offered them only one answer: just married.

To make the picture one of even greater fascination Madge was also knitting something.

All down the Adriatic it rained in grey, gloomy torrents, but 'our führer' was totally undismayed. Tomorrow, in Dubrovnik, all would be sunlight, a perfection of blue sky, the warmth of spring. Oranges would glow on the trees; narcissi and iris and anemones would greet us as we landed. And so it was. The morning was one of pure brilliance; oranges did indeed glow like lamps from the trees; mimosa glowed everywhere in yellow clouds; purple iris and white anemones shone in the gardens; and over it all glowed that amazing piece of ancient beauty, Dubrovnik, of purest white stone, its great walls encircling a city in which, I believe, there is no house later than the eighteenth century.

Some words in Tchehov's letter of 1891 cause me to pause and think: 'For us poor and oppressed Russians it is easy to go out of our minds'. Similarly, in 1939, the Germans would have us believe that they too were poor and oppressed: not enough living space, no colonies, a criminal craving to possess what belonged to others and what they supposed, by God's right or Hitler's, belonged to them. The sheep-like excursions of the party aboard the steamer had a tragi-comic air. 'Lead us,' they seemed to say, 'no matter where, and we will follow.' It is only fair to add that once or twice they kindly invited us to follow too, so that we found ourselves driving out, in large open Fiats, in freezing Yugoslavian dawns, to visit remote places inland, pausing occasionally on the way at some primitive inn to knock back, at a penny a glass, fiery draughts of plum brandy as a means of partially thawing out throats frozen solid. High beyond us lay black mountains; on the lower slopes pitiful little fields scratched from nothing and fenced by low stone walls, were all that cultivation had to show. The market places of little villages had an air of starved weariness: a few goats and hens, mules, a bunch or two of root vegetables and once what we were told, with some pride, was donkey ham. From houses no bigger and better than pig-sties pretty, laughing but unwashed peasant girls ogled and eyed us, giving the impression that for a few *dinars* nothing would be denied. The men were moustached, martial and incredibly handsome and in the streets elderly women stole furtively past, faces covered to the eyes, black-shrouded ghosts of the days of Turkish rule.

In the town, where there was still much of Turkish influence too, we discovered a restaurant that might have come out of the old Austro-Hungarian Empire. It seemed to belong to the Vienna of Strauss or old Budapest; it reminded me of an enchanting little film *Sunday Affair*, which is rather like a combination of Molnar and Tchehov: everybody having hours of time in which to sit over a newspaper, a cup of coffee and a glass of water, gossiping, arguing, doing nothing. A little scarlet-uniformed negro boy stood in the vestibule waiting to take your coat; the waiters wore the old traditional mid-European white aprons; in one corner a motley orchestra scraped away tunes from Strauss, Liszt and Dvorak. To me it was also a corner of dying Europe, a Europe whose death had been criminally advanced by having its heart, the old Austro-Hungarian Empire, forcibly gouged out, leaving a sinister crater filled by doctrinaire ferment, oppression and murder ever since.

But for us, during those all too short two weeks, the sun remained for ever brilliant, with the premature warmth of April. We wandered, one warm Sunday afternoon, into a little coastal town and heard music, from fiddles mostly, coming gaily from an open-windowed house. We stopped to listen; we even peered in at the windows. Within a second or two a joyful young man rushed out, seized my hand as if I were the returning prodigal son, and dragged us both inside, as if we were indeed the lost that had at last been found. We were at once in the centre of a wedding feast. We could speak no word of Yugoslavian, and no Yugoslav could speak a word of English. Our language for the rest of that gay afternoon consisted entirely of smiles. We ate much sweet cake and drank much champagne and were altogether the objects of so much delighted attention that we began to feel that perhaps, after all, the hotel in Venice and the Germans on the little Italian steamer had been right: that it was we, and not the bride and bridegroom, who were on honeymoon.

And perhaps, as I look back, it was a honeymoon. We had never been able to afford one anyway, but had through sheer lack of cash to go straight from church to the Granary. But if honeymoon over-romanticizes that brief sunlit visit to Dalmatia in spring it cannot and will never detract from the brilliance of the memory of that last look at Europe before its lights went out. It remains as vividly and affectionately in memory as a harvest field in childhood, the feel of wet watercress on my hands, the milk-warm touch of a thrush's egg against the mud basin of its nest in an April hedgerow.

That it was also sad there is no doubt. But just as illness magnifies and even beautifies, so sadness can itself heighten or deepen the illumination and beauty of memory. At any rate I returned to England refreshed, indeed more than refreshed. The past, even the immediate past, was a dead body that had to be buried. The erosion of confidence, that can spread like gangrene if left untreated, had to be checked. It was no time for prolonged inquests, self-recrimination, self-pity. The medicine, I well knew, was within myself.

If the lights in Europe were rapidly going out they were not yet going out, I told myself, in me. Nor were they going to be extinguished by the mere failure of yet another novel. Until the body itself is dead nothing can kill imagination. Imagination is the soul of the artist. My only way of expressing it, I told myself, was in words and there were, I felt, thank God, plenty of words left in me yet.

XIV

Readers of the poetry of the First World War will know that there runs through it a common note: the agony of the enlightened and enriched beauty of nature on the one hand and the contrast of appalling negation and the useless holocaust of blood and filth on the other. The first spring skylark singing above the craters of battlefields, the first breaking green shoot on a landscape populated by shattered ghouls that were once trees, the brief blessed salve of a few English summer days of leave, the soldier's relief from rats, lice, gas and the whole Dante-esque hell of pitiless, pointless slaughter. These excruciating, ironical contrasts are the things that give that war poetry much of its poignancy.

Though war had only just been declared in September 1939, and then not very martially, there was something of the same feeling in the air. Suddenly all of nature and its beauty, all that mattered of earth and flower and root and grass, became unbearably heightened in value. All too often, as I have said, it is in little things that memory enshrines its more precious moments; and so it is with September 1939. The weather was hot and dry. The wheat, uncut as yet in the fields, stood strong and straight, the ears untouched by rain and burned by sun until they were the colour of brandy. They seemed to me to have a great steadfastness about them, those fields of corn; and I felt that nothing could blemish them or lay them low.

In the warm sultry evenings Madge and I, she tired of being played football with by her fourth child, who wasn't to appear on the field until November, used to take brief slow walks in the falling darkness along the village green, listening to an odd plane flying somewhere, gazing at the odd white trumpet-shape of a searchlight somewhere far off, wondering if war really had begun or if, in a strange way, it was all an hallucination sent to mock us. And again it is the very smallest things that enshrine those evenings in memory to such perfection that they might have happened only yesterday. In this case it was glow-worms. I couldn't ever recall having seen glow-worms before. But there they suddenly were: tiny greenish lights in the roadside grass. Though so minute, they seemed on these taut, sultry evenings to glow like indistinguishable beacons. You felt that they were saying 'Don't despair. The lights are not out. We are small but we are unquenchable. Look at us and take heart a little.' We did indeed look, every evening, and take heart. The strange thing is that I have never seen a glow-worm since.

On a more practical level I had to do something to keep my family on the one hand and prevent myself from going mad on the other. If the times had been bad for authors at the time of the General Strike in 1926, they were little short of catastrophic now. I found it impossible to work creatively. The entire emotional and physical climate had now an air of senseless suspense about it, now a furious desperation as if you were on one of those moving staircases that are going down when you want to go up, thus trapping you into the frantic and crazy gymnastics of an escape that never happens. The so-called year of peace between Munich and September 1939 had at least seemed to be leading somewhere, even if only to the final confrontation of war. The phoney autumn of war was, instead, a trap; you were held in a vice from which you could get neither point nor escape of any kind.

The evacuation of children from London to the countryside was the first of the revolutions that were brought to us; and human nature, I fear, came out of it badly. Madge and I, she as always in the forefront of battles for good causes, proceeded to go on patient excursions about the immediate countryside, looking and begging for homes where children could stay. It was astounding how, suddenly, on these visits, the size of houses dramatically diminished. 'We only got one spare bed-room and his old mother uses that.' Ferocious old couples shut their doors in our faces. Old ladies comfortably supported by private means suddenly produced doctors' certificates for sciatica, bronchitis, bad legs, rheumatoid arthritis, stone-in-the-kidney or any of the thousand ailments that noisy children are bad for. Nevertheless the children came, estranged in a land of trees and orchards and hops and cows; and for a time their East End parents came too, but all too briefly. The horrors of rural England ('only one bloody pub, only one bloody shop') were altogether too much for most of them, so that they fled back with speed and relief to Lambeth and the Mile End Road, glad to be back in the civilised world of sand-bags, four-ale bars and street markets, leaving our Kentish cornfields to waste upon the desert air.

When winter came at last it was ferocious. Blizzards left their mark in vast carved drifts, sometimes the shape of great sea-breakers caught and frozen at their very crests, sometimes in

giant pure bosoms milkily overhanging the hedgerows, sometimes in shapes like those of huge basking white whales, their flanks ridged in long stream-lined fissures. The road clearing equipment and chemicals that now clear snow-bound roads in an hour or two were not part of the war-time scene. Snow froze in jagged corrugations everywhere, making any passage into town a nightmare. Once it snowed for 72 hours without stopping, leaving us trapped for days in an arctic prison.

In these frustrating circumstances – the winter, as I recall it, lasted at its worst for seven to eight weeks – I felt that writing of some sort was my only salvation. Still locked completely in cold, uncreative mood, I now turned my thoughts to something that I had had at the back of my mind, awaiting birth, for some time. Rich as the 1920's and 1930's had been for the short story on both sides of the Atlantic, I had continually found myself searching in vain for a book that would put this fruitful sphere of its development into words, both critical and explorative, and perspective. There had been books, most of them not good and many of them merely dealing with the aspect of stories for purely commercial markets, on how to write short stories and how to market them successfully. This was not what I had in mind. Writing, like medicine and gardening, is not an exact science. There are no rules and I do not believe that it can be taught, even basically taught, in the way for example that painters are first taught to draw. In essence it is a process of discovery and it was as a guide to this discovery of what had been done and was being done in the realm of the short story that I now began *The Modern Short Story*. It was in no sense to be a text-book on how the short story could or was to be written; it was to be illustrative of what some of its greatest exponents, from Poe to Hemingway, had achieved.

If I began the book as much as an essay in personal distraction, at a time when all creative impulse was dead in me, I can only say that I ended up by producing a critical survey which has been in constant use in schools and universities ever since, on both sides of the Atlantic. Though I had had no intention whatsoever of dispensing any plan or plans as to how a short story might be written it was inevitable that my predilection for certain methods, including my own – I had already published more than two hundred short stories – could not be kept out. The chapters on Tchehov and Maupassant, American writers after Poe (e.g. Herman Melville, Bret Harte, Ambrose Bierce, O. Henry, Jack London, Stephen Crane and so on) Gogol and Turgenev, Tolstoy and Katherine Mansfield, the Irish School (Moore, O'Faolain, O'Connor and Joyce) and the new American renaissance of Hemingway, Faulkner, Sherwood Anderson, Katherine Ann Porter and so on all served to indicate the many shapes and directions I felt the modern short story capable of taking. I had also some strong opposite prejudices. I berated the worst of Coppard while cordially praising the best; I said what I had to say of the tedium of

Henry James by saying nothing; I lambasted Kipling, who in his loud vulgarities still seems to me the Wagner of literature, than which I can think of no worse insult; and I made the discovery of an interesting piece of near-plagiarism by no less a person than Somerset Maugham.

Compare, if you will, the following two passages:

The first:

'Like other rich men at the beginning of this century he ate and drank a good deal more than was enough to keep him in health. Even his excellent constitution was not proof against a prolonged course of overfeeding and what we should now consider over-drinking. His liver would not infrequently get out of order and he would come down to breakfast looking yellow about the eyes.'

And the second:

'I fancy that life is more amusing now than it was forty years ago and I have a notion that people are more amiable. They may have been worthier then, possessed of more substantial knowledge; I do not know. I know they were more cantankerous; they ate too much, many of them drank too much and they took too little exercise. Their livers were out of order and their digestions often impaired.'

Maugham or Samuel Butler? Which is which? I really don't think that a studied reading of these two passages will give any greater clue than a cursory one. Maugham's style is so much in the manner of Butler's that one might have supposed it to be the work of a young and apprenticed hand, guided by early hero-worship, instead of that of the author of *Cakes and Ale*, from which the second passage is taken, the first passage being from *The Way of All Flesh*.

The long savage winter ended. In the middle of it our younger son, Jonathan, was born: a restless young gentleman of quick brain ungifted with an ability to sit still for more than two seconds at a time but an astonishing opposite capacity for meticulous care in the work he now does, which is to put complicated soundtracks into highly expensive films.

When the long snows finally gave way to spring, which in turn was to give way to an almost faultless summer, you felt once again assailed by the old excruciating paradox, that of beauty flourishing, heightened and refined, against a background of foreboding, fear, and impending disaster. Primroses had never looked so eternally symbolic of spring, or so pure and lovely; daffodils may have touched Wordsworth's heart back in the early nineteenth century, but they never came as near to breaking ours as in that spring, bitterly momentous as it was to be, of 1940. Everything about the land, the woods and the garden was of an infinite, searching preciousness. I remember once how an American visitor to England during war-time, when things were at their blackest and lowest, telling me of how he was impressed above all not by the fortitude, resilience and sheer guts of Londoners under stress and fire but by the way they would stand in silence by some half-shuttered flower-shop window and gaze with solemn, hungry rapture at the few blossoms on sale inside. That is much as we felt that spring.

Meanwhile, over in France (where in certain R.A.F. messes officers were known to have complained bitterly that the price of champagne had gone up from 3/6 to 3/8 a bottle) the snows too had melted and the warmth of spring had cleared and dried the roads. The stage was, in fact, set for battle; the phoney war was over. All that had been predicted in the aptly named *Insanity Fair* was now printed on the programme; it was merely unfortunate that certain readers of the programme were still either wearing the wrong spectacles or had left them somewhere in some dust-ridden pigeon-hole. The plan across the channel was well laid; its execution was dramatically, diabolically swift.

In the south country we lived all this time with a feeling of nakedness, as on stretched wires. The notion that we were also to be shot at as we lay there stretched out was not exactly a pleasant one and we never spoke of it. But it was there on the first exquisite days of May, when both hawthorn in the purity of its whiteness and oak-flower in its bountiful olive-yellow which always seem to me the great symbols of spring coming up to its great overflowing, (I wrote once of may blossom as being 'the risen cream of all the milkiness of May-time') were of excruciating tautness. It became clearer and clearer every day that France was rotten. Like a neglected and diseased tree the central heart of whose trunk was mere fungoid pulp while its outward exterior looked sound it was about to fall at the first well-directed gust of wind. It did fall; and, strange and contradictory though it may now sound, great was the rejoicing, at least on my part. I shall for ever believe that on the day that France fell in the spring of 1940 many of the people of Southern England – I do not and cannot speak for others farther north – felt that a great load had been lifted from their hearts and shoulders. They were alone at last and they were glad to be alone. Only we ourselves could now be traitors to ourselves. Nor did we need the words of Churchill, mighty in comfort and inspiration though they were, to tell us that that at least would never happen.

There followed a Gilbertian situation: serious enough at the time, terrifyingly futile and comic in memory, and now enshrined in a television show, *Dad's Army*. I belonged to it. I might have been better employed making marmalade. I was issued with a rifle. I was terrified of keeping the rifle in the house because of the children and equally terrified of taking it on Sunday morning parades in case I had accidentally left a bullet in it and it would go off and shoot somebody, probably the Major. I abhorred shooting and hunting in any case and as I crawled about on my belly on dark summer nights in woods, fields and churchyards, looking for an invisible enemy, I never once felt like a hunter but only the hunted. Sometimes in the dead of night air-raid sirens went off and I, ever eager for duty, would be up and dressed and at the ready, rifle in hand, in a matter of seconds, to report to H.Q. across the village green. Whenever I did so there was never another single soul in sight; I for ever got the feeling that I was defending England utterly alone. After an impossible interval a few sleep-drunk comrades would join me, accompanied eventually by an elderly lady from next door, so evidently eager to give her all in defence of her native land that she could scarcely walk for an armoury of gas-masks, tin helmets, stirrup pumps, buckets, spades, whistles, vacuum flasks of tea and cocoa, shawls, scarves, gas-capes and almost everything else of a defensive and offensive nature except a pike and a suit of armour. Invariably, under the weight of her defences, she fell flat on her face, by which time the siren for the all clear had sounded.

The German soldier being noted for a high degree of well-disciplined efficiency I have grave doubts as to whether Dad's Army would have lasted very long in defence of its Kentish woods and hop-fields. Resolution is not enough; I had resolution in plenty but of military tactics I knew about as much as a rabbit being cornered by a stoat. Our official warning note that invasion was or was about to take place was the ringing of the local church bells and I well remember a morning when, buttoning up my trousers in the lavatory, I was absolutely sure that I suddenly heard the dread clang of bells from our local tower. I hastily sat down again. Happily it was a false alarm.

While this tragi-farce was going on at home something of infinitely greater seriousness was going on across the channel.

There was about to be made the most momentous decision of the war. It is of course the easiest possible thing to marshal figures in order to prove points and whether the following figures are strictly accurate matters little now; the situation adds up to the same thing. At the time of the German invasion of Norway the R.A.F. probably had, with the French, some 1400 fighter aircraft as against the Luftwaffe's 1500; but in second line fighter strength the Germans were probably stronger by 1000 than British and French fighters combined. Of bombers the Germans had a first line strength of probably some 2500, or about 3½ times the R.A.F. strength, together with reserves of about 4500, or about 2½ times the strength of our reserves. On all counts, therefore, excluding the defection of France, we were very much outnumbered.

Worse still, our losses in the late spring of that year in France were frighteningly heavy: so heavy in men and machines in fact that there arrived a moment when it was clear that if they continued for another three weeks, or even perhaps two weeks, on that scale, there would be little if anything of Fighter Command left. At the very height of these paralysing losses the evacuation of British troops from the beaches of Belgium and Northern France had begun and many an embittered soldier, shelled and machine-gunned on the beaches of Dunkirk, inevitably looked up at the sky and asked himself where the bloody hell was the R.A.F.? The answer was one of the most momentous importance. The R.A.F. was back in England, having been brought back by the wise and courageous decision of Air Chief Marshal Dowding, who realised that the Battle of France had been lost and was consequently unprepared further to sacrifice his Fighter Command on the useless ashes of a burnt-out altar. He had therefore ordered Fighter Command back to England, well knowing that the Battle of Britain, the real Battle, was still to come and knowing equally that in fact there would be no Battle of Britain if there were no fighters to fight a Battle of Britain with. It was one of the great decisions of the war and there seems to me little doubt that if it hadn't been made at that moment there would have been no Battle of Britain to fight and that the war might well have ended victoriously for Germany in June or July of 1940.

By his action Dowding was able to rest, re-form and reinforce his fighter squadrons. That they were soon to be shattered not in the sky, but on the ground, on their own airfields, was the result of inexperience which laid more stress on lines of fighters looking trim and neat on their perimeters than on security and this, after some further paralysing experiences, was remedied by a system that became known as dispersal, whereby planes, intelligence staff, radio operators and so on were no longer assembled neatly in one place, like a well-ordered school, but scattered far and wide for safety and survival. That we managed somehow to survive those blistering attacks on airfields seems to me a miracle, but survive somehow we did.

The Battle that presently began in that torturingly beautiful summer will always be known as the Battle of Britain. Of its supreme importance I will say more in a moment. But geographically, of course, it covered no more than a tiny fraction of Britain. The area of combat took place in a cube roughly eighty miles long, nearly forty broad and five to six miles high. The vortex of all this was the Maidstone, Canterbury, Ashford, Dover, Dungeness area, in which Spitfires largely operated, with the further rear centre of combat between Tunbridge Wells, Maidstone and London, largely commanded by Hurricanes. Sometimes in the frontal area as many as 150 to 200 individual combats would take place in the space of half an hour.

To the civilian population below, who were able to see something of a battle for the possession of their island for the first time for centuries, the entire affair was strangely, uncannily, weirdly unreal. The housewife with her shopping basket, the farm labourer herding home his cows, the shepherd with his flock, the farmer turning his hay: all of them, going about their daily tasks, could look up and see, far, far above them, little silver moths apparently playing against the sun in a game not unlike a celestial ballet. Now and then a splutter of machine-gun fire cracked the heavens open, leaving ominous silence behind. Now and then a parachute opened and fell lazily, like a white upturned convolvulus flower, through the blue midsummer sky. But for the most part it all had a remoteness so unreal that the spectator over and over again wondered if it was taking place at all. Nor was it often possible to detect if the falling convolvulus flower contained enemy or friend, and often the same was true of aircraft: so that the battle was watched in the strangest state of suspense, with little open or vocal jubilation.

It was of course, with its combatants, much glamorised by newspapers; but Richard Hillary was right when he said 'much that is untrue and misleading has been written on the pilot of this era. Within one short year he has become the nation's hero and the attempt to live up to this false conception bores him . . . The pilot is of a race of men who since time immemorial have been inarticulate; who, through their daily contact with death, have realised, often enough unconsciously, certain fundamental things. It is only in the air that the pilot can grasp that feeling, that flash of knowledge, of insight, that matures him beyond his years'. This was just as true of the far less glamorised bomber pilots, as I was later to discover.

Remote though it may have seemed to the spectator below there can however be no shadow of doubt that the Battle of Britain was the most decisive of the war. Its closest parallel is Trafalgar. Both were the beginning and not the end of the long road to victory. A good many years were to elapse between Trafalgar and Waterloo; another five of bitter and extensive combat on air, sea and land were to elapse between mid-September 1940 and the surrender of the German armies at Lüneburg Heath in 1945. This book offers no space in which to argue over the inter-allied conflicts and duplicity that went on in those years, bitter though their results may now seem to the British mind; it simply remains to say that if the Luftwaffe had knocked out the R.A.F. in that unbearably beautiful summer of 1940 it is scarcely possible that we would have hoped to achieve another Waterloo.

Throughout it all I wrote little. It was a world in which you felt there was no tomorrow. You lived for the day; and the day, you hoped, by the grace of God, would be enfolded mercifully by a night in which men didn't kill each other. The nights, as I remember them, were of a marvellous starlit calm; the days broke limpid and soft and flowered into a perfection that mocked and pained by its beauty. Like an old hen protecting its brood I hovered protectively about my young family, holding it to be my duty, for the present, to see that they at least had a protective umbrella held above them. They, after the manner of children, grew to accept it all more readily than their parents, so that there came a day when a great blast of thunder broke out above the house and all of us dived under the kitchen table, the children weeping with fear until pacified by their parents' soothing words: 'There's nothing to worry about. It isn't thunder. Only bombs,' so that tears were silent and dried in a moment or two.

As the summer drew on, growing always in beauty, until once again the wheat was the colour of brandy in the fields, it became clearer and clearer that the climax of the battle was still to come. You felt your nerves begin to stretch to breaking point. Not only did it presently seem as if there were no tomorrows; there were no todays either.

At this moment Madge's brother paid us a week-end visit. Far away in Northamptonshire he had been as remote from battle as a nurse in Kensington Gardens might have been from Sevastopol or Khartoum. He found it impossible to believe that war was being waged above his head. I don't think he slept well; but in the morning he came forth with a marvellously sensible suggestion. We would go fishing. I myself hadn't fished for years and neither of us had a hook or line to our name. Accordingly we went out and spent some magnificent sum, about two pounds I imagine, on the two cheapest rods we could find, hooks, lines, floats and shot. We dug vast quantities of worms and mixed great puddings of paste. We then armed ourselves with beer, cheese and sandwiches and set off finally for the two pretty little lakes that lie in the centre of the village, one of them containing an island of quince trees, with the limpid narrow young River Stour running alongside them by woods of alder and hazel and here and there under big old horse chestnuts and half drowned ancient willows.

An immense peace enshrouded us; in a garden an old man placed an even older ladder against an apple tree glowing with early red fruit as with lanterns; a kingfisher streaked, copper and blue, through the dark tunnel of alders; a flight of mallards winged away above the quince trees; moorhens dived and disappeared and pranced their delicate way among the tall thick summer reeds. It was hard to believe that this was a battle-field. The paradox of war and the ethereal exquisite nature of summer dissolved together to form a sort of opiate, a state where time and its senseless, fragmentary paroxysms of pain and fear no longer existed. We simply were; we sat beside the still waters; and there was nothing else that mattered.

The little river hadn't been fished for years and as we cast in our lines it was like taking chocolate from innocent and unprotected children. Fat perch and roach, sometimes a small pike, an occasional rudd or silver bream: all came to us as if we were hypnotists. Even in the heat of the day we went on hauling them in. Then suddenly the opiate heat of noon was shattered. A dog fight broke out above us with such unexpected suddenness that I thought at first it was the boughs of the big tall poplars catching noisy fire above our heads. Machine-gun shells spattered down the full centre of the lake, rousing a thousand fish, big and small, from August slumber, so that they leapt out of the water in silver frightened shoals as if pursued by some monstrous legendary pike. We angled with a little more circumspection after that, seeking the shelter of trees; but though we heard once or twice again the rattle of machine-gun fire there was really nothing that could ever destroy the suspended beauty of that day, which had calmed at least one troubled mind and given it hope for the future.

The immediate future was in fact to be one of blackness. With the coming of September the Germans were to make another full and deliberate attempt to destroy Britain. The full premeditated nature of the attack, based on Goering's personal orders from France, was clear: it was to smash London and with it, if possible, the entire morale of the people. The first attack, on September 7th, was the heaviest the country had ever had to face. Very heavy bombers, Dornier 215s, were used, escorted by powerful fighters, including the new Heinkel 113. The Luftwaffe bomber force, outnumbering the R.A.F. many times over, was over London for hours, commanding the sky. Docks, stores, warehouses, masses of working-class houses and buildings of all kinds were smashed. By night, from fifty miles away, we could see from our Kentish fields the great red-orange light of London burning. Throughout it all the outnumbered R.A.F. fought like tigers and though in the heat of battle it is never easy to assess casualties with any accuracy we claimed to have shot down a hundred Nazi planes. Against this over 300 Londoners were dead and another 1600 injured.

This was by no means the end. On September 15th a new great mass of bombers with their fighter escorts was again pitched against us, London again the main target. In one of these desperate moments when something has to be done to hide fear from children and distract them from a catastrophe about to blow up in their faces we had trundled off, pram, kettle, food, fishing rods and all, to picnic by the lake. The quinces were already turning gold on the trees by the water and the day was as golden as the ripening fruit. We had scarcely begun to fish when the sky, from the south-east, the direction of Dover, began to blacken. It was darkened all over by what seemed to be a monstrous gathering of giant starlings. Helplessly we watched them, at no height at all, flying above our heads, in relentless formation, on their way to London. As they passed there was suddenly, among the reeds along the lake, an explosion, followed by another. Though by no means loud, it frightened us more than the bombers, even long after we had discovered that it had been caused by two addled wild-duck eggs bursting in the summer heat.

Again a small, ludicrous event, remembered after nearly thirty years, illuminates an affair of far more sinister import. In the recollection of the exploding duck-eggs lies the thought, tenuous but satisfactory, that that day, September 15th, was virtually the end of Goering's effort to destroy us. Fat duck-egg as he himself looked, it was he, not us, who was that day exploded. We claimed – again, probably in the heat of battle, mistakenly – 185 Nazi planes destroyed. The precise number hardly mattered to a dozen one way or the other. On the 18th, 27th and 30th we claimed a further 230 and after that the Luftwaffe fire was virtually expended.

Those who lived in the south-east that summer will never forget the irony of its ethereal beauty and its deathly, deathless conflict. When the weather broke at last, bringing autumn rain, it also brought an odd, repeated phenomenon. I had never seen it before and I have never seen it since.

It was a sun-dog: a kind of evanescent circular rainbow that, in unsettled weather, appears just a little away from the perimeter of the sun. It had about it a kind of ominous beauty. It might almost have been a sign from heaven: a portent, but of what you were too tired or shattered or relieved to wonder.

XV

Misery, said Coleridge, is not an exportable commodity, the market being everywhere glutted by it; and I will therefore not enlarge too greatly on it by going into that little known and other Battle of Britain, the night battle, which followed in the winter of 1940–41, when the Luftwaffe night bombers attacked London and all Britain's major ports, an onslaught of unparalleled power, up to that time, for the repulse of which we had only twelve so-called night-fighter squadrons, not one of which contained a night-fighter or even an aircraft of the required competence or even fitted with any night device for seeking out the enemy. Our fortune in escaping total destruction in this dark and little known confrontation, in which pilots were actually peering outside the cockpit in order to try to identify some object in the sky, is a mystery locked for ever in the bosom of God Almighty himself. He alone knows how we survived.

In the Battle of Britain, by day, the risk to civilian life had been relatively small; it was the pilots, five or six miles up, who had been killing each other. It was fear of invasion, that defences might be defeated and leave us naked and occupied by an enemy that induced the feeling that there were no tomorrows. When the day Battle had been won and the night Battle took its place the situation became entirely different. It was now the civilian population who were being exposed. Thousands were being killed and maimed and made homeless. Cities were being reduced to ruins. Tension, even in the south, was becoming intolerable. Much has been written of the resilience of people under campaigns of continuous air bombardment and subsequent history has proved that resilience is not necessarily a British prerogative. But perhaps one small reminiscence of those days will serve to show that in certain situations humour is the British synonym for courage.

The story was told to me by Lady Reading, head of the Women's Voluntary Service during the war: the W.V.S. who, in their neat green uniforms, drove about London and other cities dispensing help in time of trouble. That many of these ladies were from the now despised upper and upper middle classes (though many were not) is one of the points of the story. At one period the situation in London was so grave that a breakdown in Civil Defence services, through sheer weight of enemy atack, was threatened. Extra forces had to be brought in from somewhere and in this case some were called in from Newcastle, which had had little share of enemy attack. When the tough and highly independent Geordies duly arrived in London their eye fell with scorn on the green-tunicked ladies dispensing tea, cocoa, sandwiches and so on. The upper classes, with their southern accents, doing their bit, eh? Saving us from the enemy, eh? God help us, the Geordies seemed to say, if anything serious did happen. There would be a wild run for the exits.

That first night of the Geordies' visit to London all hell broke out over the city. London experienced its heaviest and bloodiest beating up to that date. In the morning the city was a burning wreck. Of this holocaust the W.V.S., well tried in battle, took little notice, but went about their appointed voluntary task of dispensing food and drink and helping injured and homeless all night long. The Geordies, on the other hand, never having experienced anything remotely like it, had

endured a night of parlous agonies. But when the smoky dawn finally broke and the W.V.S., the despised ladies, were still at it, at least one Geordie had the grace to go to Lady Reading in humility. 'Aye,' he said, 'when we saw you yesterday we didn't think much o' you. But now we know you're best bloody bitches in t' world.'

This intolerable tension of living in the south at last forced us to a decision: we would evacuate the two girls to Northamptonshire. Not that this solved another of our problems: money. I had written little or nothing except *The Modern Short Story* since war began and it was certain that this would never make me rich. I cannot recall even having written any short stories though I do know that up to that time I had never been paid as much as £10 for one. I had once, it is true, been offered £10 for one and had accepted the offer, only to be let down by the editor, who welshed on me. Nor had I now many friends to whom I could turn. Derek Verschoyle, who had given me much work for *The Spectator*, had gone into the R.A.F.; Rupert Hart-Davis had enlisted in the Coldstream Guards; David Garnett had also gone into the R.A.F. to do special work for Coastal Command. I had consequently not only lost sight of all of them but was deprived of the kind of help they had long given me.

In desperation I went to *The Spectator*, for whom I had written much in the way of reviews and articles as well as the regular *Country Life* feature, and asked the editor, Wilson Harris, if he would take me on to the staff. To my infinite surprise he said that he would and that I could in fact take over the job of literary editor. This seemed too wildly good to be true and I accepted gladly.

I will not go so far as to say that I actively disliked Wilson Harris. I will merely say that he appeared to me to have about as much humanity as a clothes prop. I once told him a slightly risqué joke, but this was received in the kind of frozen silence that would have greeted an incident of indecent exposure in the House of Lords and I never repeated it. Aloof, cold, ascetic, distant, Wilson Harris appeared to be the sort of man who had never consummated his marriage with life. As an editor he appeared to me to be a kind of bloodless public school headmaster of a long out-dated type. I used to enter his study armed with proofs, books or articles like a small boy tremblingly ready to apologise that he had failed to finish his impositions, do his Latin prep. or unravel the diabolical mysteries of his trigonometry. In consequence I never felt anything but very, very small, very, very inferior, very, very unhappy.

Against this I must set the fact that I wasn't a very, very good literary editor. Perhaps my longseated hatred of journalism, however superior, that had had its inception in the Wellingborough office of *The Northampton Chronicle* (whose present editor, by the way, has recently been vastly amused by my account of my shortcomings there in *The Vanished World*) was responsible. Fortunately for me R.A. Scott James, a very good journalist who at least had some red blood in his veins and had been of help to me on occasions in the past, was also on the staff and acted as a sort of cushion between the clothes prop on the one hand and the harassed and volatile literary editor on the other. Life was certainly not easy. I used to come into St Pancras station every morning by ten o'clock, always to find that some new part of London had been devastated in the night and that streets and pavements were crowded with apparently cheerful Cockneys sweeping up broken glass and rubble and damning Hitler in the appropriate vernacular. Most days, as soon as I arrived at *The Spectator* office in Gower Street, air-raid sirens would begin their warning wailing and all the staff would go into underground retreat, thus disrupting half the day. In this way I learned to adapt myself to an entirely new system of writing: one whereby I could shut myself away in a cocoon and go on working, whether in tube or bus or railway carriage, as if the outer world never existed.

There inevitably came a day when the new boy, not having lived up to his promise, had to face expulsion and I confess it was rather more with relief than anything else that I said farewell to the clothes prop and *The Spectator*. It is, however, not quite true that I said farewell entirely to *The Spectator*, since I continued for some time to write the *Country Life* notes, which didn't displease the headmaster and had certainly made me many friends among its readers. But I cannot forbear to say that I never now pass No. 99 Gower Street without a feeling that a headmasterly hand will stretch out and order me into the chill of the editorial study.

Where, then, to go from here? Not for the first time in my writing life I hadn't the faintest idea. If the times had been bad for writers in 1926, as Edward Garnett had well pointed out, they were now hell. That they were also hell for a lot of other people was of small personal comfort. It now seemed to me that it might be better to abandon, at least for the period of crisis, all idea of being a writer. The tension and frustrations attaching to it were becoming so great that it seemed to me better to do as T. E. Lawrence had done and seek an anonymous, part-monastic seclusion in one of the armed Services, there to bury my identity completely in a regimented life apart, uncomplicated by private struggle. I accordingly applied for a commission in the R.A.F. – and was turned down.

In this suspended, negative moment there occurred another of those small interfering pokes by the hand of fate, or whatever it may be called, that was to alter the course of my life. Cecil Day Lewis, who is now Poet Laureate, was at that time doing work for the Ministry of Information. Whether he had heard in some way of my unsuccessful application for an R.A.F. commission I have no idea or whether he had heard of an exceedingly unfortunate experience of mine with the M.O.I., I shall probably never know, but at all events I presently received a letter from him.

Before I tell of it I may perhaps tell of the unfortunate experience that preceded it. One day at lunch with Graham Greene I had mentioned to him my arid literary predicament (I hardly think his own was all that much better) and he had suggested that my talents surely had their correct place in the Ministry of Information, for which he himself was doing certain work. Very kindly he promised to put in a word for me in the right place, which he duly did, and in due course I went along to the headquarters of the Ministry, then housed at London University.

I was there ushered into the presence of a gentleman who informed me that he had been a school inspector: a tribe of whom, I understand, the teaching profession is not particularly enamoured; and after my experience with one I cannot say that I wonder why. We had scarcely begun to talk when he was called away to another room for a telephone call, leaving the interview to be carried on by an office boy. The following illuminating conversation then took place.

'What kind of work do you do?'

'I am a writer.'

'You mean you actually write?'

'I actually write.'

'Oh! really? What have you written?'

'Books.'

'Oh? You mean you have actually written books?'

'Yes.'

'You mean the sort of books that are published?'

'The sort of books that are published.'

'Oh! good heavens. And *have* they actually been published?'

I rose and walked out, not waiting for the return of His Majesty the school inspector.

Graham Greene's fury at this nonsense, when I told him of it, was so great that he may well have communicated it to Cecil Day Lewis. He certainly communicated it to someone at the M.O.I. and as Graham Greene isn't noted for using stale suet for words I do not doubt that the echoes of protest reverberated acidly.

Soon afterwards came the letter from Cecil Day Lewis. It contained the interesting suggestion that I might care to look at some portraits done by Eric Kennington, Paul Nash, Laura Knight, Sir William Rothenstein, Graham Sutherland, Keith Henderson and others of some of the pilots who had fought in the Battle of Britain. I knew of course of Kennington's work from his vividly admirable portraits of British and Arab leaders alike in T. E. Lawrence's *Seven Pillars of Wisdom*. I had long thought highly of them and ever since that brief meeting with Lawrence himself I had been specially haunted by the simple but profound sketch Kennington had done of him. Simple, economical, sensitive, it seemed to me to have touched and revealed much of the essence of the man. Some years later I met Kennington, who lent me one of the few existing typescripts of that abrasive, self-destructive, unhappy book, *The Mint*, which he carried about with him like a pot of uneasy gold.

Meanwhile it was Cecil Day Lewis' idea that I should look at the Kennington and Nash portraits of the Battle of Britain pilots, see what I thought of them and then annotate them for a small book to be put out by the M.O.I. When the portraits arrived I was instantly struck by several things: first the great variation in the faces of the men themselves, which varied from the glamorised types with their fancy neckerchiefs (one at least of these, stationed close enough to London, used to have his lunch specially sent down to his station every day from Pruniers) to Sergeant Pilots of calm and unglamorised composure and resolve and sensitive men who might have been poets, Oxford dons, picture restorers or prelates or indeed anything at all. The great variation of those faces was infinitely fascinating. I duly did my annotations and the little book was duly published. I had given it the title of *You Have Seen Their Faces*.

Little though I was aware of it at the time, the title was to a degree prophetic. The faces that had fought the Battle of Britain had been little seen or known until Kennington and other artists drew them. But behind them were many other faces of whose characteristics the greater part of the population of Britain were also entirely ignorant.

The opportunity to look at these faces too was now about to be given me, as I shall now describe.

XVI

Still in a state composed more of frustration than despair I wrote the following letter to David Garnett on the 13th of August 1941:

'I hear that you are again at the Air Ministry and I have been wondering if you can give me any idea of what chances I have of getting any special work to do in your own or any other R.A.F. department. I have until October before my exemption expires; then I am booked for the R.A.F. under special duties. Meanwhile I've been asked by Bobbs Merrill in New York if I'll do a book on the American Eagle Squadron. Unfortunately until recently the Eagles haven't been much in action, but now that they are I hope to do the book. But replies from the Air Ministry are slow, and one first contacts one person and then another. Do you know any personage of high plumage among the Eagles? I am very keen to do this book and if you can help in this or any other way it would be splendid.

'I have just done the introduction to the R.A.F. war pictures by Kennington, Nash and others for the M.O.I. and the Oxford University Press. They were pleased with it, and it seems as if this too might help to persuade the Air Ministry that I might be of some use. Will you anyway advise me as to what I might do? – if it is of any use applying to the Air Ministry and to whom and so on. I feel a bit desperate about getting my future outlined a bit.'

To all this David acted with great promptitude, so that by September 6th I was writing to him that I had been to Air Ministry and had there seen a good friend of his (and a subsequent good friend of mine) John Nerney, the Air Ministry Librarian, 'a rock of integrity', who exercised a good deal of influence on the civilian side of R.A.F. Public Relations. I do not remember much of this interview except that John Nerney was kindly and intelligent and furthermore suggested that I should come back for another interview in a few days' time.

It cannot have been many days later when I duly turned up at King Charles Street, expecting again to see Nerney alone but to be confronted instead by a trio consisting of John himself, Harald Peake, then Director of R.A.F. Public Relations at Air Ministry and now head of Lloyds Bank, and Hilary St George Saunders, deputy librarian at the House of Commons and then also attached to Air Ministry.

I hadn't the vaguest idea of why this distinguished band had gathered to meet me and when they at last began to explain why I felt I had been led into some hall of dreams. Harald Peake, who was both intelligent and charming, was the leading spokesman. There had been conjured up, he proceeded to explain to me, the idea of an entirely new concept in R.A.F. Public Relations. It was proposed to form a new department, to be known as P.R.11, and of which Hilary St George Saunders was to be the head. This department would, in essence, have as its aim something of what I had done with the portraits of Kennington, Nash and others. It would show not figures, statistics, bulletins, communiqués and so on to the public, but men, characters, faces. It would dedicate itself to the proposition that figures, if repeated *ad nauseam*, mean nothing, but that a pilot with a pint of beer in his hand and a popsie in bed can illuminate the troubled business of war in a way that will bring war and its participants vividly, excitedly, even painfully alive.

To this end Harald Peake and Hilary Saunders (my friend to the all too early end of his life) now proceeded to put forward not only a truly remarkable proposition but one utterly unprecedented in any of the armed services at any time. They proposed to commission me into the R.A.F. simply as a short story writer.

I listened aghast. Why me? My further immediate reactions were first of being greatly honoured and then of being terrified. I couldn't be other than honoured by such a proposition, I told myself, but what of the not impossible situation if I should fail in the appointed task? I knew nothing of flying, flying men, aerial combat, bombers or fighters. With such faith implanted in me by men of high rank I could hardly be other than terrified.

Hilary, Nerney and Harald Peake proceeded to allay these fears by saying that they had equal faith in both my talents and me. Even this wasn't enough for me. I proceeded to explain that one of the things you cannot do is to make a writer write; you cannot put stripes on his sleeve and call him a Flight-Lieut and put him at a desk and say 'Proceed, by the comma, quick march, and produce short stories.' Art, even in such limited form, acknowledges no keeper called regimentation.

Gifted with much intelligence as they all three were, Hilary, Harald Peake and Nerney cordially agreed. They were with me completely. They understood. I then put a further point to them. If I were to accept their proposal I should have to insist on utter freedom in time and movement; in other words I must be allowed to write when and where and how I liked, to go where and when and how I liked; to disregard authority when it threatened to interfere, to make my own rules (always within King's Regulations) and to be bound by no other commitment than to do what I was to be commissioned to do: namely to write short stories and nothing but short stories.

Again, to my infinite honour, astonishment and satisfaction, they agreed. These were precisely the things that they had in mind. They would treat me as an artist, see that others treated me as an artist and see that I was as free as a bird. I would be answerable to no narrow-minded station commander, no petty regulation, no inhibiting duties, but only to the men whose new, inspired idea this was. It was short stories they needed and it was I, and I alone, whom they had chosen to write them.

I left Air Ministry that September afternoon feeling rather as if I had been awarded a literary Victoria Cross. It was a very, very momentous day in my life: perhaps, as it turned out, the most momentous day of all.

I felt, at last, that my world had indeed blossomed. Of how it further matured, both in the R.A.F. and elsewhere, I hope to tell fully in another volume, *The World in Ripeness*.

THE WORLD IN RIPENESS

I

Burdened by an impossibly large and heavy blue cabin trunk, I set off on October 17, 1941, for the Royal Air Force Station at Uxbridge, there to engage in a three-week Officers' Training Course. The afternoon was utterly typical of an English mid-October: the air limpid, soft and warm as new milk, the distances touched with that same tender haze that must surely have inspired Keats' 'Season of mists and mellow fruitfulness'.

I only wish I could say the same for my own spirits; but I fear that for all my natural buoyancy, it was not so. Honoured though I was to have been singled out by Air Ministry to be the first writer ever to be commissioned in the Armed Forces solely as a writer of short stories I must nevertheless confess to having been slightly heavy of heart. I was leaving behind me a young wife, who had somehow to manage, on God only knew how little money, to feed and clothe and comfort four children under the age of eight, in a part of England where, even though the immediate threat of German invasion had receded, constant day and night raids by enemy bombers and fighters were still very much part of the day's unamusing routine.

I could, I think, have dodged this particular column, largely on the grounds that Officers' Training Courses do not have, as part of their curriculum, any special instructional periods for the guidance of short story writers; but I was determined in this, as in other matters, to seek no special favours, and I have ever since been specially glad that I did not do so.

The scene at Uxbridge was in part comic, in part sad. It rather resembled one of those appalling Old Boys' Reunions at which some men remember others only too well whereas others, either by design or the sheer passage of years, have forgotten. ('By God, it's old Jonesy. Remember? Upper Fifth. 1922. Gosh, you were a devil. Remember how you set fire to your Latin crib one day? Just got the damn thing burning merrily when the Old Man himself popped in. God! – talk about laugh! Remember?') Some, as I say, remembered; some, on the contrary, did not. An air of uneasy embarrassment hung over everything as the extraordinary motley company of players attempted to sort out their baggage, find their billets and beds and somehow accustom themselves to the thought of a sort of semi-monastic three-weeks' imprisonment.

Shop-keepers, schoolmasters, small business men, hoteliers, solicitors, commercial travellers, engineers, clerks, accountants: motley, indeed, the assembly was. Most were family men in their early or mid thirties. One was a Rugby International; another, rather fat and podgy, appeared to have been honoured with some special dispensation, since he wore on his sleeve not the miserable thin blue line that is the mark of the lowly entrant Pilot Officer, but the huge broad ring that denotes none other than the lofty Air Commodore. All of us treated this

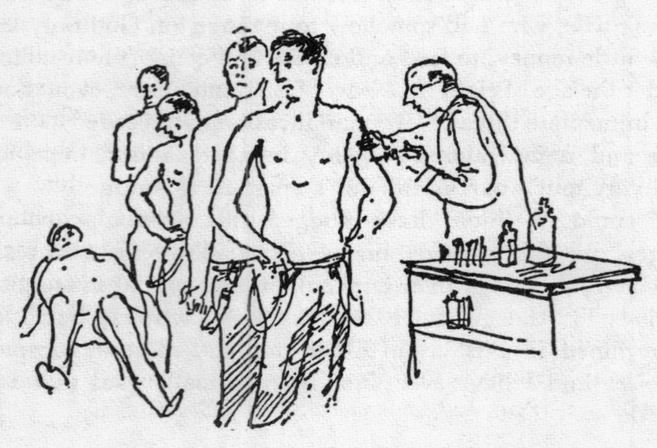

particular gentleman not only with awe and respect but a certain suspicion that he had been placed among us as a sort of guardian-cum-spy. It was not until next day that we discovered he had, unfortunately, suffered from the misguidance of an over-zealous tailor.

That night fifty or so of us were herded together as in a school dormitory. The atmosphere was in keeping; there was much farting; I slept badly. In the morning, by now turned alarmingly chilly, we paraded at an ungodly hour for the customary injection against small-pox, tetanus and so on. One of my companion officers had turned out to be an old schoolfellow, also a Rugby player, a hefty young man of some fifteen or sixteen stone. He was behind me in the queue for jabs. Suddenly I was stunned by a sound as of falling masonry and turned to see my erstwhile schoolmate flat on his back, cold and glassy-eyed.

Soon we were being addressed, in terms alternately avuncular, soothing and stern, by the Commanding Officer, who solemnly assured us that, as if we were about to enter Holy Orders, the RAF Officers' Training Course, Uxbridge, could bring nothing but physical, mental, moral and indeed spiritual elevation to our wretched and all too recently civilian souls. We listened in silence, as yet unconverted.

Presently we were led, with a sort of casual subtlety, into the curriculum itself. This consisted of a couple of hours' square-bashing after breakfast, followed by a short break, then followed by a lecture and then, after lunch, by a further lecture and more square-bashing. I didn't really mind the square-bashing; at least, on the suddenly freezing October days, it kept the blood in circulation. Of the lectures it is hard to say if they were worse than the lecturers; but on balance I should, in memory, vote slightly in the lectures' favour, little though that may mean.

One of the lecturers was a kind of stage silly ass type commonly seen in those appalling musical comedies of the 1920s; dapper and la-di-da of voice, he conceived it stupendously clever to enliven his sessions with *risqué* stories having neither point nor humour (*A Waaf had an accident; she fell out of bed. She was swerving to avoid a child*), at the same time offering us not a single improving word. Another was an ex-public school master of infinite and lofty snobbery whose constant injunction to us was 'always to remember our *Alma Mater*'. A third was a semi-illiterate whose favourite word was *personnel*, pronounced roughly to rhyme with *Rommel*. I used to listen to him, I fear, half-shrouded in sleep.

It must have been on the second or third day of the course that I fell in with an ex-hotelier from Cornwall who had earned his commission the hard way, having come up from the ranks. As a result there was nothing, absolutely nothing, that he didn't know about dodging duties, responsibilities and parades, bending or breaking the rules, always quite legitimately, and generally avoiding the harsher moments of service life. My first experience of these long-acquired ingenuities occurred on a frigid afternoon when thin flakes of snow were dismally floating through the darkening air, making the thought of an afternoon parade, without overcoats, more than a slightly forbidding one. Duty bound, spruced and ready, I was nevertheless about to leave the dormitory when to my infinite astonishment I saw my friend the hotelier lying indolently on his bed, still in his shirt sleeves. The following conversation then took place.

'It's two o'clock already. Hadn't you better get ready for parade?'

'Not coming.'

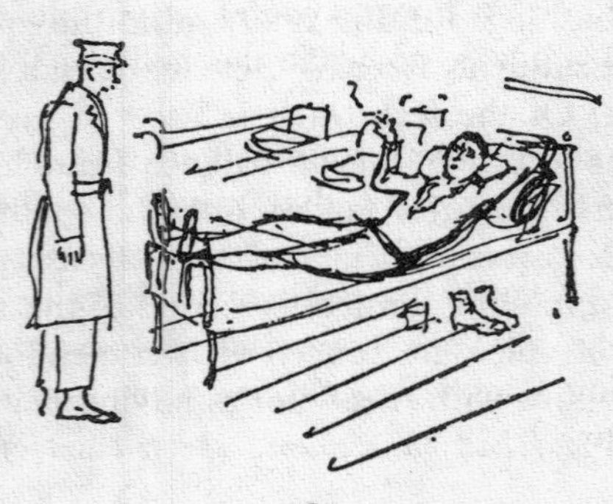

'*Not coming?*'

'No.'

'Good God, why ever not?'

'Going out.'

'*Going out?* Where on earth to?'

'Dental.'

This single cryptic word was drenched with all the distillation of long experience. Dental? Was there, I enquired, something wrong with my friend's teeth? Had he toothache?

'No.'

'Then if there's nothing wrong with your teeth why are you going to dental?'

'Well of course there might be something wrong that I don't know about and of course I shan't know, shall I, until I get the dentist to have a look? I'll be back for tea.'

The next afternoon, again snatched prematurely from winter, the word 'dental' was replaced by 'medical'. When I inquired if my friend was feeling ill he airily replied that, on the contrary, he felt as fit as a fiddle. But that didn't mean, did it, that there might not be something wrong and until you got the doctor to have a look you couldn't know, could you?

The following evening he proceeded to announce a still more audacious piece of adventure. He was going to town for the night. He had, it seemed, a pleasant little bird up there.

'But Good God, man, you can't be out of camp all night.'

'Oh! yes, I can.'

'But have you a special pass or something?'

'Don't need one. As long as you're on parade at eight-thirty next morning you can do what the hell you like with your nights.'

'But I thought we were supposed to stay in and swot up King's Regulations and all that, ready for the passing-out exam.'

'All baloney. What's the point of swotting up when you're allowed to take all your notes into the exam? What's the point of reading King's Regulations when you've got all the answers anyway?'

'I never thought of that.'

'Well, you must, old boy, you must. Listen to me. Never be too bloody diligent and all that. If you are they'll spot it like a hawk and have you posted to some Hell-hole like Aden or somewhere. That's where they send the nice, good, obedient types. Not my sort. They know we can't be trusted.'

'You amaze me.'

'Glad to hear it, old boy. And let me tell you something else. *Never be on time anywhere.* Whenever you're posted always turn up a couple of days late. Why? A thousand to one the signal about you will never have got through and even if it has the bloody Adjutant or some WAAF or other will have lost it. No, never be on time, old boy, never be on time.'

With such splendid subterfuges my friend was able constantly and easily to dodge all the more arduous or boring or irksome of duties. One of these consisted of an incredible afternoon when, herded into the camp cinema for an hour and a half, we were given a stunningly thrilling lecture on the social duties incumbent upon officers, in particular *The Art of the Social Afternoon Call on the Wives of Other Officers and the Leaving of Cards Therewith.*

When the three-week course was finally over I got the posting I expected: that of Flight-Lieutenant to Public Relations, Air Ministry. On the way out of camp my heavy cabin trunk was carelessly dropped from a truck, one of the sides bashed in. Instantly, properly inspired by the wisdom of my hotelier friend, I made it an excuse to snatch two days' leave at home. Nobody, as my friend had truly predicted, turned a hair.

II

When I eventually reported back to Air Ministry it was to find that the newly formed department of Public Relations, P.R.11, consisted of only four men, I now being the fifth: Hilary St George Saunders himself, an assistant Flight-Lieut., John Pudney and F. A. Walbank, who had produced one or two anthologies but, unlike John Pudney and myself, was not commissioned. In the various other departments of P.R. there were considerable numbers of other writers of much experience and distinction. Leonard Dodds and Dudley Barker were both later to become my chiefs and very excellent and understanding ones at that; many of the rest I never met at all and others not until some long time later. Among those I did meet, and indeed made good friends with, were Geoffrey Harmsworth, of the famous newspaper family, R. F. Delderfield, still a struggling playwright, with his phenomenally successful *Worm's Eye View* still to come, Eric Partridge, who had in fact published at his Scholartis Press a book of mine, *Seven Tales and Alexander*, Vernon Noble, Stanley Bishop, renowned as a crime reporter, John Macadam, sports writer, and Fletcher Allen, an editor. Also somewhere in the building were Alan Melville, John Strachey and Philip Guedalla, as well as artists and photographers of much distinction too.

John Pudney and I at once got on well together (indeed I can truthfully say that, with one single exception, I encountered nothing but friendliness in my entire RAF service). In sharp contrast to this was the behaviour of Hilary St George Saunders and his assistant Flight-Lieut. who daily and indeed almost all day engaged in prolonged and abusive slanging matches, carried out with a sort of rude verbal affection, love-hate, pitilessly, no holds barred. These encounters were a joy and wonder to behold and listen to. Hilary indeed was a master of fearless invective, a gift he used on not a few occasions in order to make easier the path of his newest pupil, to whom he now presently announced:

'We think we should send you first to a Bomber Station, where you can stay for two or three days in order to sense the atmosphere. The one we have in mind is at Oakington, just outside Cambridge. But first we'd like you to go to H.Q. Bomber Command at High Wycombe, where their head man will take you under his wing and see you on your way.'

There was little I could do but acquiesce in all this, though I did so with an increasing nervousness and apprehension. Once again I was assailed with the chilling fear that I might fail in my mission. Of bombers and bomber crews I knew nothing; the vocabulary and territory of that world, celestial or otherwise, were utterly foreign to me. Suppose it should happen that I boob, put up a black? Thankfully the understanding wisdom of John Nerney, that 'rock of integrity' as David Garnett has called him, was there to sustain me as I went to say good-bye to him before leaving for this, my first assignment. Somehow he managed to imply, without actually saying it, that all would be well, and my faith in myself was re-implanted.

Next day I was on my way to High Wycombe, in my car. I had scarcely cleared the suburbs of London before I was

flagged down by a Cockney gentleman seeking a lift. In true Cockney fashion he had the new, green Pilot Officer weighed up in about three minutes flat: the easy, dead easy touch. His trouble, he proceeded smoothly to explain, was that he'd been supposed to meet his brother that morning, in Ealing, but for some reason the brother hadn't turned up. They were in fact going to High Wycombe to pick up a set of car tyres and the brother, see, was the one who had the money. My Cockney passenger was now, of course, as he proceeded glibly to explain, in 'somefink of a spot'. He had three quid on him all right but he needed another five so as he could get the tyres. Did I know what? – if I could lend him the fiver he would later leave it at the *Poste Restante* at High Wycombe Post Office and I could call for it on my way back from wherever I was going to. See?

I fell. This, among the oldest of confidence tricks, was too much for, and completely mesmerised, my innocent good nature. I duly handed over the fiver and duly turned up, some days later, at High Wycombe Post Office, to emerge empty-handed. There is, however, a true and good saying, especially applicable, I think, to writers of fiction. It is to the effect that 'nothing is ever lost'. The incident of my Cockney friend and his confidence trick never left my mind, and more than twenty years later I turned it into a story, *Mr Featherstone Takes a Ride*, for which an editor paid me 250 guineas, thus showing a fair profit on a morning in which I too had been taken for one.

On arrival at H.Q. Bomber Command, High Wycombe, I was assailed by the illusion that I had, by some misguidance, strayed into the portals of the Ritz. All, it seemed to me, was grandeur. I had grown used to, in my three weeks' Officers' Training Course at Uxbridge, a certain prison-like shabbiness, even if sherry was only ninepence a glass. Here at High Wycombe the Mess Bar Steward was as impeccable as a first-class Head Waiter, dressed in a jacket as white as that of an umpire at Lord's. 'And what, sir, would you care to drink? We have everything. A little sherry perhaps? Bristol Milk? Bristol Cream? Thank you, sir. The Bristol Cream.'

After a lunch of an excellence only comparable with that of the Bristol Cream I drove on to Cambridge, guided and

accompanied by 'the head man'. It was, as I remember it, a grey, damp and dismal November afternoon which grew only greyer, damper and more dismal the farther north we got. By the time we reached Cambridge it was almost dark; at Oakington it was completely so, a circumstance that only served to increase my already wavering fears and apprehensions. Nor were these uplifted by the fact that at the RAF station, in the Mess ante-room, a radio was belting out a popular tune that has for ever remained in my mind as one of haunting melancholy: *Daddy, let me stay up late*, which to this day enshrines so much of the ephemeral nature of the lives of the young bomber pilots and crews I was about to meet and write about. It is not too much to say that I can never recall that song, still less hear it, without being very near to tears.

But before I ever got to the Mess still another experience deepened my gloom. It was my first sight of the giant Stirling Bombers, lined up like so many black broody birds, apparently either ready to roost for the night or to lay equally black and destructive eggs, all round the perimeter of the airfield. Huge, unwieldy, twenty-five feet or more high from ground to nose, not easy to fly, desperately difficult to handle in a cross wind, those monsters stood there in dark, sinister, ugly assembly. My one comforting thought, as I looked at them in the dimmed light of that November evening, was that I had been expressly forbidden, on Air Ministry instructions, thank God, to take any sort of part in Flying Operations. It was no small expression of Air Ministry's Public Relations wisdom that my job was to write stories and not, by the Grace of God, to get myself unnecessarily killed.

When at last I found myself in the Mess ante-room it was to be further assailed by the impression that I had somehow strayed into a gathering of Sixth Form schoolboys grown prematurely old. I think it true to say that of all the officers assembled there that evening scarcely more than a dozen were over twenty-five. One of these was the Station Commander, Group-Captain Adams, an extraordinarily likeable and able man who looked rather more like a sea captain from Drake's time than an R.A.F. officer; another was an American from Texas, known naturally as Tex, a rear-gunner of small stature but extremely powerful hands who had got himself into the R.A.F. in order to wage a purely personal war against Hitler; another was a Kentish man, Norman Winch, who had done some journalism but was really hoping to be a farmer and who, I am happy to say, is now a farmer and has been my good friend, together with his pretty wife, ever since; another was myself, so ancient at 36 that it would not have at all surprised me if the young pilots had called me Pop.

It was the eyes of these young but prematurely aged officers that made a first powerful and everlasting impact on me. They were not 'sicklied o'er with the pale cast of thought' or even that of fear. It was something much more elusive, profound, disturbing and hard to define. Perhaps I can best illustrate it by telling of a young Australian pilot of whom, eventually, I was to write two or three stories. He had come from a family of sheep-farmers, up country, in Victoria: lean, indeed gaunt of face, tight of lip, eyes glassy and seemingly sightless, almost, from long night fatigue. I grew very attached to him before he was finally shot down and killed over Germany.

When his parents and his sister at last read the stories that I wrote of him they had one paramount desire: to come to meet the man who had written of the son and brother they had lost. The war eventually being over, they came to see me: simple, honest, proud, rural people steeped in pride for a young man who had given his life 12,000 miles from home. With such pride as parents naturally have on these occasions they showed me a photograph of him taken when he had first joined the Royal Australian Air Force: a mere boy, starry-eyed, proud too, the new entrant on his way to the big school.

I weep as I write these words: I did not recognise him. Nor, as I handed them my own photograph of him, the gaunt-faced, glassy-eyed, weary veteran of Heaven knew what Hell had been his lot over Germany, did they recognise him either. In silence, they far more shocked than I, we realised that we were speaking of two different men.

Such was my initiation into the world of Bomber Command; and that night, as I went to bed, I knew that Air Ministry's suggested 'two or three days' would have at least to be two or three weeks, perhaps even two or three months. The immediate problem was to get these men to talk; but how? That was the question. I knew of course of that great unwritten R.A.F. law: the one that forbids the shooting of lines. But somehow lines had to be shot or extracted: whether in secret, by trickery, subterfuge or even some form of cheating I didn't yet know.

Next morning I met the Wing Commander of No. 7 Squadron, a tough young man who viewed with a certain suspicion, if not indeed resentment, the writer from Air Ministry. Nevertheless we talked; and as we talked I solved the first of my problems: I would play the game of eavesdropping. Accordingly, that morning, I got my first story, unwittingly given to me by the unsuspecting Wing Commander who, in an unguarded moment, let fall some remark to the effect that the worst of his own problems was that of writing to relatives of men killed or even of seeing them in his office as they turned up, pitifully hoping, perhaps, that by some sort of miracle he would conjure their beloved ones back from the dead. 'It's Hell,' he said, 'but then that's just the way it is.'

This, in fact, was what I called the story, *It's Just the Way It Is*, and this is how it began:

November rain falls harshly on the clean tarmac, and the wind, turning suddenly, lifts sprays of yellow elm leaves over the black hangars.

This clear, pictorial simplicity was, I felt, the right and only way that this story, and indeed any others, should be written. I wrote it the following day, in a couple of hours, and posted it straight off to Hilary Saunders, half-dreading what he might have to say about it. In no time there came back from Whitehall a stream of delighted cries and I was able to breathe again.

My next task was to make friends; and this I did, drinking with pilots and navigators, playing cribbage with them, exchanging purposely idle gossip, hardly ever mentioning ops, bombers or writing. Soon a certain air of tension that my arrival had built up began to be dissipated. In a week my presence was accepted, warmly, often with much humour, and without suspicion.

Almost the first thing I had noted about these bomber crews, and which never afterwards failed to fascinate me, was their international democracy. Canadians, Scots, Australians, Rhodesians, Tex the American, Englishmen, Irishmen, Welshmen, New Zealanders: the mixture of nationalities was great. Perhaps an even more striking thing was that of rank. It not infrequently happened that one of those great Stirlings would be piloted and captained by a sergeant, who might have under his command men of the rank of pilot-officer or flight-lieutenant. Rank in fact became meaningless as crews set out for the blackness over Germany. Many of these sergeants, in fact, neither wanted nor sought commissions. They preferred the *camaraderie* of the sergeants' mess, well knowing that a sergeant, as pilot and captain, could expect and receive utter obedience and respect from men superior, however superior, to him in rank. And this, it seemed to me, was a wonderful thing.

Beer was the main drink of these flying men and off duty they swilled at it pretty heavily. It is not a drink I greatly care for but I confess to having drunk more of it in my three months at Oakington (for three months was it to become) than either before or since. Fortunately there were more refined sources of refreshment and one of these was the Arts Theatre Restaurant in Cambridge, where the excellent cellar had been built up by wines given from various college cellars. And it was here that I presently began to take a pilot, perhaps two, to dinner so that we could talk, over a bottle of wine, far out of range of Mess ears. Again I played the game of eavesdropping, never pumping my guests for stories, content always to pick up the creative crumbs as they fell.

They fell pretty frequently and I, like an artist catching a quick glimpse of a face, a scene, a horse, a bird on the wing, made from them my quick-sketched stories, using always the simple, clear graphic approach. Almost always, I think, these flying companions utterly failed to realize that it was the casual, unsuspecting, apparently irrelevant word that I was waiting for as my inspiration. I will give two instances. One evening a pilot, an extraordinarily good and tough one, let fall the casual statement that sometimes, not returning from ops over Germany until dawn was breaking, he would see the sun rise twice, once from several thousand feet up and a second time after he had landed. I could scarcely wait to get this illuminating symbolic episode down on paper and when I did so I called it *The Sun Rises Twice*.

The second incident fell from the lips of the young Australian of whom I have already spoken, Geoff Heard, and it almost drove me wild with excitement. There had been, it seemed, on a remote sheep-farm in Victoria, a couple with an only son. So precious and useful were his hands in the running of the sheep-farm that when war broke out the parents instantly resorted to every kind of trick and subterfuge in order to keep the news from him. Newspapers were cancelled, letters were opened, hidden or burnt, the radio was put out of action. All this, combined with the extreme remoteness of the station, enabled them to keep the stark fact of war from him for an entire year. Then, inevitably, there came a day when he drove a hundred miles to the nearest good-sized town for a few days' holiday, went into a barber's saloon for a haircut, picked up a newspaper and was stunned by the greatest shock of his young life. He enlisted the very next day and I called his story *The Young Man from Kalgoorlie.*

Cambridge, besides the sheer everlasting beauty of its colleges, had other civilised pleasures to offer. Two or three times a week there were afternoon orchestral concerts and to these I often went with some fellow officers not on duty, to listen to Mozart, Bach, Schubert and others. One of these officers was a small, shy, soft-spoken young Irishman who behaved and looked more like a gentle poet than a fighting man. I admired and liked him so much that I truly believe that if he had asked me to go on ops with him I would have flouted Air Ministry rules and have gone with him. Fortunately he made no such suggestion; and after lunch one day I stood on the perimeter of the airfield and watched his big Stirling take off for Brest, there to attack the two German battleships *Scharnhorst* and *Gneisenau* popularly known as Salmon and Gluckstein. The plane had scarcely risen to five hundred feet or so when it suddenly seemed to blossom into a great orange and crimson flower. It fell in fields, wreathed in a vast black pall of smoke, a mile or two away.

It was Canadians, mostly, who provided a physical toughness far removed from the poetic gentleness of my young Irish friend. One of these, a hefty navigator named Mac, was for ever, in true Canadian fashion, spoiling for a fight. We not infrequently went out together, often with another Canadian, Ed Baker, and Norman Winch, and sometimes with an extremely pretty blonde WAAF officer named Christine to whom we were all rather attached. One evening as we sat over drinks in a hotel bar I was amazed to see the two Canadians suddenly rise swiftly to their feet, simply seize a man on the other side of the room, frog-march him through the door and hurl him with unceremonial violence into the street. The reason?

'The guy was undressing Christine with his eyes.'

But even this brief episode of violence was as nothing compared with another memorable encounter that, a few nights later, Mac enjoyed in London, where he had gone on leave. When he finally returned to Oakington his appearance was like that of a man who had been in a fifteen round contest with Jack Dempsey, Joe Louis and Rocky Marciano all at the same time. His face was a red-and-purple mass of bruises and lacerations; his eyes were mere swollen red bags; his tunic was torn and stiff with dark, dried blood.

When I inquired as to the reason for this disturbing sight Mac informed me with calmness that it was nothing. Just nothing. Nothing. Just a fight.

'Some fight.'

'No. Just an ordinary fight.'

Mac, it seemed, had gone into the men's room at the Regent Palace Hotel, there to find three big men picking on a little one. Such an excuse for a scrap was on no account to be missed and Mac merrily mowed in.

'And how did it finally turn out?' I wanted to know.

'Oh! they took 'em away in ambulances.'

Looking at the lacerated face of my Canadian friend I could only marvel and wonder, trying to guess the state of his defeated adversaries. Ordinary fight indeed.

Not very long later Mac was on ops over Italy, where he was shot down, wounded and taken prisoner-of-war. In typical fashion, after a few days in hospital, he mesmerised a young Italian nurse into letting him have slightly more than the regulation amount of freedom and thus instantly escaped and, having escaped, promptly proceeded to walk to Rome, where he knocked on the door of the Vatican.

There he was given a suit of civilian clothes, a seat on a plane and a day later was back in England.

At lunch one day, trying to force down my throat a dreary plateful of bully beef and potatoes (the food at Oakington was on the whole sadly uninspired) I was called to the telephone. At the other end of the line was Hilary Saunders, informing me that I had been summoned to the immediate presence of no less a person than the Secretary of State for Air.

When I finally reached Whitehall, filled with a certain apprehension at my summons there, and was shown into the ministerial presence, it was to find Sir Archibald Sinclair, a man of highly distinguished appearance, indeed aristocratic of presence without being aloof, and of great personal charm and impeccable politeness. His American mother and Winston Churchill's American mother were cousins. I consequently felt no little honoured that he had not only greatly admired my stories but had sent for me personally in order to offer his congratulations. It gave me satisfaction to feel that, in spite of all my doubts and forebodings, I had gone some way towards justifying the faith that Hilary Saunders, Harald Peake and John Nerney (and also David Garnett, the original moving spirit behind it all) had had in me. At the same time I was told that the stories were soon to be published and that Hilary had been inspired to invent for me the pseudonym *Flying Officer X.*

The stories duly appeared in *The News Chronicle* under that *nom de plume*, which in fact hid my identity for just about a single day. My imprint, it seemed, was on every word. When I got back to Oakington the first of the *News Chronicle* stories had already been widely read and I felt a sense of inexplicable unease. There was much leg-pulling; and the Wing Commander, I was told, was gunning for me. The Station Commander was fortunately far more tolerant but even so I took the first opportunity of making some excuse to go back to Air Ministry, with the avowed intention of begging Hilary to give me a few days' leave, which in his typically generous fashion he did. Later it was of no little satisfaction to me to know that the men of Bomber Command themselves approved of the stories; it seemed that the right, authentic, unheroic note had been struck; the stories were also much read, I understand, in prisoner-of-war camps and today, I am assured, still offer much interest to a generation unacquainted with either Bomber Command or the war.

When I again got back to Oakington the air was calmer, my unease had disappeared and I even found myself being congratulated by the WAAF telephone operator who had all unwittingly provided me, sometimes, with material for stories too, often in circumstances painful to her, when she had to inform me that she was afraid 'Flight-Lieut. so-and-so had bought it, over Bremen last night'. She was a girl of much quiet charm and I fear there were often tears in her eyes.

But now a momentous event occurred. The chief Station Intelligence Officer, an agreeable man who had done much to make my early passage smooth, one day suggested that I go and have a talk with him. He had, he felt, something to tell me that might be of considerable interest. We duly talked, I being sworn to secrecy. It appeared that the Captain of a Wellington Bomber shot down over France had escaped by devious routes and was now back with his Squadron, which though not specifically stationed at Oakington, nevertheless shared our Mess; and it seemed that he had a remarkable story to tell.

The point about secrecy arose from the fact that in those comparatively early days any mention in public of pilots escaping after being shot down over the Continent was strictly taboo. But, the Intelligence Officer informed me, I could if I wished talk to the pilot, though only on the absolute condition that I neither breathed nor wrote a word of what he had to tell. Next day I met and talked with the pilot and the seed of *Fair Stood the Wind For France* was sown.

Partly because of the immediate excitement of this, partly because so many of the men I had first known in No. 7 Squadron had now either been killed or taken prisoner (there were some deeply dark days on that often fog-shrouded fen-land that winter) I felt it a propitious moment in which to leave Oakington and seek new stories elsewhere. I also felt that, regardless of all rules and swearing to secrecy, the Wellington Bomber pilot's story must, somehow, be got down on paper. I therefore resolved to tell Hilary that I needed a change of scene and a break before we could decide on the exploration of 'fresh woods and pastures new'. Hilary, ever understanding and in any case pleased that he had put his money, by some good chance, on a horse that wasn't quite an also-ran, duly gave me leave and I went home, my brain and imagination positively bursting like a ripe seed-pod under the heat and fervour of the story I wanted to tell.

I wrote as in a fever, the words nevertheless cool, simple, graphic, restrained. The seed given me by the Wellington pilot was seed only; it now had to be sown and nurtured in the soil of imagination, as of course all fiction has to be. I had first to invent the bomber crew; then their disastrous moment of being shot down; then their being hidden and aided by a French family, among whom the young daughter was of supreme, proud and electric importance. Indeed I saw the entire story as one epitomising the youth of two countries, on the one hand England almost alone in battle, on the other France alone in humiliation and defeat. I wanted to extract from this, if possible, the beauty, the pride, the courage and, if the word is not now too suspect, the patriotism of the young of two civilised countries determined that they would in no circumstances be slaves to an oppressor. If there was also an air of fatalism about it all so it had to be; it was just the way it was.

Dates and times are now a little difficult to recall with accuracy, but I think I had a fortnight's leave, in which I wrote, I can only suppose, very nearly half the novel. One more thing I had to invent was that particular part of the French countryside in which the events, especially the escape of the pilot, had to be set. The northern part of France I already knew; but south of Paris I had never been. Nor, of course, had I ever been to the city of Marseilles, where the final scenes of the novel were to be enacted. All this too had to be conjured from imagination, but at the same time with topographical accuracy and, in the case of Marseilles, with some sort of urban accuracy. I duly read my maps, my guides to France and my Baedekers. I like to think, now, that I got most of these things right, though eventually Hilary, who knew France far better than I did, informed me that I had caused sugar-beet to be grown in a part of France where, in fact, it never was.

So, at week-ends, in odd moments, in a few days of leave, I wrote *Fair Stood the Wind For France*, taking the title from the immortal words of Michael Drayton, Shakespeare's contemporary who, in fact, wrote at least one sonnet comparable in quality with those of the great man himself: *Since there's no help, come let us kiss and part.* He also wrote, in the poem beginning *Fair Stood the Wind For France*, the perfect plan for the prevention of the D-Day invasion of France by Allied Troops, a plan fortunately ignored by the stupid Hitler and his advisers and generals:

> '*But putting to the main*
> *At Caux, the mouth of Seine,*
> *With all his martial train*
> *Landed King Harry.*'

So indeed we did land; it was by no means the first time that Englishmen had landed at that particular point in France or, in fact, defeated their enemies there.

In this way I left Oakington and the grey, fog-bound and so often dismal fen-lands. The countryside, except for the colleges of Cambridge and the superb cathedral at Ely, had not inspired me; the men of No. 7 Squadron and their ugly, difficult bombers had.

It was now decided that I should go to No. 1 Fighter Command Station at Tangmere, just outside Chichester, midway between the luscious Sussex Downs above Cowdray Park and the sea. The weather was bitterly cold and the atmosphere in the Mess, alas, hardly less so. I wandered about for days in a state of lonely misery, scarcely speaking to a soul. There was, it seemed to me, in contrast to the warmth of Oakington, a certain chill snobbery in the air. I once tried an approach to an Australian, who merely turned on me a cool

deaf ear. I tried chatting to New Zealanders and felt myself to be in the presence of aloof, petty provincials. My one and only contact with a South African merely revealed the presence of a Boer who was a boor. I was uneasy in the company of the Station Commander, who viewed my invasion of his hitherto jealously guarded kingdom with a certain high suspicion. Nowhere could I detect a keyhole, still less a key, that would grant me entrance into a world containing stories. I felt near to despair. In addition to all this there was no bed for me in the base and I was put into an otherwise empty house some distance away and there slept and brooded alone.

I developed a strong suspicion that this lack of co-operation stemmed from the Station Commander himself. I accordingly went back to Air Ministry, there to speak with Hilary about it. Hilary was vexed and firm. 'You are beholden to no one but Air Ministry and if your precious Station Commander fails to co-operate we shall deal with him appropriately.' After that I went back to Tangmere with spirits slightly lifted and then, by a piece of good fortune, things improved.

One day in the Mess I noticed a young Squadron-Leader, standing well over six feet, whom I hadn't seen before. He had

no left hand. In its place he had been fitted with a metal gadget which looked rather like a complicated egg-whisk. Perhaps the shattering experience of losing his hand combined with a fanatical determination to go on flying, in spite of it, had given him more humanity than some of his fellows. At all events we talked; his name was McLauchlan; and presently he was inviting me to meet some of the pilots of the renowned No. 1 Squadron, of which he was leader. No. 1 Squadron was by now a night fighter squadron and perhaps it was the experience of flying by night that gave its pilots some of the warmth and kinship that I had so much liked and admired at Oakington. At last, I felt, I had my keyhole and my key.

One of these pilots was a Czech named Kuttelwacher. He too had had a shattering experience: namely that of escaping from his native country by the most devious and adventurous of routes through Southern Europe, Turkey, the Mediterranean and Heaven knew where. He was a man of much humour and gaiety and McLauchlan had dreamed up the idea of shooting up trains and airfields in France at night, operations the two of them carried out with joyous rivalry and glee. I too felt joyous, seizing on these events like a hungry dog long deprived of bones; and this is how, at the time, I described it all:

'It was one of those periods in a station when the unity and life of a good Squadron becomes too strong to remain a local thing, compressed within itself, meaning something to only a few people. It breaks out, and spreading, warm and energetic and fluid, becomes a large thing, meaning something to many people.

'It was one of those periods when everything was good. The weather was good and calm and sunny, the sea-light lofty and pure over the sea by day. The nights were good and starry, with no ground mist and just the right cover of cloud. The Squadron was good and proud and knew itself. The things it did were good and the news of its doings was in the papers. Whenever you came into the Mess or the billiard-room or the dining-room and heard laughter boiling over too richly you knew it was that Squadron laughing. You knew by their laughter that they wanted nothing else than to be kept as they were, flying by night together, shooting up trains on the flat lands of Northern France, shooting down careless Dorniers over their own aerodrome. They had found each other. The positive and exuberant feeling of their discovery spread over the Station, from Erks to Waafs and from Waafs to officers, until all of us felt it there.'

By this time, too, winter had broken, letting in spring at last to the luscious Sussex hills, to which I used to repair with another kind of hunger, famished for the sight of bluebells and primroses, may-blossom and oaks in green-gold flower. To roam those hills was an experience of heart-breaking beauty, infinitely precious. Our bodily hunger was also well taken care of at Tangmere. The Mess Fund was rich, carrying an enormous surplus by means of which the Mess Secretary was able to fill us with out-of-season delights. On my arrival he had even apologised for the fact that dinner in the evening had unfortunately to be cut down from seven courses to a mere five, a difference that after Oakington's sparse fare did not in the least depress me.

Unhappily there came a day when, going back to Air Ministry, I found Hilary Saunders no longer there. He had been transferred to Combined Operations. Worse still, P.R.11 had been disbanded and I found myself in a new department, P.R.3, among new faces. In Hilary's place, however, was an extremely agreeable officer, Leonard Dodds, with Fletcher Allen as a sort of second-in-command. On my very first afternoon at P.R.3 I gave Fletcher, affectionately known as Fletch, a not inconsiderable shock.

At half past three I was preparing to leave the office when Fletch stopped me.

'And where, Bates, may I ask, do you think you are going?'

'Home.'

'*You are going where?*'

'Home.'

'Good God. May I inform you that no one leaves this office until seven o'clock?'

'You may inform me but I am nevertheless still going home.'

'Good God, are you out of your mind? Are you due for leave or something?'

'No.'

'Then what the hell are you going home for?'

'I am going home to write.'

'Very interesting. *Most* interesting. Is it too much to ask, perhaps, that you write here? Couldn't you, perhaps, do that?'

'No. Not the sort of writing I want to do.'

'And what, may I ask, is the sort of writing you want to do?'

'A story.'

'And how long, if it is not too much to ask, will you be away?'

'A week. Very probably two. You see, it's a very long story. And I think a very important one.'

Thereafter Fletch was speechless but, being also human, he relented and let me go. A couple of weeks later I came back with the longest *Flying Officer X* story I had yet written, *How Sleep the Brave*, and Fletch, having read it at one gulp, went into raptures of excitement. So P.R.3 accepted me on the terms Hilary had long since promised. I was a free agent, moving and writing where, how and when I liked.

Some time before Hilary had left Air Ministry he had put his own enthusiasm for the *Flying Officer X* stories into the practical proposition that they should be published in book form. I felt much honoured by this but rather less pleased when he told me that he thought the firm of Macmillan should be the publishers. I said that, on the contrary, since Jonathan Cape had been my publishers for sixteen years, they should be offered the book instead. Hilary at once agreed and immediately picked up the telephone to talk to Cape. I then remembered that Jonathan Cape himself was ill and said that Hilary should talk instead to Wren Howard, his partner.

'Right,' he said. 'And why not listen on the extension?

Hilary and Wren Howard duly talked and I listened. The attitude of Wren Howard, at first, could only be likened to a hard frost. There were long periods of silence, clearly denoting a strong air of suspicion touched with an equally strong lack of enthusiasm. Then Hilary played, quite casually, a trump card.

'You would, of course, be given all the paper you need. Unlimited paper.'

Paper being, at that period of the war, as precious as platinum, the change of atmosphere at the other end of the telephone was instant and miraculous.

'What we have in mind,' Hilary then said, 'is that our edition should be a sort of Penguin, selling at sixpence, but that you may do your own hard-back edition at, perhaps, half-a-crown.'

The temperature at the other end of the telephone rose as in a heat-wave.

The ultimate results of this conversation I shall describe in more detail later.

Meanwhile there came a day when Group-Captain Dodds,

affectionately known to us all as Doddie, as indeed he still is today, sent for me one morning and said:

'Old boy, they are going to publish your *Flying Officer X* stories any moment now. And guess what?'

I had nothing I could possibly guess.

'First printing will be 100,000.'

Never having heard of a book, except the Bible and *Gone with the Wind*, selling such figures, I nearly fainted.

III

In periods of leave, at week-ends or whenever I could snatch a spare day I now worked on *Fair Stood the Wind For France*, writing in a frenzy that fitted the mood of the times yet always striving to keep the style of the novel, as in the stories of *Flying Officer X*, clear and vivid in its pictorial simplicity. What exactly would happen to the book if and when it was finished I was as yet unable to tell. It might have been that if I had shown it to Authority I could well have incurred much displeasure since I had flouted regulations on security about escapes, which were still very strict. It might also have been that even if I incurred no such displeasure or reprimand the appropriate department in charge of security might not have been given the necessary clearance for publication. A third possibility was that Air Ministry might well have said that, since the book had been written in service time and from material provided by another serving officer, they would claim the book as theirs, leaving me without a penny profit; and Heaven knew that I needed every penny I could get.

Fortunately there now began to be slight signs that security regulations relating to escapes were relaxing; and soon, as they still further relaxed, I decided to show the now finished novel to Fletcher Allen. Ever since I had written *How Sleep the Brave* Fletch had shown an increasing tendency to regard me as his own *protégé*, covering me with an increasingly protective wing. I therefore thought I could rely on his discretion.

When Fletch had finished the novel he instantly jumped into a new ecstasy of admiration and excitement. Not only was the book marvellously good, he declared, but come Hell or high water it was going to remain my own. The business of clearance ought not, he thought, to be difficult, after which he declared with every ounce of conviction that the book would be a best-seller. The pleasure at hearing this was presently slightly tempered by a mild reprimand. To Fletch's infinite astonishment he discovered that I had not, and never had had, an agent to handle my affairs. Such folly was unthinkable and had at once to be rectified. 'I will arrange at once that you meet my friend Laurence Pollinger.'

So, for the first time, I met the man who has handled my increasingly complicated affairs ever since. We instantly got on extremely well together and it can truthfully be said that that first meeting, like that with Edward Garnett, was dramatically to change the course of my life. Among other things it also led to my changing, after some seventeen years, my publisher.

Laurence Pollinger has ever been a tireless and watchful champion in the battle for the protection of authors' rights and the rectification of the injustices that are often done to them. He had, of course, heard of the wide success happily attained by the *Flying Officer X* stories and he now inquired how well, financially, I had done with them. When I replied that I had of course received not a penny other than my officer's pay he was both astounded and angry. But what, he inquired, about Cape? Had Cape not slipped a guinea or two into my hand? A box of chocolates into my wife's? They had not, I declared, nor had they slipped a drink, a lunch, a case of wine; indeed they had made no material gesture of thanks whatever, though they had sold countless thousands of copies of *The Greatest People in the World* and *How Sleep the Brave*.

This further fanned the flames of Laurence's anger. 'Do you then propose,' he asked, 'to let them publish *Fair Stood the Wind For France?*' I replied that I had firmly and irrevocably decided not to. This pleased him. And to whom, he asked, did I think of taking the book? He had only to show it to any one of twenty publishers and he was sure they would, like Fletcher Allen, jump for joy. Without hesitation my mind went back to my first meeting, nearly ten years before, with

Michael Joseph. M.J., I declared, was to be my man.

Instantly there was set up, at No. 30 Bedford Square, the house of Cape, a strong resistance movement. Was I not aware that my last contract, in its final clause, gave them the option on my next two books? I said that I was well aware, but it so happens that such a clause has no validity in law. It is what is termed 'a contract to make a contract' and is not, I fear, worth the paper it is written on. So came my parting with Cape and not, I think, without good cause.

Michael Joseph, at this time, wasn't enjoying the best of health (my own, at the same time, was deteriorating rapidly, the old abdominal pains getting more and more severe, leaving me all too often grey of spirit, sleepless at night and haggard with exhaustion) and the man in charge at No. 26 Bloomsbury Street was Robert, now Sir Robert, Lusty. Bob treated me with sense and generosity, giving me a fat, unbelievably fat, advance on the book. As Laurence Pollinger was also able to sell the serial rights of it to both England and America and negotiate yet another excellent advance from *The Atlantic Monthly* I found myself, almost for the first time in my life, free of financial anxiety.

After twenty years of writing, with its several disasters and constant struggles, *Fair Stood the Wind For France* was my first wide success. The book was translated into many languages, and indeed is still being further translated, and at least one perceptive reviewer saw it, as I had intended it to be, a story epitomising the youth of two countries at a period of great conflict and agony. Part of the story concerns the amputation, in great and dangerous secrecy, by a French doctor, of an English R.A.F. pilot's arm, and I hope I shall not appear guilty of self-praise if I say that, many and many a time, not only in England but abroad, I met admirers of the book who took one look of astonishment at me and marvelled that I still possessed *both* of my arms. This is, or should be, a verification of Thackeray's dictum that 'the work of fiction contains more truth in solution than the work which purports to be all true.' It is indeed true to say that there were times when I was writing the description of that amputation I really felt that it was, in fact, my own arm that was being cut off.

By this time the war had reached a strange, tense, darkening phase. In some ways it was rather like being trapped in a powerless train in a long, black suffocating tunnel. One felt gripped by a ghastly inertia, a ghoulish nightmare in which the end of the tunnel could not only not be seen but seemed as if it would never, never be there. There appeared to be neither daylight nor hope. Destruction of shipping by U-Boats piled up to a scale excruciating, savage, vastly perilous. There used to be a pair of lady comics, Gert and Daisy, who sang songs of cheer on the radio, interspersing them with remarks such as 'We go to bed hopeful and wake up thankful'. To this day I wonder how, at times, we had the heart to continue with either hope or thanks.

Yet, all this time, more and more people were returning to the capital. The vortex of the whole grim unease was there, in London's heart, and one felt that one had to be part of its agony. Now and then I returned to Tangmere or to other Stations, hoping, as a man mushrooming or birds' nesting on a summer's day, to find a scrap of treasure that would translate itself into a story. It rarely happened. A sortie or two over the French coast, an enemy fighter shot down, one of our own pilots lost: of great drama, as in the Battle of Britain, there was little or none. On occasions pilots went out over the Channel to have a 'look-see' and either saw little or, as in the case of the Station Commander of Tangmere one fine summer afternoon, got themselves killed. An era of apparent pointlessness, of pacific or half-pacific pause, seemed to have arrived. Where were we going, if anywhere? I used to ask myself. Why the hell, indeed, were we doing it at all?

Somewhere about this time, to my great dismay, Group-Captain Leonard Dodds was posted to India. He had been a wholly understanding chief, urbane of humour, understanding in matters such as giving complete freedom of movement to a writer of imagination, never once confusing a uniform with a strait jacket. We had got on supremely well together and I knew that I should miss him greatly. My fear was, I think, that some narrow-gutted tyrant, a petty king, might take his place.

Happily it was not so. Doddie was presently succeeded by Group-Captain Dudley Barker, an experienced and very able journalist who also, very fortunately, understood that writers of imaginative ability cannot be regimented even if and when you put them into uniform. Dudley and I also got on, I am glad to say, supremely well together and it was to him, some time later, that I was to owe a great debt. He, like Edward Garnett and others before him, was to accomplish yet another revolution in my life: of which I shall have much more to say later.

One day I received a summons to Dudley Barker's desk, there to be told that no less a person than Air-Chief Marshal Portal (later Lord Portal) wished to see me: in fact not only to see me but to take me out to lunch. I had instant visions of having committed some appalling misdemeanour, which in turn would involve demotion (by now I was a Squadron-Leader), severe reprimand or a dismissal to some arid diabolical post, such as Aden, far from my beloved England. Happily, again, it was not so.

The meeting with Portal proved not only to be pleasant; it confirmed once again, in my experience at any rate, that the higher one got in the realms of Service Rank, the more impressive were, with very few exceptions, its members. I had already been much impressed by Sir Archibald Sinclair; I had been equally impressed by Lord Willoughby de Broke, who had always shown me, even in my modest rank of Pilot Officer, all courtesy, understanding and friendliness. ('Hullo, Bates. Sit down. Take a pew, old boy. What now? Splendid stories of yours, dear fellow. What can I do to help?') It was only when one met people of the middle orders – what in Northamptonshire language we should call piss-quicks – that there was aroused in one a disquieting sense of inferiority. The aristocracy did not, I found, wave their flags of superiority.

The middle and lower orders, I fear, very often did. For this reason their few members shall be nameless.

I do not now recall where Portal took me to lunch but it was most probably, I think, his club. If I had any lingering disturbances of thought as we met they were soon dispersed. I found myself in the presence of a man of intelligence, charm, good conversation and width of vision. I think I am right in saying that we had reached the stage of the coffee before he disclosed exactly the reason why he had singled me out from the company of my fellow Public Relations officers for some specialised purpose; and when it came I was slightly surprised. It was his idea, he proceeded to explain, that someone should write the story of the Night Battle of Britain, a perilous affair whose near-catastrophic events had already been allowed to slip back into a darkness as Stygian as that in which it had in fact been fought in the winter of 1941. Whereas the Battle of Britain had been blown up by infinite publicity into a sort of *Boy's Own Paper* adventure serial (and I am not attempting by one iota to detract from its formidable and high significance as a battle, comparable as it is with Trafalgar, with which it alone shares a day specifically named after it in the British calendar) the Night Battle had somehow slid away into the limbo of nightmares apparently best forgotten.

It was Portal's idea that this state of affairs should be put right. He proceeded to elaborate by comparing the two battles: the day battle an affair largely waged by one force, one section of the populace so small that its members had already been honoured as the Few; the night battle waged by comparison with scores of varied units drawn from all sections of the community, both service and civilian, as I have already described in *The Blossoming World.*

How we survived these deficiencies and their attendant and bloody ordeal, as I have also remarked in *The Blossoming World*, it is impossible to tell. Small wonder that Coventry was soon a blackened heap of masonry, its Cathedral a burnt-out skeleton, that London burned like tinder, its underground stations packed with thousands of refugees hoping and hoping for a bloodless morning, or that the ancient and beautiful cities of Canterbury, Exeter and Bristol had the flower of their long heritage destroyed. The great and eternal wonder is that it wasn't a thousand times worse. But, as the subsequent history of aerial warfare in various parts of the world has proved, the dropping of vast quantities of wickedly explosive material on civilian populations, of whatever colour, class or creed, may kill but does not necessarily and finally destroy. In precisely the same way as Jewry has resisted and even flourished under centuries of persecution (in Britain it is at present in decline precisely because it is *not* persecuted) so a populace scourged and persecuted by bombs may emerge from the ordeal fewer in numbers but greater in resistance and strength, determined in spite of all odds not to be crushed. Whether you call this a triumph of mind over matter, of dignity over savagery, of civilisation over the jungle, it is exactly what happened to Britain in the Night Battle of Britain in 1941. We emerged bloody but unbowed.

The pamphlet was duly finished but, though approved in high places, was never published. Today it is safely filed away in the Public Records Office, from which it will doubtless never emerge. After I had finished it the war entered, as far as I was concerned, a new phase of inertia. Nor was this alleviated by my health, which continued to deteriorate, so much so that I endured almost constant abdominal pain, was unable to sleep at night and eventually was driven to beg Leonard Dodds, before his departure for India, to give me leave to go home and see my own doctor. This cry of despair followed innumerable visits to R.A.F. doctors who, after all the usual routine checks, one by one pronounced me A1, Grade 1. Never was a verdict on man's health a greater travesty.

In due course I found myself in hospital, attended by an embarrassing number of nurses and swallowing a revolting concoction known as a Barium meal, in preparation for an X-ray. This having been done I requested to be given the plate in order to report back to Group-Captain Dodds with proof that I had in fact been under hospital scrutiny. Not the least part of Doddie's endearing qualities is a certain wry sense of humour and when I duly reported back to him with the X-ray plate of my stomach, which incidentally revealed something known as a *duodenal diverticulum* he immediately sent it to the photographic department of P.R., which then spent the better part of an afternoon trying to elucidate from it which part of Berlin had been bombed the previous night. My own doctor's verdict sounded a rather more ominous note: 'One day we shall have to take a little peep inside you.'

All this, combined with the fact that I now had few if any stories to write, made me feel that the war had come to a premature dead end. It hadn't of course; but the plain fact was that the writing of pamphlets and articles was dull stuff compared with the stimulating, gay and often tragic days at Oakington, when I had been at the vortex of a whirl of action and comradeship the impact of which I knew would never fade. I longed for some opportunity, such as another *Fair Stood the Wind For France*, to use my imagination, but none was to come for another year or two. Meanwhile I did my best with bread-and-butter jobs and once even wrote a parliamentary speech for Sir Archibald Sinclair which he duly praised and delivered in the Commons.

This is not to say that our galleried room at P.R. was dull; very far from it. My friend and colleague R. F. Delderfield has well described it as a sort of Writers' Club, where rank counted for nothing and an atmosphere of great friendliness prevailed. Nevertheless I felt considerably frustrated, a situation in which I was certainly not alone. For what we were all waiting for at that time, I suppose, was the invasion of Hitler's Europe and there were times when the prospect of that event seemed a thousand years away.

Eventually, however, it began to build up to its inevitable climax. The air began to be full of rumours; the woods of the south country were filled with camouflaged guns and tanks. Soon, together with the rest of my colleagues at P.R., I was being given my assignment for D-Day. To my great joy I was to go back to Tangmere, there to cover, in a series of despatches designed specifically for American eyes, the first fighter assaults across the Channel. The actual date of the invasion still being a closely guarded secret, I again went through a period of much frustration, idly kicking my heels between Air Ministry and home, until eventually the tension of waiting grew unbearable and I at last took the road to Tangmere.

When I arrived there on a warm June afternoon I found every inch of space occupied by fighter squadrons, many of whom were aggressive, seething Canadians, raring for battle. There was not a bed to be had. Accordingly, after receiving the inevitable hypodermic jabs for this, that and the other, I drove into Chichester and got myself a room at the Dolphin Hotel, then suddenly started to feel uncommonly ill and repaired immediately to bed. There, remembering my friend the hotelier's consistent injunction never to be on time anywhere, I resolved to sleep late the following day. It was in fact a mere half past nine when I woke, feeling much better, and went placidly downstairs to what I hoped would be a leisurely breakfast. Sitting waiting for it I was, however, horrified to hear two ladies at the next table loudly discussing the fact that invasion had begun. I instantly swallowed a cup of tea, dashed out of the hotel to my car and drove at breakneck speed to Tangmere, cursing myself all the way for being fool enough to chance my luck once too often and considerably scared of the wrath of Air Ministry to come for my having failed in my assignment.

I needn't have worried; if invasion had indeed begun there was little sign of it at Tangmere. It is true that several squadrons had taken to the air but none were yet back from the scene of the battle they had so long thirsted for. It must have been eleven o'clock before the first of them began to appear from over the sea, their gay red-and-white candy striped wings brilliant against a deceptively hot blue sky that was to be darkened, before the day was out, by a storm that came perilously near to wrecking the entire enterprise.

As soon as possible I sought out crews and pilots for interview, only to find everywhere nothing but angry, frustrated men.

Not one of them had a story to tell for the simple reason that there was no story to tell. Not a single German fighter had left the ground that morning in answer to our attack. The difficulty of defending a perimeter as vast as that which Hitler held from the Atlantic coast of France up to the Baltic is that in addition to not knowing where exactly the invader will assault you it is virtually impossible to decide, in the early stages of attack, whether the first strike is a feint or the real thing. To commit yourself too soon in these circumstances could be tragic folly. Goering had therefore not committed either himself or his fighters: hence my furious, frustrated Canadians, denied the blood and battle they had waited so long to taste.

Nevertheless a despatch had to be written and sent off by plane to Air Ministry by mid-afternoon. At first I conceived the task of writing a despatch about nothing to be utterly hopeless; then I woke to the fact that the very nothingness of it was of high significance. Accordingly I dashed off the piece, took it to catch the special Air Ministry plane at four o'clock and then crossed my fingers. Less than a couple of hours later a delighted Dudley Barker was on the phone to me, warm in his praise of a piece I had considered hopeless.

For a week or more I wrote a despatch every day. As invasion progressed there was more and more action to cover and my confidence in my ability to cover it grew in parallel. Every piece was well received in London and I have rarely enjoyed an assignment more. If its beginnings had been clouded by apprehension its end had given me some of the satisfaction of 'something attempted, something done, has earned a night's repose'.

Our foothold on Europe having been secured it was reasonable now to begin to think in terms of the war's end. In fact a whole year was to go by, a great deal of it bloody and bitter, before it did end and for my own part there lay ahead of me an adventure totally unlike anything I had experienced before and which was to make the year 1945 the most significant of my life, in some ways, since that damp January day when I had walked into Bedford Square to meet Edward Garnett.

Before I tell of this particular and exciting adventure, however, I must deal with another which, though briefer and less significant in its effects, nevertheless had its own measure of excitement.

IV

Some time before D-Day at last occurred I had been home in Kent on leave for two or three days when I woke in the middle of the night to a great and hideous noise and the sight of what was clearly a burning aircraft flying low over the roof of the house. I had never before seen a burning aircraft flying so low at night but within minutes it was followed by another and then another and yet another. All were flying in the same direction, that is north-westwards, towards London, at the same height and with the same hideous racket. I was greatly mystified and, with four young children in the house, not a little frightened.

Morning solved the mystery; these were the first of Hitler's malevolent flying bombs, aptly named doodle-bugs, launched in formidable numbers, without respite, and with the object of causing infinite disaster to London and infinite damage to the morale of the civilian population. The flying bomb has been called an instrument of despair on the part of Hitler, who undoubtedly cherished the notion that what the blitz of 1940–41 had failed to achieve the impersonal evil machine of 1944 would. Undoubtedly he saw it as a softening-up device preceding the inevitable Allied invasion of the Continent. Equally undoubtedly we were unprepared for it (by 'we' I mean the civilian population; authority may have had its own information) and were taken greatly by surprise. It was not long, however, before we learned to listen for the sinister cut-out of the bug's power, the dreaded after-silence and the final inevitable bang: moments which were not funny but which had about them a dark and chilling air of doom.

At first our defences against these evils were badly deployed. For a few days London bore the blistering brunt of the attack and then defence chiefs moved quickly. It was swiftly realized that doodle-bugs must be intercepted either before they reached

England's southern coast-line or in the immediate hinterland between the coast and the neighbourhood of the North Downs. Fighter squadrons were accordingly re-deployed and pilots suddenly found themselves engaged in a riotous and unreal sort of circus in which they were fighting an enemy as impersonal and ghoulish as any robot. The doodle-bug in fact proved easy meat and many were the devices said to have been used by pilots for knocking them down, one being the use of a fighter's wing-tip to flip the bug off balance and send it reeling on its earthward way.

This is not to say that the bugs did not do untold damage; nor to deny that the populace were very frightened, wearied and highly tense from nervous strain, irritation and lack of sleep. Nor was London alone in this; the Kentish countryside had the unenviable experience of being the graveyard of thousands of bugs shot down before they reached the capital. A shot-down bug was not, of course, a dead bug; as it hit the earth, whether in cornfield, village street, meadow or churchyard, it exploded just the same, all too often with fatal results. On my own piece of pastoral England more than 3,000 of these intercepted bugs fell in a few weeks, so that a map showing each fallen bug looks like a settlement of black flies on a dead carcass. Perhaps the most remarkable of these was one which on a beautiful July evening floated over my house, cut out half a mile away and fell after the usual sinister silence with an almighty bang, having ended its flight on the top of the church tower under which, so many years before, Madge and I had paused to watch a flock of sheep safely graze. The moment was a doubly sad one, since Little Chart Church was, unless I am gravely misinformed, the only Protestant church in England that contained within its walls a Roman Catholic chapel. Today the ruined and empty tower stands as a stark grey monument to one of war's more senseless stupidities.

From all this racket and tension I was immensely relieved, in August, to be given a couple of weeks' leave. We accordingly went to Scotland, where Edinburgh's calm and beauty formed a haven of bliss after the dreary dread and gloom of the South.

The Trossachs seemed as lovely as the very Elysian fields and Edinburgh itself seemed hardly to know that a war was on, let alone that London and the South were living out a nightmare. For me, however, the respite was short-lived. After a few days there arrived from Dudley Barker a telegram ordering me immediately back to London. As I received it I instantly remembered my friend the hotelier's injunction about never arriving anywhere on time and I decided that 'immediately' meant at least another twelve hours. This was eminently sensible, since to have caught a morning train would merely have meant arriving in the capital at night, when all but air-raid wardens and their various brethren would have gone to bed. Far more sensible to catch the night train and arrive for breakfast, which I accordingly did, only to be woken in the dead of night by a guard calling 'Squadron-Leader Bates, Squadron-Leader Bates!' and ultimately to be handed a second telegram, couched in terms considerably more severe than the first.

I confess to fearing some extremely stern reprimand when I turned up, sleepy-eyed and not at all well-shaven, at Air Ministry that morning; but Dudley Barker, most amenable of men, had no word of reproach to offer and merely informed me that he wished me to fly to France on a mission the sole object of which was to seek out, and report on, doodle-bug launching sites in the area of Picardy and the Pas de Calais. I was to take all the time I wanted, go where I wanted and, if I thought fit, as Dudley obligingly put it, have a look at Paris while I was there.

I departed from Northolt the following afternoon in the usual tin-can Dakota. My wretched stomach, never any good at the best of times, revolted violently on the flight and I was miserably sick for most of the journey, which finally ended at Amiens, where groups of the French Resistance Movement were still rounding up sorry-looking bands of Nazi prisoners from the surrounding woodlands. Presently I was piling into a truck with various other officers and men, to be driven out of Amiens to an encampment on the town's outskirts. All was

Little Chart
Church

infinitely dreary; the camouflaged tents might have been prisons; the food, if food it could be called, was ghastly.

Happily I fell in with an Australian Air Force officer, who turned out to be as depressed as I was. 'I can't bear this bloody place,' he said. '*I want to smell France. The real France.*' These were thoughts so much after my own heart that I suggested we beg, borrow or steal some kind of transport and go and spend the night in Amiens. This we accordingly did, finding ourselves a room in a crumbling little hotel which I strongly suspect was also a brothel. However, we slept well and, as my Australian friend had so devoutly wished, smelled the real smell of France again: and very good to smell it was.

Early next day I set out to seek transport for the purpose of executing my doodle-bug mission. There was no transport. I then discovered a young R.A.F. driver who informed me, with a confidence and assurance that would have done credit to my old friend the hotelier, that of course there was transport. He could lay his hands on a jeep in no time; you just had to know. Within a quarter of an hour he was back with the promised jeep and I was, as I thought, on my way to the early execution of my mission. I was, as it turned out, almost on my way to another kind of execution, since we had scarcely driven half a mile when we were abruptly halted by two service policemen who irately demanded to know what the Hell we were doing with the Group-Captain's jeep? I duly sought out the Group-Captain and proceeded to eat, before him, the largest piece of humble pie I have ever had to consume.

All this, however, did little or nothing to deter my young driver, who in no time at all was back with another jeep, at the same time full of assurances that this time it had not been filched from higher authority. So we set off, not knowing quite what we were looking for or where to look for it. My French, far less adequate even than it is now, helped a little but not much as we stopped a peasant here and a peasant there in order to make our needs known. Finally we tracked down the first of our flying-bomb launching sites.

It was of almost frighteningly simple construction, consisting as it did of two lengths of railway line poised in the air at an angle of 45°. Up this track the doodle-bug was launched, to float away, if all went well, in the direction of England. Often, in fact, all did not go well. Not infrequently the doodle-bug stalled, spun backwards and fell back on its unfortunate launchers, blowing them to exceedingly small pieces. On other occasions a bug would execute a much larger loop, falling on the equally unfortunate citizens of Amiens, with similarly ghastly results.

These launching pads were all of identical construction. The only difference was in the sites they occupied. Some were well hidden in woods; others in orchards; a few in back gardens; and one at least occupied a village street. I suppose, that morning, I saw and inspected perhaps twenty of them, arriving at last at the conclusion, fortified by complete boredom, that having seen one I had seen them all. It must have been about two o'clock when I finally decided that the sight of one more doodle-bug site would drive me scatty and I remembered the words of Dudley Barker.

'Ever been to Paris?' I asked my young driver.

'No, sir. Never.'

'Well, you're going now.'

We drove southward. If I thought that the road to Paris was to be an easy one I was shortly to be much disillusioned. I

knew, but had failed fully to appreciate the fact, that every bridge in France had been blown up in order to frustrate the Nazi retreat; but it was not until we reached our first river that I came to a moment of an awful realization that it was one thing to decide to go to Paris but quite another to get there. On either side of the river there appeared to be utter chaos: groups of service-men, French citizens carrying bundles, bags of all kinds of motley belongings wrapped in newspaper and so on. There appeared to be no hope whatever of getting across that river.

Then to my infinite surprise I saw a pontoon consisting of several insecure-looking planks lashed to empty petrol drums slowly being punted on its way across stream from the opposite bank. This was a welcome enough sight in itself; but what was even more welcome and astonishing was the sight of a beautiful woman standing on the pontoon, beside a black Citroën car, waving a bottle of brandy. Clearly she was very excited.

'Hullo there, England!' she shouted, in English. 'Lovely to see you! Have a brandy.'

As the pontoon touched the shore she leapt to the bank, excitedly waving the brandy bottle, and at once proceeded to embrace me with rapturous fervour. Her charm and vivacity and her unmistakable Englishness were matched only by her husband's charm and courtesy and his equally unmistakable Frenchness.

'First time we've been able to leave Paris since the occupation.' She first introduced herself as a Countess and then inquired where I was bound for. When I said Paris her excitement mounted. Where was I going to stay? When I said that I hadn't the remotest idea she at once said: 'Then you must stay at our apartment. The concierge and his wife will look after you and will be thrilled to have you. I'll write down the address. It's in the Place des Etats Unis, just off the Avenue Kléber, not far from the Etoile.'

We drank more brandy; she wrote down her address; and then I asked where she and her Count were going.

'To our Château. Not far from Amiens. Haven't seen it

since 1940. Will you be coming back that way?' I said that I supposed we would. 'Then you must call and stay with us there. I insist. No formalities. Just drop in. God, it's great to speak to an Englishman again.'

We parted, brandy-filled, as rapturously as we had met, she warmly insistent that we used her apartment in Paris and equally urgent that we call on her at her northern Château. I promised fervently to do both and then we drove on our respective ways.

As we approached Paris, however, I began to have misgivings. Had the Countess been talking or was it the brandy? On cooler reflection I decided it was the brandy and in consequence told my young driver to take me to the Hotel Scribe. This, as I understood it, was being used as a centre for radio and newspaper correspondents and innocently I trusted I should find some kind of succour there. Instead I found a madhouse. Nobody knew anything about anything. Nobody had time either to speak or listen. All was bedlam and chaos.

Then by pure chance I ran into Richard Dimbleby. Though I didn't know him personally but only by reputation I knew that he knew my agent, Laurence Pollinger, very well. I accordingly introduced myself, explaining at the same time that I could get no change out of anybody and that I had nowhere to sleep.

'You must bang the bloody table!' said Richard. 'It's the only way to get anything done in this damn place.'

By this time I was more than a little weary and in no mood for table-banging. There was nothing for it, therefore, but to navigate to the Place des Etats Unis.

This square, I should explain for the benefit of those who do not know it, is one of the most exclusive in Paris, and much of my apprehension returned as we drew up to the Countess'

Place des Etats Unis

grand establishment. I need not, however, have worried. The joy on the faces of the concierge and his little wife was comparable only with that of the Biblical shepherd rejoicing over his one lost sheep that had at last been found. Fortunately I was armed with a plentiful supply of 'K' rations and a pound or two of real coffee. This in itself was pure gold and soon, in return for it, the wife of the concierge was cooking us an omelette as only the French know how to.

But before this she showed us up to our rooms. I have rarely seen anything in such palatial, perfect taste. Rare Persian rugs, fine old masters, exquisite china and glass, sumptuous period furniture: I felt myself to be in a miniature Renaissance palace.

One thing, however, disturbed me. To my considerable consternation Madame now and then referred to a 'Monsieur Barker'. Did she, in some way, know about Dudley; or did Dudley know about me and my tendency to truancy? I failed to decide. Then by chance the word 'Granville' was dropped to join 'Barker' and the mystery was solved. The sumptuous apartment really belonged to the celebrated Granville Barker, man of the theatre.

Next day the wife of the concierge was insistent that I meet the wife of another concierge. Madame Martin, who lived on the far side of the Place des Etats Unis, was, it seemed, English, though her husband was a Frenchman. Great would be her joy at meeting an officer of the Royal Air Force.

That afternoon I accordingly went to call on Madame Martin and found a tiny red-haired woman whose diminutive stature perfectly matched the tiny concierge rabbit hutch in which she and her husband, like thousands of others of their kind in Paris, somehow existed on the ground floor. The pathetic nature of this tiny box contrasted painfully with a house where grandeur was even more palatial than that of the house of Monsieur Barker. But of Madame Martin's joy there was no shadow of doubt. Her red letter day, long prayed and hoped for, had at last arrived. With touching, tearful insistence she begged that I would take tea with her; and take tea I did, the tea being made from a few pathetic ounces jealously hoarded ever since the Nazi legions had triumphantly tramped into Paris.

As we took tea Madame Martin referred on several occasions to *la Duchesse*. It was the greatest pity that *la Duchesse* was away in the country. *La Duchesse* would have been greatly honoured and delighted to have met an English officer. In her excitement Madame Martin frequently forgot her English, the opportunity to speak which had been denied her for nearly five years, and lapsed into a mongrel language composed of three parts French to one of almost broken English, so that sometimes I had difficulty in understanding her.

Many years later I saw her again. The occasion was one at which my French publishers were giving a cocktail party in honour of a new book of mine. The *rendezvous* was in the Place des Etats Unis and great was Madame Martin's astonishment when I walked into her tiny rabbit hutch and handed my hat and coat to her. But greater still was my surprise to find that my hostess was *la Duchesse* herself. I will refrain from giving her name but will be content merely to record that it was that of one of France's most renowned and aristocratic families. Not that it is she I remember. The figure that still haunts my mind is that of the tiny Madame Martin, with her red hair and precious ounces of tea, by no means happily married to her French husband, living a life of virtual imprisonment under conditions that many an animal lover would have found intolerable for a dog, her life sweetened at last by liberation and the sharing of a cup of tea with an English officer. Somehow she personifies France's war-time agony more deeply than any Frenchwoman could have done, just as *la Comtesse*, so rabidly English, personifies her joy.

I cannot now recall with any accuracy how long we stayed in Paris. My acutest and most abiding memory is of wandering, in a hazy day-dream, by the Seine, stopping to browse over book-stalls or to chat with an occasional fisherman and then of wandering up and down the Rue de Rivoli, the windows of whose shops were astonishingly filled with goods that had long since disappeared from England.

Finally, with fond farewells, we left for the north. As we drove out of Paris we saw, at every street corner, hordes of hungry faces – hungry not for food but for a lift to somewhere out of Paris. As the jeep would hold only one extra passenger I decided that the fairest thing to do was to give a lift to no one, a resolution in which I was frustrated by a young woman who athletically leapt into the vehicle while it was moving, shouting, 'Lille, Lille, Lille!'

In vain I told her that I was not going to Lille and that I had certainly no intention whatever of doing so. She implored me, in typical Gallic fashion, to change my mind. I was quite adamant. She then offered me money. I declined more firmly than ever. Then, as we again reached the river where *la Comtesse* had jubilantly waved her brandy bottle at me, she begged me to walk along the river bank with her while we waited for the pontoon to cross. We walked as far as a stretch of woodland and here, as she paused, I realized that if only I would take her to Lille another kind of bribe could be mine for the taking. This too I very firmly declined and we finally left her in a state of tearful and angry frustration on the riverside.

Some few miles farther north we then came upon a sad sight. A young man and woman, bearing a long stout pole from one pair of shoulders to another, were wearily plodding along

a road as long and straight and barren as only certain French roads can be, the pole bearing two large and clearly very weighty suitcases. The pair looked fit to drop. The good Samaritan in me that had with apparent callousness rejected the girl from Lille, rose up at once, greatly touched. We stopped the jeep and the exhausted couple fell into the back.

'*Où allez-vous?*' I said in my primitive French.

'*Amiens.*'

'*Moi aussi.*'

The noises from the back of the jeep were a strange chorus of tears and laughter.

As we drove on they explained that they had left Paris riding a single ancient bicycle – a machine which, under the prodigious combined weight of two grown people and two vast suitcases, had promptly and inevitably broken clean in half.

So we took them to Amiens, where they too, like Madame Martin, had hoarded a few precious ounces of tea, which we now gratefully shared with them, at the same time declining an offer of an evening meal and a bed for the night.

'No,' I said to my young driver, 'we have to get on.'

'Where to now, sir?'

'We are,' I said, 'going to call on the Countess.'

We duly found the Château of the Countess, a typically grey turreted house of the kind to be seen all over France, only

to discover that there was, alas, no Countess. From below the low hillside on which the Château stood there were, however, sounds of village revelry, and it was here, the servants of the Château informed us, that we should find the Countess, dancing.

The astonished Countess, vastly enjoying herself at a village hop, was even more jubilant and excited at seeing us than when she had first waved the brandy at me from the pontoon. She at once insisted on leaving the dance and repairing to the Château, there to kill, if not the fatted calf, at least a bottle or two of precious wine. This we did and very soon the four of us were sitting down to an extremely good dinner, we full of our gratitude for all the hospitality at the Place des Etats Unis, she eager to hear how we had found the people and the city. I had in fact been greatly excited by the city; so much so that many subsequent visits to Paris have never quite matched my simmering fervour on that first post-war, or almost post-war, return. The evening continued and ended gaily.

Memory again serves me poorly here, since I find myself quite unable to remember if we spent one, two or three nights at the Château. I recall only that it was all infinitely pleasant, that I promised I would telephone the Countess's father when I got back to England and that finally, when we did leave, I went away burdened with gifts that seemed comparable with those borne by the three Wise Men, among them a superlative handbag for my wife. There was further a parting injunction that we shouldn't fail, on any account, to visit an Anglophile friend of the Count and Countess, some fifteen miles away. She too was a Countess and her arms, we were assured, would be open to infinite widths to receive us.

Having enjoyed the company of one countess so much, we had no hesitation in seeking out the second. This we quickly did, to discover that her house was not a Château, in the grey, turreted, almost prison-like French tradition, but a big four-square stone manor house, a true French farm *manoir* built round a huge central stone-flagged courtyard. Here, when we arrived, a number of women servants were sitting in the evening sunlight on hard kitchen chairs, very much in the French summer fashion, knitting, sewing and gossiping. After I had introduced myself my primitive French once again elucidated the fact that, alas, *la Comtesse* was not at home. However, I was assured, she soon would be and would we be pleased to wait?

I spent the waiting time wandering in the huge, square, typically stone-walled garden. Here, on the walls, glowed ripe crimson peaches of luscious magnificence; I fancy there were also deep purple figs; and in glass frames there shone, like green-gold suns, cantaloupe melons of such opulence that you felt they must surely burst and, like over-full cornucopia, spill out their golden juicy riches. Seeing it all I began to have certain doubts as to whether in fact the French had starved under the German yoke or if some, if not all of them, had lived in little insulated rural paradises, lushly as medieval nobles: a suspicion that, as I shall presently explain, was well supported next day.

In due course Countess No. 2 arrived: a rather older woman than the first but equally attractive, equally excited, equally delighted to have the honour of entertaining an English officer. It was she who graciously took us into the house which, inside, was even more a true French *manoir* than it appeared from the courtyard. Vast rooms, vast beams, vast doors, a vast oak refectory table laid for supper: it might all have come straight out of some story by Maupassant. One felt in it the very breath of a France feudal, burdened with a centuries-old rural tradition, self-contained and self-supporting, cut off not only from any urban, outside world but from that more sinister one of Nazi occupation.

These first impressions of mine grew stronger and stronger as we collected round the great refectory table for supper. What further astonished me was the extraordinary number of people who had now gathered for the evening meal. It was not merely that we were suddenly *en famille*, with *grand'mère*, *tante* this and *tante* that, the Count and Countess and a sister or two, but there was also the farm bailiff and several other retainers whose exact *rôles* were not clear to me. Again the scene might have been one out of a story by Maupassant;

again, as in the garden, there was no hint of things impecunious or impoverished; you felt indeed that war and all its attendant trials and atrocities had passed this lovely *manoir* and its opulent oasis completely by.

In the morning, at breakfast, my suspicions about the fullness or emptiness of at least some French bellies under Nazi occupation were finally and fully confirmed. In the centre of the big breakfast table I found myself gazing on a large square yellow object weighing perhaps two or three pounds. After gazing at it for some minutes in wonder and disbelief I was at last moved to inquire what it was. '*C'est du beurre, naturellement.*'

Butter! A block of not much less than three pounds of it. Fresh farmhouse butter. I couldn't recall ever having seen so much butter before except long ago when, as a boy, I used to go for my mother to the local dairy, there to watch with fascination the white-coated attendant slicing lumps of butter from a great block and smacking it into shapes with wooden pats on cold marble counters. But in war-time – the thing was a mocking miracle. The piece of butter on the breakfast table seemed soon to assume the size of a yellow tombstone and I could only wonder how large an English family, pitifully eking out its meagre rations, it would have fed and for how long.

I was then further moved to tell the Countess that I had never, or at least for a very long time, seen so large a quantity of butter: an admission which seemed to amuse her much. I was then emboldened to ask if I couldn't, perhaps, buy a pound or two of it in the village to take back to England with me.

'Today it is doubtful. Today is not a butter-making day. But tomorrow will be. So if you will stay with us another night – and we do hope that you will – we will round up a decent quantity for you. I hope you will stay for another reason – I know that some of the French Resistance boys would be greatly honoured to meet you.'

I duly met some half dozen of the French Resistance boys – and they were really not much more than boys – who promptly invited me to lunch with them in Amiens the following day.

We were to meet at midday in the central square. I was very happy to accept but breakfast the next morning made me happier still: for there, waiting for me, was my miracle of butter, about four pounds of it, together with a great box of luscious peaches, several melons and a number of pairs of pure silk stockings for my wife. I don't think I wept at the sight of these riches, but I am not ashamed to confess that as I said farewell to the Countess, her opulent garden and her Maupassant-like *manoir* I was very near to tears.

At midday, having met the French Resistance boys, I was taken off by them to a modest and typically plebeian restaurant called *Restaurant des Cultivateurs et Voyageurs*. And here, once again, I found my suspicions about French bellies well confirmed. Having eaten a large and excellent dish of *tomates provençal*, I was just preparing to relax, fully replete, when I was astonished, if not indeed dismayed, to discover that this was merely what is sometimes called a starter. To follow *les tomates* there arrived an equally large and equally excellent dish of *blanquette de veau*, with which I confess my poor war-shrunken stomach found it hard to cope.

That afternoon, laden with riches and feeling almost as if returning homeward from some fabulous Samarkand instead of from a France stricken and divided, I hitched a lift on the beer-plane to England. I name it the beer-plane because that is precisely what it was: a small hedge-hopping machine, probably a D. H. Rapide, which jumped from one air-field to another, depositing crates of beer and taking empties away.

My trip had been one of much reward and excitement. If I hadn't learned much of great importance about doodle-bug launching sites I had learned, or had more truly confirmed for myself, much else. The descriptions of rural France in *Fair Stood the Wind For France* had had necessarily to be done, almost all of them, from imagination. Now my visit had proved, not for the first or last time, that imagination can take a writer nearer to the heart of truth than any amount of observation, and that instinct, rather than sheer reasoning, will often guide him just as surely. Once again indeed Thackeray's celebrated dictum had been justified: 'the work of fiction contains more truth in solution than the work which purports to be all true.'

I had now ahead of me another adventure, larger and of far wider import than the mere interlude in France; and of this I must now proceed to tell.

V

As the winter of 1944–45 came on my health grew infinitely worse. The abdominal pains I had had to endure with increasing misery since my schooldays had now become a scourge. Pain not only tortured me by day, but kept me agonisingly awake at night. I wrote little of any consequence and derived little or no pleasure from what I did. It was clear that one day surgeons would have 'to take a little peep' inside me but no such operation would be possible until a more critical stage in my physical condition had been reached. I simply had to grin and bear it.

When therefore Dudley Barker summoned me to his desk at Air Ministry one day in mid-January 1945 it was to greet me with something like these words:

'We all know what a miserable time you've been having with your health and if you want to say "No" to the proposition I'm going to put to you we shall all understand. It's entirely up to you. If you feel you must decline please decline. Nothing more will be said.'

'What is the proposition?'

'We'd like you to go to Burma. You would actually be based in India, at Calcutta, where Doddie will look after you.'

'How long for?'

'Entirely up to you. The object of the exercise is to write half a dozen pieces – even some short stories – specifically for the American market. It's felt that the Americans should be made aware that there is in fact a war going on in Burma, and a pretty desperate one at that. But, as I say, you don't *have* to go. It's neither a posting nor an order.'

'May I think it over?'

'That's exactly what we want you to do. In fact buzz off now, talk it over with your wife and tell us later what you feel. But remember – there's no compulsion.'

Oddly enough, I felt excited. My feelings were very much akin to those I had experienced when Hilary Saunders, Harald Peake and John Nerney had first proposed that I should be commissioned into the R.A.F. solely to write short stories. Here, now, was a new field to explore, a new theatre from which I might extract stories and drama. Once again I felt excited, honoured and no little apprehensive.

For a day or two I talked it over with Madge and she, like me, felt it was clearly my duty to accept the proposition. She knew that, with four very young children, my absence would be hard for her; and I knew it too. But neither of us ever really felt otherwise than that I should go to India and Burma, and within another day or so I went back to Dudley Barker to tell him so.

Dudley, though pleased at my decision, nevertheless warned me: 'We probably won't be able to get you away before early February, so if in the meantime you decide to change your mind you are perfectly free to do so.'

I replied that I didn't think I would change my mind and I may even have said – I certainly thought it – that healthwise the trip might even do me good. The only further comment I had from Dudley was the simple one that 'India is a mess'. Little did I know.

So on a day in early February Madge came with me to B.O.A.C.'s air terminal in London, where we said a fond but rather dejected farewell. Scarcely had she waved her hand for the last time and disappeared into the street than a loudspeaker announcement told that my flight had been cancelled. I was home ten minutes after Madge and we were able to have one more evening together.

Next day I entrained for Swindon and thence to Lyneham. There a positive horde of service-men and women had been waiting for an entire week for February's fogs to clear and they were full of mocking laughter at the new buoyant contingent just arriving. Nevertheless, that night, the fog did clear; morning broke white with hoar-frost and by half past eight we were air-borne. An hour or two later I could see the far

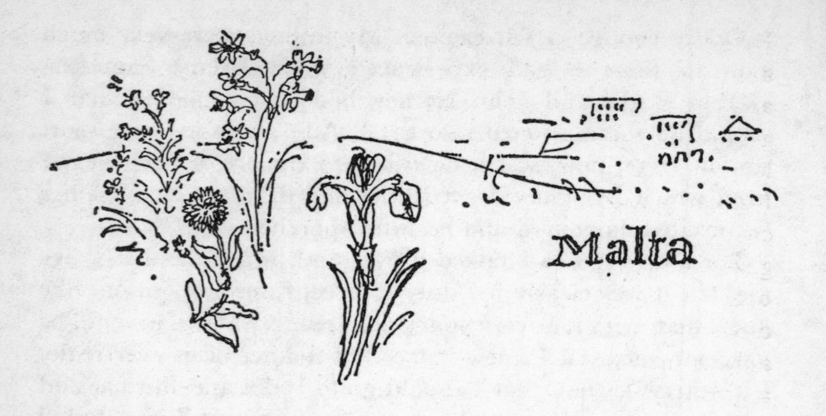

distant line of the Alps, looking like a crowd of pink sugar mice nestling together in the low, brilliant morning sun.

Eventually, on the dark blue sea below, a rock appeared: of such apparent and unexpected smallness that I simply couldn't believe that this was our first stop, Malta. But Malta it was and soon half a dozen of us were wandering among Valletta's white and sparkling ruins. Malta indeed was a sad sight; there was little to do or buy; and we ended the day by taking a moth-eaten gharry and driving to some remote black market restaurant and there eating what I strongly suspect was some species of dog heavily flavoured with garlic and herbs. If however I give the impression that Malta was a scene of utter desolation I must at once correct it. Its ruins apart, it was a little paradise of flowers; arum lilies, narcissi, irises, stocks, sweet-peas, marigolds and trees of fruit blossom. I marvelled and revelled greatly in that premature touch of spring.

Next morning we flew on to Cairo, arriving in time for a lunch which my tiresome stomach rejected, so that I spent most of the time slowly sucking at an orange and gazing dreamily at a vase of sweet-peas. After lunch, since our flight wasn't due to continue until the small hours of the morning, six of us, including I think two army brigadiers, thumbed a lift in a truck and made for Cairo. One had the immediate impression that that city had been shipped straight from

Paradise. I recall a shop window full of sponges, a sight which so awed and transfixed us that we spent an unconscionable amount of time simply staring at it in total disbelief, not like a group of grown men but like schoolboys outside a tuck-shop long out of bounds. Then there was the famed *confiserie* of Mr Groppi, sparkling with riches long denied us: chocolates, cakes, tarts, sweetmeats of every kind. Here we didn't merely gaze; the latent schoolboys in us leapt to life, positively falling over each other with mouth-watering greed. Finally we discovered – the city now as brilliantly lit as a fair – a restaurant in which two dozen chickens revolved on a spit over a glowing charcoal fire. Small wonder that we drove back to base more than a little heady on Palestinian wine.

We flew off in early morning darkness. I invariably find it impossible to sleep in an aircraft and I sat awake for several hours, merely staring at the blackness ahead. Suddenly the blackness sparkled with jewels: diamonds, rubies, emeralds. This was our airfield; we were about to come down in Persia.

Dawn was breaking as we touched down; then we washed, shaved and breakfasted briefly. Sheiba airfield looked like any other airfield in the middle of a desert: sandy, wind-swept, desolate. This in fact was my one and only glimpse of Persia, yet many years later I had the strangest dream: I dreamed that I was a magistrate-cum-tax collector in a small remote Persian town and that I was to preside over the magistrates' court. The year was 200 B.C. (this perhaps was the oddest part of the dream, since one couldn't know, in 200 B.C. that in fact it was B.C.). Another vivid fact was the blinding, blistering heat of the day: a fact that made me decide to start holding the court immediately after dawn. Still more vivid was the sight of the shadows in the narrow Persian streets shrinking and shrinking until, at midday, under the perpendicular sun, they existed no longer.

The first strange thing about this dream is that, unlike so many dreams, it has never faded; it still has the same indelible brilliance as on the night when I first experienced it. The second strange thing is that I had not, beforehand, been reading or talking of Persia or seeing anything of the country on the television screen. My entire acquaintance with Persia consisted solely of one hour, in war-time, on an R.A.F. airfield. How to explain it all? My friend Ann Todd, the actress, a woman of much intelligence, entertains no shadow of doubt about it. I *was* once a Persian magistrate and am now reincarnated.

After Persia we flew on to Karachi. My first experience of India (this was before the birth of Pakistan) was to drink the vilest cup of tea that has ever passed my lips and as I threw it away my heart for some reason, sank to my boots. I suddenly felt bitterly, depressingly homesick, a sensation that wasn't in any way lessened by the fact that when the aircraft took off again I found myself to be the one remaining passenger. The fact of that isolation, as we flew over India's vast desert interior, filled me with a dark and desolate gloom.

We came in to land, stickily, in a cross-wind at Dum-Dum

airfield. Perhaps it was merciful that Dudley's comment 'India is a mess' had remained cryptic and unexpanded. I knew, in fact, nothing of India; its history had largely passed me by; I hated Kipling; of the sub-continent's many languages and dialects I had heard only of Hindi, of its rivers only the Ganges. Ignorance may indeed, at times, be bliss, but as I stepped out into the afternoon's torrid heat on Dum-Dum's tarmac there was to be no bliss for me.

Nor was I suffering merely from ignorance. I cherished several fond if not idiotic illusions. One was that Doddie, if unable to meet me himself, would surely have sent someone, with the necessary transport, in his place. I soon realized that there was in fact no Doddie and no transport. Desperate inquiry at several offices purporting to be sections of the R.A.F. merely brought, from young Indian servicemen, that curious sideways tilt of the head that seems to indicate something half way between yes and no but which experience finally teaches simply means damn-all. I then realized that I hadn't the faintest idea where Doddie's Headquarters were; nor had I fully grasped the fact that the day was Saturday, nor the still more discomforting fact that in Calcutta the war stopped, every Saturday, at noon. All I knew, or thought I knew, was that Doddie was somewhere in Calcutta, then a city of $4\frac{1}{2}$ million people and some twenty-five miles in diameter. This in fact was another fond illusion, since Group-Captain Dodds was, in fact, not in Calcutta but in Hastings, twenty miles northward up the River Hooghli. Nor did I then know that the reason why neither Doddie nor anyone else had come to meet me was that authority – and this at a time when it was almost as difficult to get out of England as out of Wormwood Scrubs – had neglected to include me on the manifest of any aircraft leaving England during the three previous days. Officially I was lost.

By this time I also felt personally lost. Eventually I hitched a lift in a truck going into Calcutta, the centre of which, another fact I didn't know, was twenty miles away. In a recent article a celebrated journalist has called Calcutta the most degraded and disgusting great city in the world, a description the full taste of which I was to savour as I now drove through twenty miles of what are indisputably some of the most revolting, most stinking, most rat-ridden, most sickening and most depraved slums in the world. A dead cow rotting on the roadside in the grilling heat of afternoon, giving off the stench of putrefaction and the charnel house; a mad rush of gharries, cars and rickshaws; an old woman, a mere shrunken bag of bones, dying in the gutter without a soul bothering to spare her a second glance; a great mass of rotting filth choking every pavement, gully and alleyway; the evil stench of poverty, of hordes of unwashed bodies, of burning dung: these are merely a few of the more obvious, more odious, more sickening features of that seemingly endless journey through Calcutta's slums on that torrid afternoon.

Eventually the truck-driver dumped me, bed-roll, bags and all, on the pavement outside the Great Eastern Hotel, in the very centre of Calcutta. The hotel, used as a sort of transit camp, teemed with servicemen, a complete madhouse. Lost in utter bewilderment, I suddenly spotted an Air Commodore and asked him if he possibly knew where I might find Group-

Captain Dodds? He stared at me as if I had asked for Jesus Christ himself. I repeated the experience with several other people, always with the same result, until I suddenly knew, exhausted and drowned in sweat as I was, that I was going rapidly and irrevocably mad.

Presently, in this utterly desperate state, I spotted an R.A.F. sergeant in a jeep. I went over to him and begged, yet again, if he might possibly tell me where I could find Group-Captain Dodds.

'Dodds? Never 'eard of 'im. What mob's he in?'

'Public Relations.'

'Gor blimey, why didn't you say so the first time? 'Op in.'

I threw my kit into the back of the jeep and hopped in. We then drove crazily round several back streets, crushing water-melon rinds as we skidded round corners, honking at the usual press of dhoti-clad Indians, all looking like lazy brown-and-white moths. It was by now five o'clock and to my horror the sergeant suddenly muttered something about we'd be 'bleeding lucky if the office wasn't shut by now'. Eventually, however, we drew up in a narrow alley and the sergeant said:

'This is it. On the first floor. I'll keep an eye on your kit while you go up.'

Near to utter exhaustion, I crawled upstairs. At the head of them a thin Squadron-Leader, accompanied by a woman companion, was in the very act of locking an office door.

I introduced myself and he almost fainted.

'Good God, Laddie,' he said in strong Scots accent, 'we've been searching high and low for you all day. Where've you been? Do you not know you're not on the manifest of any aircraft that's left Great Britain for the past three days?'

No, I said, I didn't know; nor did I care.

At this point the Squadron-Leader introduced himself as Nickie, then his companion as Mrs Henderson. 'Mrs Henderson and her husband Tom are old friends of mine. Aye, they're Scots like me.'

I shook hands with Mrs Henderson, a small bright-eyed, cheerful woman who eyed me up and down keenly – purely because, as she afterwards explained, she simply couldn't believe that I could possibly be as weary as I looked.

'Talking of manifests,' I said, 'it's manifest that I get a room somewhere. Is there a hotel you can recommend?'

The Squadron-Leader laughed uproariously.

'Listen, Laddie. Calcutta's a city of four and a half million people and it has three hotels. One is a sort of transit camp, one is a brothel that when it isn't a brothel is closed because of dead dogs, cats or rats in the water supply. The other has so many bugs they eat you alive. Hotels? – you must be joking, Laddie. Joking.'

Then where the devil, I wanted to know, could I stay?

Mrs Henderson gave me another long, searching, pitying look. 'Ye dinna need worry your head about that tonight. My husband and I'll see ye have a bed for tonight.'

I thanked her warmly and a few minutes later I was piling my kit into the Squadron-Leader's car and the three of us were retracing the sordid miles of Calcutta's slums that had so sickened and revolted me an hour or so before. The second sight of them seemed only to reveal a greater squalor than the

first; the dead cow putrefying by the roadside had entered an even more evil, sickening state of putrefaction; on trees and fences about it vultures were already gathering, evil-looking themselves, in readiness for tomorrow's scavenging gorge; everywhere in bazaars and streets and alleyways there seemed to be greater crowds than ever; rickshaws, both man-powered and bicycle-powered, dashed precariously among huge open taxis, all driven by dark turbanned Sikhs; trotting, sweating coolies bearing loads on the ends of long poles, so that they looked like pairs of human scales; women with great bundles on their heads; all seemed noisier, more chaotic, more miserable to look upon.

After a long period of all this we came to a more or less open road bordered on each side by dusty bullock tracks along which both bullocks and water-buffaloes were lugging heavy wooden carts, lumbering like Biblical beasts through deep rainless dust. Above them great tall palms threw long shadows, their high motionless fronds looking as if cut out of black steel against a sky almost colourless in the last half hour of daylight preceding India's swift short twilight.

Presently we came to another squalid settlement with the everlasting crowds, among which barbers sat in gutters cutting their clients' hair, and the everlasting squalor. Then suddenly we halted at a pair of enormous wooden gates, which were duly flung open in obedience to irate honkings on the car horn. A pair of obsequious Indians salaamed as we passed through into a biggish courtyard, on three sides of which stood a prison-like factory. 'Jute,' said Mrs Henderson and I then remembered that jute was the main artery of Calcutta's life-blood.

On the other side of the factory flowed the wide stewy Hooghli, its far bank already glittering with a thin scattering of lights. On the near bank, taking advantage of the last daylight, a gang of kneeling Indian women and girls were planting grass on a newly prepared stretch of red-brown earth, dibbing in each green tuft swiftly, as rice is planted. Behind them it was possible to pick out the patch-work of previous days' plantings, the nearest pale and wilting, the farthest already a brilliant emerald green.

The Hendersons' flat was on the first floor of a block overlooking the river. We climbed up an outside iron staircase, an Indian bearer, a boy of perhaps thirteen, lugging my kit up behind us. The flat was far from large and out of it appeared Tom Henderson, shortish, of typical Scots countenance, looking slightly but patiently aggrieved that his wife, as I discovered was her habit, had brought home yet another weary R.A.F. waif-and-stray who could not find himself a bed. Tom Henderson had in fact lost an R.A.F. son by an earlier marriage at some earlier stage of the war and in consequence, like his wife, was ever-ready to play the good Samaritan.

'Will ye no be takking a wee chota peg, mon?' Mr Henderson said.

My weary brain failed signally to translate this sentence of thick Scots, with its peppering of Hindustani, into any kind of sense and in answer I could only stare stupidly.

'Tom means would you like a drink?' Mrs Henderson said and I came suddenly to my senses, causing laughter.

For the next half an hour I drank much gin-and-tonic, well iced, and nothing had ever tasted so good. As we drank, Nickie announced that I was a writer, a piece of information that caused great surprise to spring into Mrs Henderson's face, as if she were unable to believe that such a species not only existed but had actually appeared in her home. But being also a practical soul, she almost at once suggested that I would surely like a bath, to which I responded with something like:

'God, that would be Heaven.'

It was indeed Heaven and thus refreshed I went early to bed, at last to slumber like a child under my mosquito net.

I woke early next morning, shaved, bathed again and then went out on to the terrace of the Hendersons' flat. The scene laid before my eyes in that exquisite first hour or so after sunrise was the perfect example of the fact that 'distance lends enchantment to the view'. The far bank of the Hooghli lay bathed in a

soft, delicious, opalescent light, as from a 'faery land forlorn' its temples and towers and houses rising from an assortment of trees and palms in infinitely tender shades of pink and cream and green and yellow and even lavender. That there lay under this sublimely beautiful, ethereally unreal curtain a dark sink of putrefying squalor seemed totally fantastic. I could only wonder which had cheated me most, the evening of the previous day or the sweet opal loveliness of my first Indian sunrise.

India, ruthless as ever towards human life, soon mocked me with an answer. Just below me, in the river, beyond the new-planted grass, a pale object floated past, twisting in slow curves on the downstream current. It was the swollen body of a man, the first but by no means the last I was to see of the wide Hooghli's victims.

It wasn't long, however, before the first fond illusion of India's fairy dawn was to be burnt in the cauldron of rising day. In an hour or two the sun was scalding; by noon the flat was an oppressive oven in which I sweated and wolfed at iced gin-and-tonic like an exhausted animal at a stream. 'Och! this is nothing,' the Hendersons said. 'This is only February. We've no begun to warm up yet. This is really the winter.'

Afternoon wrapped me in a long siesta, from which I emerged to the blessed refreshment of tea flavoured with fresh green limes. Soon afterwards Nickie appeared, announcing his readiness to drive us all up river to Hastings, there to find Group-Captain Dodds. It was growing dark as we left in his car and the air was alternately sweet and noisome with the heavy fragrance of what may have been incense trees and the fires, in villages, of burning dung. Something about this combination of the sweet and the acrid very much depressed my spirits. Sunday in time of war, as any serviceman would tell you, was the week's worst day, when families are most missed and most thought of and homesickness sits on the heart like a grey blight. That first drive up the Hooghli on Sunday still lives with me, vivid and gloomy as ever.

Headquarters at Hastings was housed, as I think I am right in saying, in a converted jute-mill. Its personnel consisted, I should say, of ninety per cent American, the rest British. As always, the Americans lacked for nothing: iced beer, drinks of all kinds, a club-house, a bar opulently built of bamboo, and girls and all the rest of it. (There is a story telling of how, at one period of the war in New Guinea, the morale of American troops dropped far below zero. The cause of this phenomenon was searched for far and wide. More beer, more hamburgers, more jazz, more women – these and a score of other opiates were investigated and rejected. It was then discovered by chance that what the troops were pining for were the comic supplements to American newspapers. These were duly flown out by the thousand in special aircraft and morale immediately rose like a moon rocket.) Not that we, the poor British, with a beer ration of one can a month, had cause to grouse at American affluence. Though they sometimes behaved with that singular insularity that is one of their less endearing characteristics (I once spent a night sharing a dormitory with seven or eight American officers, not one of whom spoke to me, as if fearing that mere conversational contact with a Limey might prove unpleasantly contagious) they were on the whole generous to their poor relations, conferring on us generous gifts of beer, a drink I am not normally very fond of but which, in Calcutta's sweltering cauldron, was sheer nectar.

It was good to see my old Commanding Officer again and his dry humour caused my spirits to rise and sweeten. Tomorrow we would meet, lunch, talk, make plans; I must get myself effectively kitted out (I was still wearing my thick R.A.F. uniform and mightily uncomfortable it was) and he would show me where. He also reminded me that another colleague from P.R.3, an officer named Chadwick, was also in Calcutta, together with one or two others I had known in London, including the journalist Andrew Rice, so that soon there would be no lack of friends. Chadwick was also a member of the Bengal Club, then probably the most exclusive club in the world, so that at least one avenue of civilisation would possibly be open to me. There was also the Swimming Club, a blessed haven as it proved, and Doddie would see that I was made a member of that.

If I have given the impression that Calcutta was wholly and irremediably squalid I must now make some effort to correct it. The east side of Calcutta was, as with so many great cities, its worst; its West End, as with London, Paris and many other cities, was infinitely superior. Here there is a wide park-like space, the Maidan, in which stands Government House, built by Lord Wellesley in 1799 and closely modelled on the great Adam house, Kedleston Hall, in Derbyshire (it must be remembered that Calcutta was once the capital of India, before New Delhi was built, being preferred to its rival Bombay because of the prevalence of plague in Bombay, a disease from which Calcutta, for all the nastiness of its climate, was relatively free). Government House was, when I first saw it, not only a fine Adam-like pile in itself, but more glorious than Solomon himself in its vast brilliant garment of red, salmon and magenta bougainvillaea: an exotic and amazing sight. And as if this vivid lustre were not enough great beds of cannas, six feet or more tall, in scarlet, crimson, yellow, orange and pink, flaunted their trumpets on the emerald, well-watered lawns in front of the great house, like companies of severely drilled soldiery on stiff and solid guard.

Alongside the Maidan runs one of the most famous streets in the world, Chowringee, once a row of palatial mansions, but now more like another Knightsbridge, filled with shops large and fashionable. Behind this were streets of colonial houses and gardens of considerable wealth and charm. Nor, indeed, would it be true to say that all of Calcutta was poor. Its large port ensures that it is a city of great wealth; though, as so often happens, its wealth abides with the few, its poverty with the many.

There is no doubt, however, that the atmosphere of Calcutta was confused, enervating and parochial. Calcutta's sister in the world of jute is Dundee, a fact which meant that a considerable part of the British resident population of the Indian city came from the Scottish one. Some, like Tom Henderson, had been there for the better part of 40 years – 'and I'm tellin' ye, mon,' they were fond of saying, 'I still don't know India.'

Here, I realized after less than a couple of weeks' acclimatisation, was my problem. If residents of 40 years' occupation didn't know the sub-continent how was I to fare? The problem, I realized, was not wholly unlike that which had confronted me on my first acquaintance with Bomber Command. Now, as then, I found myself in a world totally unfamiliar to me, its idiom strange, its people apparently unapproachable; yet from this difficult and unpromising material it was my job somehow to extract and translate into lucid form articles and stories which would convey to far distant readers a picture of what India, and later Burma, were like in the turmoil of war. What had seemed a task of apparent simplicity – namely that of writing half a dozen short pieces for American consumption – now began to seem of disturbing complexity.

This is precisely what I had felt at Oakington, but there, fortunately, I was living with the battle and with the men who were fighting it. In parochial, steaming Calcutta, in spite of the presence of thousands of servicemen of innumerable nation-

alities, there was no battle. The war, on its several fronts, was not only far away; it might not have existed. Where, then, was my material coming from? I appeased my conscience a little in that direction by writing what I think was a vivid piece on Calcutta itself which was well enough received, writing it in the comparative cool and quiet of the Swimming Club, in the morning, when the club was virtually deserted. For the rest I knew that I had, as I had done at Oakington, to keep my ears cocked for those stray crumbs of gossip which are so often enough to set the imagination of writers on fire.

Presently one of these crumbs was unwittingly let fall at the Hendersons' flat. Evening after evening there used to appear there a man of perhaps forty or so, clearly of much experience in the East, apparently hard-bitten and without doubt a hard drinker. He struck me as being very much like a character out of Conrad, a writer on whom in my extreme youth I had been strongly suckled and whose interpretation of the East, both atmospherically and otherwise, had long seemed to me infinitely superior to both that of Kipling, the Imperialist, and Maugham, the pretended cynic who was often a sentimentalist in disguise and whose world was in many ways as narrow as that of Surbiton – as parochial as that of Calcutta itself.

The apparently hard-bitten visitor to the Hendersons' flat belonged neither to the Imperialistic nor suburban world. He generally arrived at the flat about six o'clock, when he would talk civilly and coherently for perhaps half an hour or so, during which time he would ferociously consume a positively fearsome quantity of liquor. As this began to work he became progressively more introspective, maudlin and then almost tearfully truculent, even abusive. I had never seen a man drink so much in so short a time or with less evident enjoyment; here, it seemed to me, was a man setting out either deliberately to destroy himself or to drown some undrownable sorrow or to expiate or try to forget some unforgettable personal disaster – a kind of wartime Lord Jim.

I was so troubled and mystified by all this that I was moved eventually to ask Mrs Henderson what lay behind it all. 'He was a planter in Burma,' she said, 'and he was on the long march to India when the Japs moved in.' Great though the disasters of that march had been, as I knew well enough, they hardly seemed to me to justify a sort of alcoholic death-wish. There must also lie in that distressed mind, it seemed to me, the bitter kernel of some greater, more personal disaster. And so it turned out. His sorrow – and sorrow it was, profound, bitter and unforgettable – rose from the fact that his personal bearer, a mere boy, had died on the journey. The severance of this deep personal bond, born of mutual love and loyalty, had had so great an effect on him that he had been crushed into a state of morbid melancholia.

From this bitter crumb there was eventually to emerge *The Jacaranda Tree*. The birth of that book, however, still lay some years ahead and for the moment all I could do was to let the seed lie dormant, though by no means dead, in the deeper recesses of my mind.

Meanwhile, as Doddie was presently to remind me, Burma itself was very much a reality. Did I feel prepared, he asked, to fly across and have a look-see? A large, formidable map of the country, a jam-like mess of purple and green, secretly told me I was not so prepared. There was in fact a certain chill in my heart. I had a discomforting feeling that I was about to go out into the wilderness and that I might never return. The prospect of such banishment seemed not only harsh; it had the further effect of making even steaming, sordid, insalubrious Calcutta seem like a piece of Heaven.

Naturally, however, I said that I was willing and ready to go, and a few days later I was flying out over the Bay of Bengal.

VI

Sometime before this event, however, I had had my one and only quarrel with a fellow officer: nothing more than a flaming, stand-up row with Nickie. Squadron-Leader Nickson was the arch-type of that kind of middle-rank officer who by virtue of that rank sets up his own personal kingdom which he then proceeds to rule by threats, fear and even terror, petrifying all of lesser rank. In Nickie's case Erks, Waafs, Indian clerks, bearers and drivers were all held in terrifying thrall. The king in his kingdom, ruling by shouting, abuse, invective, foul language and often sheer bullying, was a law unto himself, and woe betide any who dared think otherwise.

Among other things Nickie was in charge of P.R. transport, both in the air and on the ground. Accordingly I went to him to request that I be given a jeep, it having been sensibly recognised at Air Ministry that I should, and must, have my own transport. With this firmly promised arrangement Nickie flatly refused to comply. In vain I pointed out that this was an Air Ministry instruction. 'Jeep? Ye'll have no jeep here. I've no jeep to spare and even if I had ye'd not get it.' Again I protested strongly; again I insisted that these were Air Ministry promises and instructions; again Nickie yelled 'No jeep! I'm tellin' ye for the last time – no jeep.' It was then my turn to yell, livid with lost temper as well as being no little nauseated by the conduct of the petty king-dictator. Presently the air grew flaming hot, then molten, and it was only when it had cooled a little that I saw the virtues of reason and swept coldly out of the office.

Outside, with no hesitation, I commandeered the nearest truck in sight, and promptly ordered its Indian driver to take me to Doddie. He, being the sort of man he was, listened to me with good sense and reason, saw the cogency of my arguments and told me not to worry. He would telephone Nickie. He duly did so and I got my jeep next day.

In the aftermath of this tempestuous atmosphere I now had to approach Nickie again on the question of air transport to Burma. The king-tyrant was again unco-operative, indeed offensive. There were no aircraft, or if there were they were all completely full. A great number of transports were U.S.; others, in case I didn't know it, were being eaten by termites. It would be days and days, perhaps weeks, before anything could be found. I knew all this to be stalling, if not deliberate enmity, but I was both impotent and powerless to do anything and the king-tyrant knew it well. For some days afterwards I turned up every morning at Nickie's office to inquire after my passage, but always with the same result: no aircraft. Finally I got a seat on a Dakota, a Dakota so ancient, so rickety, so tied up with string and, unless I was much mistaken, so eaten by termites that it would surely never, I thought, make the passage from Bengal to the Arakan. Ever since that day I have in fact nurtured the unpleasant thought that Nickie, by that shambles of an aircraft, hoped to kill me.

But reach the Arakan, along the Burma coast, I eventually did. It was mid afternoon when I arrived on the wide dusty airfield, far beyond which, to the north, a range of mountains smouldered in a vast heat-haze. On the ground itself, as I stepped thankfully from the aircraft, the searing, blinding sun struck down on me like a blow from a mighty white-hot steam hammer. Never had I felt anything like it; even the heat of Calcutta seemed temperate by comparison.

I was then assailed by a mirage. The dusty, barren airfield seemed suddenly to flower. Then the flower became a woman, a white woman, tall, shapely, elegant, very beautiful. I could only stare and wonder. Such things simply didn't happen on remote, sizzling Asian airfields. Then she moved and walked and I knew that this was no mirage. She was, as it turned out, an actress who had flown in to entertain such few servicemen as were left in Akyab.

My *Encyclopaedia Britannica* describes Akyab as the third

largest port in Burma, lying on the coast where three fertile valleys, watered by the rivers Myu, Koladaing and Lemyu, reach the sea in an intricate network of tidal channels, creeks and islands. The hinterland is described as rich with forest, the fertile alluvian valleys yielding inexhaustible supplies of rice.

Alas, when I saw it on that first burning, blinding afternoon, Akyab and its fertile valleys presented only a scene of bitter desolation. No rice had grown there for three years or more; Akyab was a half-swallowed ruin – swallowed by Mother Nature in all her torrid tropical vigour. The jungle ruled and dominated all. Vines, creepers, trees, elephant-grass twice as tall as a man, bamboos, palms – fed by tropical suns and watered by monsoons, the once thriving port of Akyab had disappeared under a kind of corruptive natural splendour.

All this had on me an impact as powerful as that of the sun had been; it drove deeply and permanently into my consciousness. At the same time it provoked in me a singular sadness. India seemed a senseless, seething mess; yet I felt that Burma, by contrast, must have been simple, ordered and happy, its people gentle, charming and reserved. Now, like Akyab itself, it was a mere husk, a dusty ghost, its people like trousered and half-broken wanderers in a dream.

Little of apparent significance seemed to happen to me on that first Burma visit. I say 'seemed' advisedly, since once again it was little things that dropped into my mind and lay dormant there, waiting to germinate and flower at some distant, even far distant, date. A large, rambling temple outside which young Burmese boys were pouring a cement-like mixture into small moulds which when baked hard by the powerful sun turned out as miniature Buddhas; a pretty little Burmese girl sitting on the step of a bombed pagoda, playing with a lizard, at first gently, merely teasing it, then with deliberate cruelty, wounding and finally killing it. Little and apparently insignificant episodes, yet the one stuck in the mind as epitomising the futility of religion, the other as an exposure of all the callous futility of war. The second of these episodes haunted me so uneasily that I went immediately back to my small hot

tent and tried, before the brilliance of its impact faded, to get it down on paper, I hoped as my first short story of the East. Not a word resulted: for reasons which I shall later set out in detail.

I flew back to India some ten days or so later, to re-enact there the stupid and exhausting merry-go-round I had been through on the first day of my arrival. A young half terrified native truck driver drove me desperately round Calcutta's sleazy suburbs in an attempt to find, in the dingy darkness, the Hendersons' flat. Just as I knew that we were irrevocably lost and he seemed about to go berserk we were stopped by an R.A.F. sergeant M.P. in a jeep, who had the good sense to order the boy back to his unit and then kindly gave me a lift in the right direction in the jeep.

That crazy drive gave me, however, a chance to see another side of Calcutta: Calcutta by night. If I now used words of my own to describe it I might well be accused of biased and deliberate falsification. I will therefore content myself with quoting from a recent article describing not the Calcutta of 1945, but the Calcutta of 1970, a quarter of a century after every wall in India had *Quit India* scrawled across it and India's millions couldn't wait for the British Raj, the hated Western imperialist, to be driven out. After heading the article *Oh! Calcutta! World's Greatest Urban Disaster*, the writer goes on:

'Millions have the pavements as their home. Miles of streets are strewn with sleeping families at night. But the pavements remain almost as littered during the day. It is evident that thousands of people either lack the energy or the need, being unemployed or unemployable, to move from their gutterside homes.

'Many, clad in filthy rags or nearly naked, loll about obviously starving or half-dead. In the city centre scores of lepers and cruelly mutilated unfortunates beg unheeded . . . Roadside stalls sell food openly exposed to dust and flies which carry cholera germs. Huge garbage dumps remain uncleared and pavements are strewn with rotting trash. The gutters are the public lavatories. Dead and dying dogs as well as humans lie about the footway . . . In the suburbs, conditions are far worse, with hundreds of thousands crammed into disease-breeding bustees, hutments built in foetid areas which lack sewage or running water . . . Diseases like cholera and plague are endemic. Malaria, once nearly contained, is spreading again due to failure to spray mosquito-breeding swamps. Tap water is unsafe to drink and often runs black . . . Trams built for 75 people carry 200 and hundreds daily risk their lives by hanging on to the footboards of overloaded buses.'

All this and more I saw in 1945. More? Trains loaded with desperate, yelling, shrieking human cargo, every inch of roof thick with bodies, every grippable piece of rolling stock precariously clutched by a desperate figure; women crawling on hands and knees along railway tracks, pathetically searching for a few walnuts of dropped coal; in the huge central market, a vast cornucopia of limes, oranges, bananas yellow and red, papayas, guavas, persimmons, pineapples, water-melons, tomatoes, grapes and indeed every kind of fruit and vegetable, tropical and temperate alike, fat rats sit with lascivious boldness among the piles of fruit while stall-holders merely laugh at them; the eternal stinking dead cow being stripped by vultures on the roadside, the eternal bloated human body floating down the Hooghli; and every morning, or almost every morning, the

sickening report in the newspapers of some young infertile Indian bride being given a can of petrol by her mother-in-law and being told that she knew what she could do with it: another human torch mercifully released from the indignity, the unforgivable sin, of not being productive, as if India's sorrowful sordid millions were not already enough.

By now it was March and India's heat was already comparable to that of a furnace; only in the first couple of hours after breakfast, in some shaded corner at the swimming pool, did I ever feel cool and fit to work. It was therefore with great relief that I met yet another of Calcutta's many Scotsmen, a tea-planter but also a public servant of integrity, a member of the Bengal Assembly, who was kind enough to invite me to spend a week-end on his estate, far to the north, within sight of the Himalayas and the foothills of Bhutan.

Before this visit could be arranged, however, he invited me to do something else: to attend a session of the Bengal Assembly. I duly went and was duly shocked. In revolting contrast to the starving, mutilated and miserable populace on the streets outside the Indian members of the Assembly were fat, oily and well-fed. They were also callous; never, in fact, had I seen the mark of evil and corruption so indelibly bitten into so many human faces at one time. Only the face of my Scottish friend and a few other specimens of the hated British Raj stood out with incorruptible integrity, like good deeds in a very naughty world.

A few days later we entrained for the north, I not having the remotest notion of what other side of India would greet me there.

VII

The scene at the railway station, on the evening of our departure, was exactly as I have already described: crowds of near-hysterical Indian bodies covering the platforms, smothering like clusters of white-winged moths the roofs and buffers and running boards of trains; an almost riotous assembly and altogether a certain air of disordered and almost childish madness. Of all this, however, my friend and I were not obliged to become part. Our first-class compartment was not only reserved but reserved for us alone. Our bearer attended to our baggage, at the same time loading into the compartment vast hampers of food and drink and other comforts.

The railway going northward through Bengal finally ends at Darjeeling, but our destination was some way to the south of the Sikkim border, at a place called Jalpagur. It was, as I remember it, only an hour or so after dawn when we arrived there, in a morning of exquisite freshness totally free of Calcutta's oppressive, sweaty humidity. So far north we could, anyway, be sure that the sun would, at that time of year, never have the implacable power it had in the south. The country air was in fact delicious; the distances were hazy, so that the peaks of the Himalayas were wholly hidden, but the foothills of Bhutan, looking strangely mysterious, brooded almost colourlessly against the northern sky.

We washed, shaved, changed and breakfasted at a club house. Smart army officers, some Indian, were breakfasting too, many of them, as I guessed, going on leave to Darjeeling. On the station platform I had already seen several people clearly coming back from Darjeeling and very refreshing it was to see two young English nurses carrying little baskets made of slender strips of wood and planted with roots of the common primrose in cool, lovely and happy flower.

After breakfast we got into my friend's waiting truck and

began to head eastwards, under the foothills. A considerable number of streams flow down here from the great Himalayan range and at that season of the year many of them were totally dry, mere beds of white sun-scalded rock. We crossed these by wooden bridges which, in the eventual monsoon season, would be swept away by torrents of flood water of prodigious power and would in due course have to be built up again.

But at one point we reached a river of considerable size, far too wide to be bridged, and over this we ferried the truck on a precarious arrangement of planks and petrol drums which had to be powerfully handled by numbers of natives with oars and poles in order that it didn't drift helplessly downstream. My recollection is that the men sang loud and vigorous chants, as Indians so often do when doing a job in concert, as they punted and rowed, all looking, in contrast to the miserable bags of bones in Calcutta's foetid streets, as happy as sand-boys enjoying some huge lark.

From the far river bank we eventually bowled and bumped along in a cloud of white dust which gave the impression of rising and sweeping away to the north, there to blanket the foothills in deep haze. This haze however was not of dust but already, in mid-morning, of heat. Not that the day had lost its freshness; on the contrary it had a certain spring-like air, an impression that was much strengthened when we reached my friend's tea estate and bungalow, in the garden of which sweetpeas, marigolds, petunias, sweet williams, stocks and phlox Drummondii were all in delicious flower. In the tea gardens little Indian children were picking some predatory orange-coloured bug off the camellia-like bushes, a task for which they would be paid a few annas a dozen, and occasionally an enormous and brilliant butterfly, more like bird than insect, would fly over with captivating splendour.

The bungalow itself was beautifully furnished, complete with billiard table, its furniture polished to perfection. Bare-footed Indian servants glided about everywhere, silently, and soon ice was clinking away in long glasses of gin, tonic water and green moons of lime. It was all very comfortable, very affluent, very respectable and very orderly: yet I gained an uneasy impression. It was that my friend lived a life of great loneliness. He lacked for nothing; a clap of the hands, the tinkle of a bell, would instantly bring him all he wanted, and yet the house was, it seemed to me, haunted by a great emptiness. Some few years later I put all this into a story called *The Frontier*, but even today I cannot totally rid myself of that atmosphere of empty loneliness, any more than I can expunge from my mind the heat-haze on the foothills, the giant and splendid butterflies or the little Indian children collecting their bright bugs from the bushes of tea.

That afternoon, being Saturday, my friend set off to the estate offices to pay his workers, including the little Indian children who sat outside, cross-legged, with their orange captures of bugs neatly laid out before them in the dust. My friend didn't claim that his was an exclusive or even very good brand of tea, certainly nothing resembling the nectars of Darjeeling; it was his job to produce a tea that would make 'the good strong cup' so beloved of many Britishers, whether the housewife struggling with her cooking and her washing or the truck-driver at the 'good pull-up for car-men'. But what he also produced, and which in turn I found fascinating, was a brand of brick tea made especially for Tibetans. This was compressed and solidified into black blocks the shape of thick saucers, some five inches across; they were immensely hard and heavy and would, if thrown at a man from short range, have inflicted no little injury. The interesting thing about these iron-like shapes of brick tea was that they were used by the Tibetans not only for brewing tea on long treks in wild mountain country (the tea was not only heavy and durable but almost indestructible) but also as a form of currency. My friend kindly gave me one of these formidable slabs but I must confess that I never put it to the test of boiling water.

Next morning, Sunday, we toured the estate and its environs by car. The air was again delicious, the scent of flowers in the garden tenderly exotic, as in some perfect warm English May.

Again too the foothills were shrouded in heat haze, the Himalayas completely hidden behind them. And now and then, as we drove through narrow jungle roads, the high dry elephant grass on both sides tunnelled by cavernous paths made by rhinoceros, we occasionally passed little groups of trotting Indian men, near-naked and very dark in colour, their bows and arrows slung across their shining backs as they set forth to hunt and kill something for the Sunday pot. They looked totally innocent, totally primitive, totally unsullied by what we are pleased to call civilisation. I found them most attractive and touching.

When we left a couple of days later to entrain for Calcutta I felt no little sense of regret; I would like to have seen more of the foothills, the jungle and its birds, the rivers and the dark trotting little men. Yet I was more than glad to have seen what I had seen and to know that there is a side of India that is lovable and in its own special way as unforgettable as the 'world's greatest urban disaster'. It is in fact not far from the truth to say that for a good twenty years after that visit to the hills and the tea plantation there were few days when I did not think of them and always with affection; and I think of them still.

Perhaps my pleasure at that week-end was the greater because I knew that the road to Calcutta also meant once again the road to Burma, and I have to confess that it was a journey I did not, at that moment, relish very much.

As it turned out it resolved itself more happily.

VIII

Never a lover of Kipling, I have often been puzzled by his lines 'on the road to Mandalay, where the flying fishes play'. It has always seemed to me odd that there should be flying fishes at a Burmese town many hundreds of miles inland from the sea but perhaps, since Mandalay is on the great Irrawaddy, Kipling may have been right after all. It was not, however, to Mandalay that I was going on my second trip to Burma, since the town was still in Japanese hands, but to Monywa, once a pleasant little country town but now a pathetic heap of ruins and overgrown jungle and also on the Irrawaddy.

It was now almost April and as I stepped from the aircraft on to the dusty airstrip the sun once again hit me a vicious, white-hot blow. As quickly as possible I hitched a lift in a jeep, piled my kit into the vehicle and drove off to the R.A.F. camp on the edge of the ruined town. At the encampment I left my belongings on the roadside, leaving a little book of Elizabethan lyrics, bound in white vellum, on the top of them, and then went off to find the camp adjutant and if possible a tent and a bed. The adjutant, when found, was helpful but not hopeful. It might mean, he explained, that I would have to share a tent with at least one other officer if not two. I thanked him and he duly took me off to find the tent. It then turned out that only one other officer was in occupation, although not at home at that moment, and I immediately went off to collect my baggage. When I got back to it the little book of Elizabethan lyrics presented an amazing sight. The furious heat of the sun, in only a quarter of an hour or so, had had such a powerful effect on the vellum that both covers were completely and tightly curled up, like a brace of white brandy-snaps.

I had scarcely begun to unpack a few things in the tent than my fellow tent-sharer, as if already warned by the swiftest possible message, arrived in a state of what I think is best described as possessive agitation. One of those born fuss-pots with an inordinate passion for tidiness, he was clearly scared stiff that I, the new intruder, would besmirch the sacred precincts of his ordered world.

I, wanting only to be friendly, showed him the strangely transformed book of Elizabethan lyrics, adding something about 'this God-awful heat', in which I was sweating ferociously.

'Heat, old boy? You don't call *this* heat, do you? I mean this is the cool season, the winter. Wait till it really warms up, say June and July – no, old boy, don't put your stuff there if you don't mind. There isn't an awful lot of room for two and I'd rather you didn't clutter things up.'

No tent in the whole of Burma could have looked less cluttered up. My companion, fussy, belly-aching, slightly effeminate, finicky of eye, had carefully seen to that. He had also carefully seen to it that every precautionary bottle of

pills, tablets, powders and so on was laid out on his bedside bamboo table in neat order ready to do battle with malaria, the common cold, heat sickness, diarrhoea, lack of salt and all the other ills which a tropical climate may, or may not, inflict on a man.

'I hope you brought your mepacrine, old boy? Terribly important. You need the proper dosage every day. I never miss.'

'Mepacrine? What's it for?'

'Good grief, old boy, you don't know? Malaria, of course. You must take it. Absolutely essential. There are chaps out here who've had malaria a dozen times, even twenty. Might never have happened if they'd been regular with the mepacrine. No, old boy, do you mind not putting your tooth brush into that beaker? It's sort of my preserve, that one.'

Hot though it was, I went outside for air. The hope that I should find it was a vain one, but I felt that if I didn't get out of that tent at once I should suddenly scream. There is no type more liable to drive me crazy than the slightly effeminate male fuss-pot, especially when the power behind it is the orderly mind. It produces in me a violent sense of impotent frustration.

Another five minutes of 'don't put your stuff there, old boy, do you mind?' and injunctions such as 'it's only fair to both of us, old boy, not to clutter the place up. There's hardly enough room for one as it is, I mean' – once again drove me out of the tent, this time in search of the Mess and a possible cup of tea. This, I thought, might at least refresh my frustrated spirit but to my infinite revulsion all I got from a diminutive Burmese bearer was a cup of what must be the world's most revolting liquid, namely tea made in the pot with sugar, condensed milk and all, the whole looking like pale liquid toffee.

Eventually I splashed about in two inches of water in my canvas field-bath, put on a clean dry shirt, my bush shirt, and a pair of slacks and then went back, in the twilight, to see if the Mess could provide anything stronger than toffee tea.

Fortifying myself with gin, I found myself being addressed by the camp Padre. This too depressed me. My long standing dislike of things parsonic at once put my back up. This, as I presently realized, was another mistake, since the Padre turned out to be neither patronising nor hearty, neither pompous nor obsequious, neither saintly nor, as I had once discovered in another Padre in another Mess, a drunk.

'Are you here for long?' he wanted to know. 'What's your particular field, if you don't mind my asking?'

I told him, explaining about the pieces I had to do for America.

'Very interesting. Perhaps I can help in some way.'

I thanked him and he suddenly said:

'I tell you what. I'm driving out to a Burmese village tomorrow morning. Christian community. Methodists. Care to come? You might find it interesting. We're going to choose the hymns for Easter Sunday.'

'April the first, isn't it?' I said, but he had character enough to ignore the intended joke. 'Well, it's very kind of you. I'll see what it's like in the morning.'

'I can tell you what it'll be like in the morning. Pretty damned hot. Anyway come by all means if you feel like it. I'll come and look you up after breakfast.'

That night I lay awake listening to what must be the world's most grievous, dismal, haunting sound: the wailing of a pack of jackals. The sound is like that of a crowd of imprisoned human souls suffering all the tortures of the damned, wailing in unappeasable misery, in the depths of hell.

The Padre called for me next morning, in his jeep, about ten o'clock.

'Oh! you've decided to come, have you? Good show. I think you'll find it interesting. They've some astonishing stories to tell, some of these Burmese. Pretty hair-raising too, a lot of them.'

We set off across the wide, empty, dusty, sun-scalded plain. A single-track railway, long since disused, went across it at one point, the red rusting rails ghostly in the burning sun.

I suppose we might have driven for an hour or so across the plain, on which a few white egrets looked like ghosts too, and then at length an oasis of palms, peepul trees, giant bamboos and palm-thatched huts appeared in the yellow glare ahead.

'This is our village,' the Padre said and a minute or two later we were mercifully enveloped in tree shade.

Almost at once there sprang out of the bamboos a shrieking chorus of children's voices, followed by the children themselves, their brown Asiatic faces grinning from ear to ear with explosive delight. How many of them clambered on to the jeep I simply couldn't count. Those who couldn't clamber dropped in the dust, then picked themselves up and, laughing hilariously at the enormity of the joke, ran on behind.

We finally drew up at a compound surrounded by low, palm-thatched houses having shaded verandahs decorated with a few pots of creepers and flowers. Children flopped on their bottoms in the dust as the jeep drew up sharply and the air was joyous with shrieking. This chorus of sound brought three or four Burmese women from one of the houses to shake hands, joyous themselves, with the Padre.

In turn he introduced me to the women, whose reaction was one of polite, sometimes smiling, but mostly grave shyness. Soon we were sitting on the verandah, there to be served with what was, in the rising heat of the morning, absolute nectar: long glasses of fresh lime juice, miraculously cold.

I had been happily sipping at this for perhaps five minutes when I became aware of a vision. A Burmese girl of extraordinary pale skin and very black hair and eyes, her oval face very grave, shy and statuesque, had suddenly glided silently from the house to be among us. She was wearing the simplest of white blouses and a purple wrap-over skirt. She looked every inch a dignified, beautiful, aristocratic goddess.

'This is Dorothy,' the Padre said. 'Dorothy is from the University of Rangoon, or rather she was. But she'll go back there one day, won't you, Dorothy?'

'I shall go back,' she said.

Something about the finality and certainty of these words,

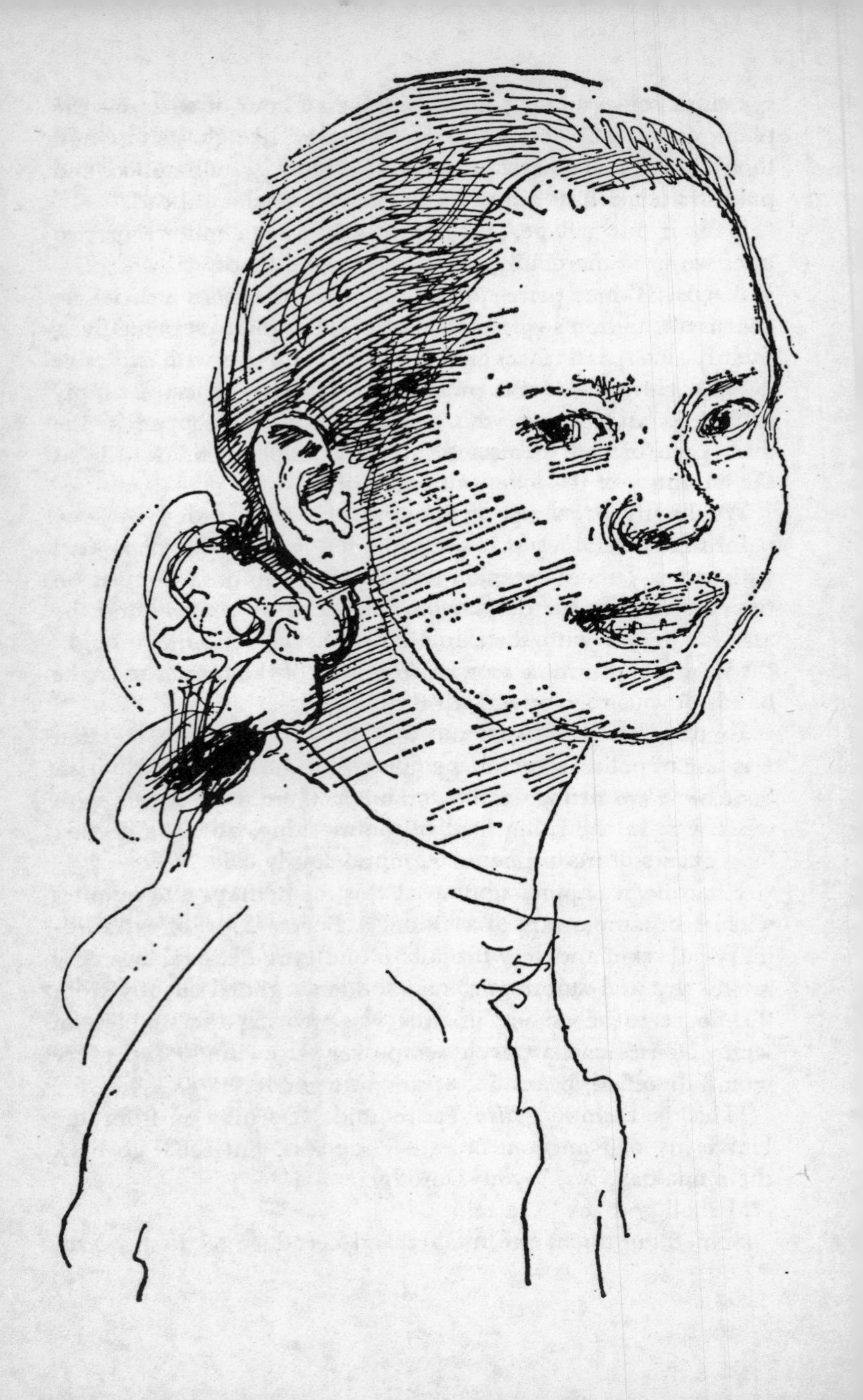

spoken in quiet perfect English, was very touching. I did not then know that she, together with the other women and many hundreds of other Burmese, had undergone a journey of sheer Hell as they trekked north for hundreds of miles in their escape from Rangoon and the pursuing Japs; nor was there any way of guessing it from that grave and exquisite young face, marvellously full of repose.

Presently, as she refilled my glass with lime-juice, the Padre said to me:

'I suppose you're not interested in jewels, are you? Almost all these villagers have stones to sell. Rubies, emeralds, amethysts, zircons, all sorts of things. Some are the genuine thing, some are what they call reconstituted, I think. You have to be careful. But if you'd care to see some Dorothy would take you to one of the houses where you'd get a fair deal.'

I confess I am not very interested in precious stones but out of politeness I said that I should like to see some. Dorothy at once put down the jug of lime-juice.

'Very well, I will take you. The house is not far.'

Dorothy and I left the verandah and walked round the compound until we came at last to another house, lived in by a rather elderly Burmese couple, and went in. What struck me at once about the interior of this house was its air of intense, provincial, almost Victorian respectability. It reminded me of the half-sacred front-room parlours of my boyhood: neat antimacassars on chairs, useless trinkets, admonishing Christian texts on the walls, a portrait of the King and Queen of England.

Presently the two Burmese were showing us a few, very small precious stones: rubies, an emerald or two, some amethysts, some sherry-gold zircons, laying them out on neat white cloths on little trays. I wasn't greatly impressed, or even greatly interested, and presently Dorothy, sensing this, began to make polite apologies for us, so that we might say good-bye.

Outside the house she gave me a quick, grave smile.

'I think the stones were not very good. You didn't want to buy?'

'No. I am sorry. I think they were not very good.'

'The pity is that so many bad ones are sold. The English boys buy them as souvenirs to take home without troubling even to find out if they are genuine or not. It gives us a bad name.'

'You haven't a bad name as far as I am concerned.'

'Thank you. That was very kind of you.'

We walked back to the house of Dorothy's sister. There we talked again, drank more lime-juice, and the Padre discussed the hymns for Easter Sunday. My recollection is that I talked little but listened much. 'Little pigs have big ears,' I could hear my grandmother saying and certainly, on that hot April morning I sat listening very much as I used to sit listening on cool rainy days far back in England, in the tool-shed, the hay-barn or under the cart-house, listening to my grandfather and his cronies talking politics, cursing governments, arguing, swapping stories, scandal and 'remembrance of things past'. Now, as then, I was the picker-up of unconsidered trifles, scraps of what may well have seemed to the Padre and Dorothy and the other Burmese trivialities of little or no importance but which I hid away, like precious stones themselves, in the recesses of my mind. I cannot now remember if I made any suggestions as to Easter hymns, but it is possible; my long arduous Sunday School training would certainly have stood me in good stead, since even today I can, if necessary, reel off the lines of countless hymns without ever a glance at a hymnal. But it was really not hymns that were in my mind that morning; it was largely the long trek of Burmese going northward from Rangoon and the grave dignified beauty, the courageous calm and the exquisite pallor of the young Dorothy's face.

Readers of *The Purple Plain* will not need to be told, I think, that the incidents recorded above are part of the early fabric of that novel: the drive across the scalding plain, the laughing Burmese children crowding on the jeep, the little Burmese house, the lime-juice, Dorothy and her sister, the talk, the precious stones. They will know that in the book the Padre becomes a doctor, that my fuss-pot tent-sharer becomes Blore, that Dorothy becomes Anna, that my place is taken by Forrester, a shattered R.A.F. pilot whose only wish is to die. The little ideas and pictures I gathered up that morning, the unconsidered trifles, were the genesis of the book.

But ideas alone, as I have frequently pointed out before, are of themselves not enough. The single idea that at first seems so good is more often than not sterile; it is a negative needing a positive to fire it into life – or, if you prefer it, an ovary needing to be fertilised before it can produce a living offspring. So, though the incidents and pictures of that morning were pictorially vivid and exciting enough, the truly vital part of it all, the positive agent of fertilisation, was still missing. Nor was I to find it, and then quite by accident, until I got back to the cooler, calmer pastures of England.

IX

I left Calcutta by flying-boat, for England, a week later, on April 8th. It is, I think, important to record here what the feeling in both India and Burma was, at that time, about the future of the Burma campaign. It was a bog of pessimism, a hundred miles deep. Not a soul, I think, doubted that the war would last a good ten years longer. Worse than this, and the pessimism it engendered, was an evident sickness of morale. In the Mess tent at Monywa I had heard officers, to my incredulous astonishment, openly talking what I could only tell myself was pure sedition; they were luridly blasphemous about government, higher command, the long futility of the war itself, above all the fact that the people fighting that war seemed to have been brutally forgotten. They were probably saying no more than the German infantryman said in *All Quiet on the Western Front*, what Sassoon and Graves said in *The Memoirs of an Infantry Officer* and *Good-bye to all that*, what Wilfred Owen exposed in his poems or what a million soldiers had said or thought in the holocausts of Passchendaele, Ypres, the Somme, Hill Sixty and Verdun, but its effect on me was nevertheless shattering.

This bitterness, the age-old bitterness of the deluded fighting man cursing war's futilities and politicians' duplicities, seemed finally to crystallize in my mind as the big Sunderland flying-boat flew westwards over the Hooghli River and the great scarlet steel span of the Willingdon bridge and set course for Karachi over India's deserts, rivers and palms. It crystallized; and then I put it, like some evil thought by which I didn't want to be haunted, aside. Burma, in all its vividness never to be forgotten, suddenly seemed part of an unreal past. Now I was merely glad, indeed near-exultant, to be going home.

The old Sunderland flying-boat was a huge comfortable

vehicle and that morning there were men and officers of all ranks, many time-expired, on board. There were also wives and children, the children running noisily about the spacious cabin decks, shouting and playing games as in a nursery at home. Officers were segregated by rank, the top brass enjoying the most superior of the boat's comforts, the rank and file herded in the tail. Thanks to this arrangement I found myself sitting next to, and finally making friends with, a young army colonel, a campaign veteran of twenty-five with five years' service in the East, a good example of the swiftness that war offers in the field of promotion. I can best describe him, I think, as the utter antithesis of my tent-sharer at Monywa, the belly-aching fuss-pot, Blore. His character was writ large, the character of a man of action, of a good talker, a good soldier, a lover of life, a bender if not breaker of rules. I liked him very much and we spent a good deal of time together, both in the air and on the ground, on the long journey home. Five years' campaigning had caused him to collect a vast amount of gear, including an enormous amount of tobacco, of which more later. This accumulated tonnage of his made my own modest suit-case, bed-roll and huge stick of still green bananas seem pathetically small. (My younger children had never even seen a banana and I was carrying home that precious green loot – of exactly the same green as the flocks of small shy parrots that I describe in *The Purple Plain* – as something infinitely more precious than all the rubies in Burma.)

In Karachi swallows were nesting under the roofs of houses and even flying about the high open-eaved rooms of our hotel. The town was not unpleasant and the people, so far as one could gather in so short a time, seemed far removed from Bengal, that 'low-lying country occupied by a low-lying people'. It was another side of India I would much like to have seen more of, but next morning we were flying on to Bahrein, a narrow-gutted town of mean, narrow streets, much dust and wind, miserable-looking Arabs huddled in what seemed to be white winding sheets, and perfectly hideous food.

This, however, only prepared us the better for Cairo, to

which we flew on next day, the flying-boat splashing down in brilliant sunshine on the Nile in a great spume of spray among the white scimitar sails of a crowd of Arab dhows. Here again was Mr Groppi's renowned *confiserie*, an El Dorado of cakes, *pâtisseries*, and every kind of sweetmeat from chocolate beans to Turkish delight. The girls behind the counters were, however, less sweet than the sweets and it wasn't until the colonel and I tried French on them that we got from them the glimmer of a smile. In the evening Cairo glowed in all its incredible brilliance, the chickens turned sizzling on their spits, and the wine glowed in our veins.

We flew on next day to the tip of Sicily, to Augusta, and another dose of contrasts. Unlike Cairo, Italy had not had a cosy war; and though Augusta's streets were brilliant with mimosa and many cherry-red geraniums the air seemed to me dark with blight. As we sat in a *café* drinking some impossible concoction or other I became aware of a low scurrying, as of mice, at the foot of the doorway. This, we discovered, was the work of three or four ragged Sicilian urchins, fishing for cigarette butts from the floor of the *café*, their rod and line being a length of wire twisted into a ring at one end, the ring finally hooking the cigarette end and dragging it under the door. The desperate poverty of all this was repeated in doorways and on doorsteps in the streets outside, where mothers were offering their own and their daughters' beds and bodies to all who cared to pay and pick. It was a moment of degradation that I found more sickening even than Calcutta's rancid iniquities.

Next day we flew into Poole Harbour on an afternoon of such exquisite warm brilliance that it might well have been that we had packaged the weather in Cairo and brought it home. An Egyptian on the plane, clearly all-prepared for England's notorious and traditional gloom and fog, simply sat staring in stunned disbelief at a sky that in its deep azure made even Cairo's look pallid by comparison. I confess I could hardly believe it myself and I underwent a small earthquake of emotion.

Continually, on that last section of the flight, my young colonel friend had held discourse on the delicate question of H.M. Customs and Excise and the equally delicate question of 'knowing the ropes'.

'It's a cinch, old boy. Leave it all to me. I've got the whole ruddy thing taped.'

'You've got rather a lot of tobacco, you said. What about that?'

'Piece o' cake. Nothing to it, old boy. Leave it to me. Had all the gen in a letter from a type who flew home a couple of weeks ago. Loaded with jewels, rugs, silks, tobacco and all the riches of Samarkand and all that and just sailed through like an innocent. Never touched him for a farthing. It's all a question, old boy, of knowing the ropes.'

We were eventually called to the customs' desks in order of rank, so that my colonel friend preceded me, going to a room upstairs. 'Back in a jiff, old boy,' he called and waved a cheery hand. The jiff became ten minutes, then twenty. At this stage I was called for customs' examination and duly declared various bits of silk and clothing and chocolate and sweets, but no tobacco. The duty turned out to be trivial and I was cleared in, I should say, five minutes. At the end of it I looked and waited, in vain, for my friend. His jiff became half an hour, then three quarters. Then slowly a shattered figure came downstairs, pale and haggard, all confidence drained away. Positively groping his way towards me across the customs' hall, he finally halted, shaking his head.

'Wanted thirty-five quid for the tobacco alone, old boy. Sixty-five for the lot. I just hadn't got it. Had to leave the whole bloody lot in bond.'

Fortunately he was able to drown his sorrows on the train. There, to our infinite astonishment, we found a Pullman car – the only Pullman car, as I understood it, still running in war-time England. Several times on the flying-boat journey my colonel friend had wagged his head sagely at me and declared that we were, in his opinion, a couple of ripe old bastards. Now it was obvious that we were a pair of kings, wining and dining at the Ritz. We luxuriated; the steward found us a bottle of wine and even, I think, some brandy.

Thus bathed in refreshment and contentment I gazed out on England, my beloved England. Never, I kept telling myself, had it looked so beautiful. Green meadows, woods rich with golden sallow and white with 'loveliest of trees, the cherry', gardens alight with daffodils and tulips and even, so early in the year, lilacs in pink and white blossom. This was my own, I

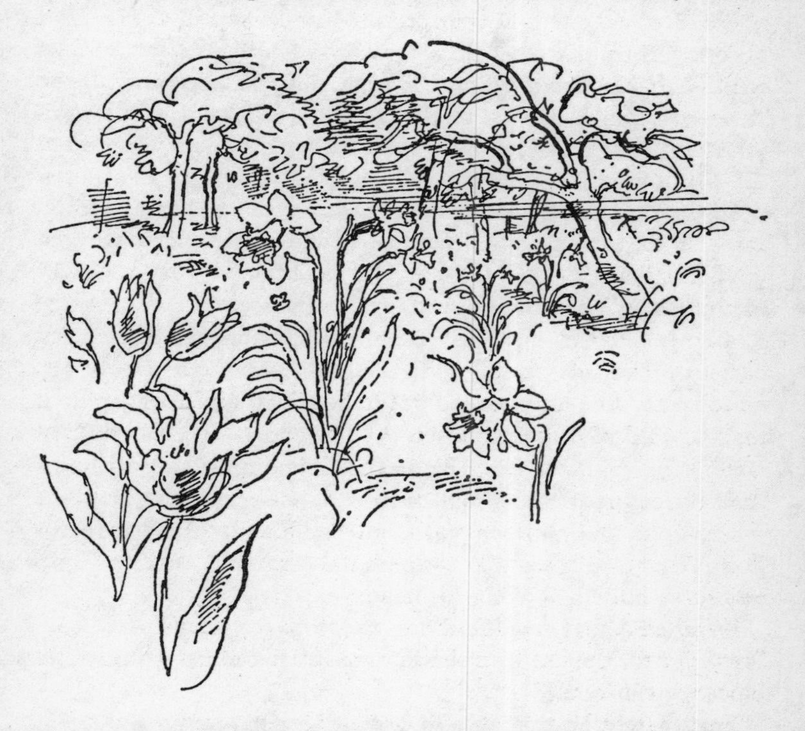

kept telling myself, my native land, and unashamedly let my eyes fill with tears, so that the countryside slipping by the train windows in the golden glory of evening light became a trembling evanescence of green and blue and gold.

It was late when I arrived home in a night as balmy as in a perfect July. The air was sweet breath on my face, the garden full of scent. I gazed for a few moments on a luxuriant bed of polyanthus that seemed like the very epitome of all that was loveliest in an English spring, then gathered my suit-case, my bed-roll and my bananas from my car.

The kitchen door was unlocked. I dumped my stuff by the stove, then tip-toed upstairs and folded a wakeful Madge in my arms.

X

Old and worn though such clichés as 'living in a dream' and 'walking on air' undoubtedly are, there are times, I think, when even they are permissible. Certain it is that for the next few days, even the next few weeks, I felt myself to be living in a dream, walking on air. Both the dream and the air, of purest April Englishness, were as sweet as spring water after the drought of a desert. I couldn't drink enough of them.

The weather in that still taut-stretched brittle April of 1945 continued to be miraculous. Every day the temperatures, steadily in the eighties, were more like July than April. Dudley Barker, glad to see me back again, I think, and pleased enough with the pieces I had written, generously gave me leave and day after day Madge and I took the children to the sea. The sense of liberation was also miraculous; so that I couldn't have cared a tinker's cuss whether the war ended or not. Certainly, in Europe, it looked like ending, but such hopes had risen before, only for the resilience of the Germans to put us again in jeopardy.

But soon, on a day when the world was half-jubilant, half-ashamed, the first atomic bomb was dropped on Hiroshima and the apparently endless war in Burma was incredibly over, as the war in Europe already was. After that stupendous event a great sense of pointlessness prevailed; an occasional visit to Air Ministry induced nothing but boredom and irritating frustration. There was nothing to do. Nor, I found, could I work at home. Indeed I frequently feared, as writers often do, that I might never write any more, that the spring waters of imagination had dried up and would never flow again. During the war I had in fact written precious little outside such writing as I had done for the R.A.F.; indeed, all I had to show for the past five years, on my own account, was *The Modern Short Story*, a critical study of the *genre* and some of its exponents, a *novella*, the first I had written but by no means the last, called *The Bride Comes to Evensford*, a few reviews and *Fair Stood the Wind For France:* hardly a rich harvest, nor a great source of revenue until *Fair Stood the Wind For France* achieved its welcome success.

Then, towards the latter part of the summer, came my papers for demobilisation. On the appointed day I drove the car up to Air Ministry, there to discover, to my joy, that R. F. Delderfield, already bursting with the phenomenal success of *Worm's Eye View*, together with some others from P.R., had forgathered for demobbing too. We all piled into my car and drove jubilantly to Uxbridge. Incredibly, when we reached the R.A.F. Station there, I found myself in the very same room that had been my dormitory on my first day in uniform, a totally unexpected completion of the circle that immediately caused the comedian in me to jump out, as R. F. Delderfield has well described in his *Overture for Beginners:*

'It had been a day for new beginnings, or so H. E. Bates declared as he pranced about the Demob Centre in his Squadron-Leader's uniform, topped by a loud coster-type

civvy cap, and looking as incongruous as a pantomime comedian in Ascot rig. Bates and I had been two of the first P.R. men in the game, scoring heavily on the points system that controlled demobilisation. He was forty and I was thirty-three, with five and a half years' service, so we said our farewells and trundled down the spiral staircase to the lift, schoolboys on the last day of term.'

The spiral staircase referred to was at Air Ministry, but before we reached that high point of our jubilations something of much greater significance had occurred. On the way to Uxbridge, before the fooling began, someone casually asked me if I had ever met a certain fighter pilot whose name I have long forgotten. I replied that I didn't think I ever had.

'Remarkable type. Had more gongs than anyone I ever knew. And got them all for trying to kill himself.'

I asked to be enlightened on this unusual situation and was told that the pilot had taken his bride, only a few hours after they were married, to a celebratory dance at a night club in Leicester Square. Suddenly, as they danced, a bomb scored a direct hit on the club, killing scores of people and also blowing the young bride out of the pilot's arms, killing her outright without injuring him. The grievous shock of all this was so great that when he went back to duty it was with the avowed intention of getting himself killed. Instead, by the bitterest of ironies, he merely succeeded in collecting a fabulous number of medals – and remained alive.

In a flash I realized that this was the positive I had been seeking for my Burma negative. This was the key that would wind up the spring that would set the mechanism ticking, so that Blore, the Padre, Dorothy, the Burmese girl killing the lizard, the laughing Burmese children and all the rest could come to life in new identity. My secret jubilation at this was infinitely greater than the jubilation at merely getting out of uniform, so that I could scarcely wait to get my hands on a white virgin ream of paper and begin to set down my version of the Burma scene:

'Shy flocks of small banana-green parrots had begun to come back to the peepul trees about the bombed pagoda. But across the rice-fields, scorched and barren now from the long dry season, only a few white egrets stepped daintily like ghostly cranes about the yellow dust in the heat-haze. Nothing else moved across the great plain where for three years no rice had grown.'

So for the next three months or more I was in imagination back in Burma, inventing, remembering, re-enacting scenes, incidents, people; nursing Forrester, the pilot, through his grief and cryptic bitterness, redepicting Dorothy as Anna, the salve to the pilot's unhealed wounds, the Padre as the doctor and my insufferable fuss-pot tent-sharer as Blore. Some of the white heat of Burma got into my blood as I wrote, so that the words came out as if driven by a blow-torch. The subsequent book trebled the success of *Fair Stood the Wind For France*, bringing me a vast new readership. It also became a film in which Gregory Peck was wholly admirable as Forrester ('Your damn book nearly killed me,' he told me, referring to his long foot-slog with his shot-down companions, Carrington and Blore, through Burma's pitiless heat;) with a young unknown Burmese girl from Rangoon playing Anna with all the beauty, restraint, withdrawal and gravity so necessary to the part.

Not that the book pleased everybody. Certain of my friends, whose critical acumen I highly esteem, made deep noises of disapproval. They referred me back to such books of mine as *The Poacher* and *The Fallow Land*. 'This,' they lectured me, 'is what we want from you. Not your hot, wretched Burma plain.' Useless for me to try to explain the powerful and almost catastrophic impact the East had had on my sensitivity; hopeless to try to convey the blistering effect of its fatalism, which Conrad had seen and interpreted so well, its callous contempt for life, expressed in the episode of the little girl and the lizard, or the blistering, pulverising heat; pointless to protest that this was an explosive revolution in my life that simply *had* to be set down, or that, God being my helper, I would surely return to depicting 'England's green and pleasant land', which assuredly, in due time, I did.

If I claim nothing else for myself as a writer I will not deny myself versatility. The same hand that writes *My Uncle Silas* also produces *Fair Stood the Wind For France;* the same imagination that produces the Chaucerian farces of the Larkin family is also responsible for the unremitting tragedy of *The Triple Echo;* the same brain that is responsible for *The Poacher* also produces the stories of 'Flying Officer X'. No: if I claim nothing else for myself I will certainly claim that I am versatile.

So it was that within a year or so the hand that had written *The Poacher*, *Uncle Silas*, *The Bride Comes to Evensford*, *The Fallow Land* and the two books into which I have perhaps best distilled my love and feeling for the English countryside, *Through the Woods* and *Down the River*, turned its attention to a second novel of Burma, *The Jacaranda Tree*. This I approached with no little trepidation. For whereas I had seen the terrain and the people of *The Purple Plain* and had absorbed the electrifying atmosphere of central Burma through not only my eyes but the very pores of my skin, I had seen not one inch of the far distant territory over which the long and tragic trek to India had been made in bitter and horrifying circumstances when the Japanese had occupied Singapore and invaded Burma in 1942. I could only imagine what it could be like. But, I asked myself, was imagination enough? Could I possibly re-create the journey that had caused the planter in the Hendersons' flat in Calcutta such alcoholic remorse, and its terrain and atmosphere? I had asked myself very much the same question before writing *Fair Stood the Wind For France*. In that case too I had seen no more than a fraction of the terrain; I was largely unfamiliar with French provincial life even in peace-time let alone in that of war; all, or mostly all, had to be invented. Now I could only hope that, since the earlier novel had achieved the necessary authenticity, my imagination and instinct would again carry me towards the heart of the truth.

The surrender of Singapore and the invasion of Burma by the

Japanese were two inglorious moments in British imperial history, though certainly no more inglorious than the cataclysm that overtook America at Pearl Harbor, an event which, in my experience, few Americans to this very day care to discuss. Nor were they as great a humiliation as the fall of France in 1940; but let us say that they were in all conscience grim enough. Thus when I came to write *The Jacaranda Tree* I felt I could not, so to speak, overdo its agony. Through the experiences of Patterson, the planter, his boy Tuesday, and other characters, I told myself that, sparing nothing, I must re-create that agony. Again, to this end, as in *The Purple Plain*, I wrote in white-hot heat.

Some few years later I met a lady who asked me, quite simply:

'Were you on the retreat from Burma?'

'No,' I confessed, 'I was not.'

'But I feel you must have been.'

A great foreboding suddenly took hold of me. Had I painted the scene in *The Jacaranda Tree* well or falsely? Had I over-painted it or not?

'You mean,' I said, 'that I have – '

'My sister and I,' she said, 'were in that retreat. If you had exaggerated ten times over what you wrote you would still have been a hundred miles short of the truth. It was truly more ghastly than you could possibly imagine.'

When the book finally appeared it achieved an even greater sale than *The Purple Plain*, again greatly enlarging my readership. But again there were also dissentient voices from friends whose critical judgement I had learned to respect. Yet again it was useless to point out the compulsion of all the circumstances that lay behind the book – the East's unforgettable vividness of scene, the catastrophic nature of the retreat itself, the fatalism, the relentless heat, the provincial pettiness of colonial types such as the Portmans and the devotion to duty and causes as exemplified by Major Brain. Nor would it have profited me to point out that I was by no means the first European, whether writer or painter, to have been so fascinated and seduced by the East as to turn his back on Europe, if only temporarily. Maugham, the young doctor of *Liza of Lambeth*, had found himself under a comparable compulsion to write of Malaya; D. H. Lawrence, brought up on pit-baths in front of kitchen fires in Nottinghamshire, had found himself similarly compelled by Mexico; Gauguin, seemingly content enough to portray the lace-capped peasants of Pont Aven and surrounding Brittany, had suddenly abandoned it all to paint the languorous naked ladies so free with their charms far away in Tahiti.

Nor was it at any time my intention to make my severance with English ties anything but temporary. 'He's finished!' one of these friends cried as he wholeheartedly fell on the two Burma novels, little realizing that in many ways the best in me was yet to be, as he himself later readily admitted. Apart from the fact that it was surely singularly unjust to judge a writer on two books alone it was also singularly silly, in my view, not to recognise that so great and explosive an experience as the East had afforded me could by no means be cast aside and forgotten as if it were some trivial summer tea party. The effect of my visit to India and Burma, brief though it may have been, had been almost to give me a disease. Its toxins had somehow to be got out of my system or paralyse me for ever, and writing about it all was, as I saw it, the only cure.

If I had ever felt any conscious compulsion to rehabilitate myself with these dissentient friends – and I certainly never did – I could have pointed to another war-book of mine, *The Cruise of the Breadwinner*, which the critic James Agate was good enough, to my intense satisfaction, to compare with Conrad's *Typhoon*. This, the second *novella* I had attempted, was a sea-story that I readily admit had drawn some of its inspiration from Stephen Crane's *Red Badge of Courage*, surely the prime example of the triumph of imagination over observation, for the simple reason that Crane hadn't even been born when the American Civil War of which he wrote with such cauterising brilliance and realism was being fought – a realism and brilliance that had caused ecstatic English critics to compare the young American with Zola and Tolstoy. Truly imagination had carried Crane nearer to the heart of truth than observation could ever have done.

The theme of my long-short story was not wholly dissimilar to his. Whereas his starry-eyed hero goes out, as so many before and after him have done, to seek the glory of war on battlefields, only to suffer the cruellest disillusionment, my similarly starry-eyed hero is a mere boy who goes out to sea in a rickety fishing boat, manned only by a fat skipper and a jaundiced engineer and armed only with an impossibly absurd Lewis gun, to seek his glory and to find his particular disillusionment in the lamplight of the little cabin of the vessel, in a darkening afternoon in the English Channel, as he watches two pilots, one English, one German, die together, indistinguishable in death as enemy or friend but merely representative 'of all the pilots, all the dead pilots, all over the world . . . And there rose up in him a grave exultation. He had been out with men to War and had seen the dead. He was alive and *The Breadwinner* had come home.'

The little story is certainly one of which I am not ashamed and perhaps this is as good a place as any in which to discourse briefly on the fascination the *novella* has long had for me. I was first drawn to it through Conrad, whose *Youth*, *Heart of Darkness* and other essays in the form are in classical mould. These had had the greatest possible effect on me in my youth. Later came Tolstoy, with the incomparable *Death of Ivan Ilyitch*, the grave beauty of *Family Happiness* and others. Side by side with them I read such pieces as Tchehov's *The Party*, Maupassant's *Boule de Suif*, James Joyce's *The Dead* and later Hemingway's *The Snows of Kilimanjaro*, Sherwood Anderson's *The Triumph of the Egg* and Katherine Anne Porter's *Noon Wine*. These all caused me to reflect what a marvellous achievement it is to pack into a hundred pages what many another writer would spin out diffusely into five hundred and in doing so perhaps achieve an even greater and more memorable impact.

To reach this difficult and desirable end requires, without doubt, great technical skill. 'The *novella*,' a critic wrote recently, 'is a form of notorious difficulty. It must combine the shock or finality of the short story with the psychological complication and density of medium available to the novel.' This is well said; but what is highly astonishing is not how few but how many writers of recent times have been eager to accept the challenge, to the singular enrichment of modern literature. Pushkin, Poe, Tchehov, Maupassant, Kipling, Maugham, Mann, Bunin, Crane, Wells, James, Sherwood Anderson, Knut Hamsen, Hemingway, Conrad, Thornton Wilder, Katherine Anne Porter, Graham Greene, D. H. Lawrence, Oscar Wilde, Joyce – the list of brilliant exponents in the form is as rich as it is seemingly endless.

I now resolved, therefore, to try to add to it myself. The challenge having been taken up I presently produced a volume of four *novellas* called *The Nature of Love*, only to be warned by my publishers that 'of course it won't sell. You must resign yourself to that.' In fact it did sell and indeed so well that I have ever since been more and more attracted to the form, so that I have now written some twenty *novellas*, the most recent being *The Triple Echo*, itself a supreme example of the form's 'notorious difficulty'.

The Triple Echo in fact took precisely twenty-five years to write, its genesis having begun in the darker days of the war, in 1943, its completion coming in 1968 – shades of 'the path of art endlessly difficult', of which Edward Garnett had warned me long ago in his preface to *The Two Sisters*. I will not of course mislead the reader by pretending that every day of that twenty-five years was spent in wrestling with that one particular story; it is enough to say that the challenge, the problem and the complexity were always there, constantly kicking away at the womb of the mind, the story apparently unwilling to be born but ever restless in its tireless determination finally to come to life.

Any writer of fiction will tell you that inevitably, from time to time, he finds it necessary to invent a new character to do the work of unravelling his narrative for him. In the case of *The Triple Echo* the exact reverse was true. What had so long inhibited the birth of my story was not the lack of a character but the fact that, as I belatedly discovered, I had one character too many. This superfluous character having been removed, light instantly flooded in on to a canvas that had been so long irremediably dark, and in a mere three weeks the story was extracted from the womb it had apparently been so reluctant to leave. 'The path of art endlessly difficult' indeed.

In 1947, however, *The Triple Echo* was still in the womb and it looked as if nothing less than an operation would ever get it out. Instead of which another crisis in my life occurred.

In the early spring of that year, on a visit to my parents in Northamptonshire, I became aware of a curious lassitude. My arms and legs began to feel as if made of lead; I could scarcely drag myself about. For a time I put this down to the fact that my native town, Rushden, is a town of steep hills and that since I hadn't paid a visit to the town for a considerable time I wasn't at all used to them. But as we drove back to Kent in the car, with snow falling dismally on the Downs, I felt no better. If anything the heavy lassitude seemed worse. Nor did it improve matters to discover, next morning, that my youngest son looked all set for a bout of measles. We accordingly called in the doctor.

When he arrived, however, he scarcely looked at the boy. Instead he asked what was the matter with me, at the same time looking at me seriously and very searchingly. In reply I told him of my extreme lassitude; in fact he didn't need to be told. He had already guessed what was wrong. He murmured something about samples of this and that and that he would call to collect them later. Next morning he telephoned me with the news that he had spoken with a surgeon; the fact was that I had had an internal haemorrhage and the time had come 'to take that little look inside me'.

It was now Easter Sunday, exactly two years after my trip across the Burma plain with the Padre. I do not recall that the news that I was to have an operation, and with all speed at that, in any sense depressed me; I felt rather a sense of blessed relief, glad that at last there might be some chance of ridding myself of the gnawing abdominal pains, with their attendant greyness of spirit, that had troubled me ever since my teens. I therefore surrendered willingly to hospital and the surgeon next day.

The operation having been completely successful I made the swiftest possible recovery and was home again within ten days. In less than another two weeks I was in Switzerland, convalescing, carrying with me words of great assurance from the surgeon. 'Diet? Fiddlesticks. You don't suppose I've taken away seven-eighths of your stomach so that you can spend the rest of your life on a diet, do you? No, I've done what I have done for precisely the opposite reason.'

From that moment my pains vanished; the greyness of spirit was dissipated; I was a new man.

XI

A great many first novels, as I have remarked before, are autobiographical, if not wholly so then at least in part. My own first novel, *The Two Sisters*, was a marked exception. Not a single syllable of it is autobiographical; in no sense, physically, emotionally or otherwise, can the identity of any of its characters be confused with mine. It is a work, as I have also pointed out, of wild, youthful imagination: an imagination not knowing quite where it is going or what exactly it wants to say. If the result is therefore sometimes confused that is the inevitable fruit of inexperience; I felt much, imagined much but at the age of eighteen and nineteen, simply didn't know enough.

In 1950, however, at the age of forty-five, I at last began to turn my attention, for the first time, to a subject that was autobiographical. It had been many years since I had seen the figure of a strikingly beautiful young girl in a black cloak lined with scarlet arrive at the station at Rushden in a smart pony-drawn gig in order to catch a train and almost as many since, on a freezing winter night, I had gone on an assignment as a young reporter to Rushden Hall, totally unaware at the time that I was sitting in the same room in which the poet Robert Herrick must have sat, three hundred years before, on his visits to the ever-hospitable Sir Lewis Pemberton. The two incidents in fact provide another good example of a negative, in this case the unknown young girl, needing a positive, in this case the draughty Elizabethan Hall where I had sat as a nervous young reporter, in order to bring it to life.

Now, at long last, the fusion of these two episodes was complete and I began to feel life flowing from it strongly. The novel I had in mind was to reflect, in part at least, my own youth, its ecstasies and uncertainties, its impatient disposition to judge people (as I had judged my friend the Reverend Bernard Harris) by prejudice, before giving them a chance, its love and love's attendant agonies, its inevitable disillusionments and pain and its final awakening. The theme and spirit of *Love for Lydia* may perhaps be best expressed in a couple of lines taken from the book itself: 'it had not occurred to me that the pain of love might be part of its flowering . . . With inconceivable stupidity I had not given love to her simply out of fear of being hurt by its acceptance; I had not grasped that I might have made her suffer'.

I set this tortured piece of self-examination against my native Nene Valley, where I had skated in winter in meadows of frozen flood water, had wandered in spring and summer with my grandfather, seeing the April unfolding of blackthorn and hawthorn and king-cup and cowslip, watching kingfishers swoop across the river and pike sunning themselves in smooth waters, and had later so often wandered alone, trying to escape

the drabness of my native boot-and-shoe town, wrestling with ideas for my earliest stories, unable to share with another soul the problems they continually created. If certain of my friends had entertained grave doubts about me after *The Purple Plain* and *The Jacaranda Tree* they could certainly find no cause for complaint here; all the distilled essence of the countryside I had so loved as a boy went into *Love for Lydia*, together with the bloom of youth, with all its beauty and tender, tenuous fragility.

Not that the completed book was achieved without much heart-searching. A novel may be autobiographical, either wholly or in part, but this does not at all mean that its execution is merely a question of dipping into memory and fishing out a fact here, an episode there; the birth pains of imaginative creation have still to be endured, the path of art is still endlessly difficult.

Even at the risk of my seeming to be repetitious on the subject of art's difficulties I feel this may nevertheless be a good moment to point out one of the chief sources, indeed perhaps *the* chief source, of these difficulties. It is all too often forgotten, I feel, that all art is ultimately a physical act. Art does not consist of merely dreaming dreams, of hearing the music of the spheres or, as Ibsen was fond of repeating, 'wearing vine leaves in one's hair'. As with love itself the ultimate moment of art's expression is, and must be, physical. This is not merely 'a consummation devoutly to be wished' but one which must at all costs be accomplished. Until the writer puts his pen to paper, the artist his brush or pencil to canvas or paper, the sculptor his chisel to stone or wood, until the composer gives his musicians the opportunity of making music physically possible, there is nothing. This may sound a truism; but it does much to show, I think, that while artistic creation has its own special exhilarations it can also be, and very, very often is, both physically and mentally exhausting. A great amount of self-discipline is needed to accomplish these things and this too increases the tensions and problems constantly facing the artist. Altogether it is a highly complex business and one about which, I often feel, the public knows little or nothing. Perhaps only the artist, struggling to discipline himself, seeking his tortuous way through the maze of thought and imagination and finally arriving at his final moment of exhilarating but exhausting consummation, knows exactly what price art extracts from its executors.

If my world was now achieving ripeness in many directions, some of them totally unexpected, there were still parts of its territory where this had not proved possible. One of these was the theatre. It is true that my first published book was a play, although an extremely short one, in one act, to be followed within a short time by another in one act for radio. It is also true that, nursing fond ambitions, I had as a young man read almost as voraciously of drama as I had of the short story. Ibsen, Tchehov, Turgenev, Bjornsen, Pirandello, Shakespeare, the Elizabethans, Congreve, Sheridan, Shaw, Maugham, O'Neill, Coward, O'Casey: I had swallowed them all, and more, with the keenest appetite. I sought desperately to be a dramatist. On this score Edward Garnett, never forgetting his own disastrous crash with his play *The Breaking Point*, a disaster so remorselessly predicted by Conrad, was for ever trying to turn me away from this course, but I fear I hardly listened. In consequence I wrote other one-act plays, following them up with three-acters, of which I have, I suppose, written seven or eight. Some of these have been performed and are still being performed; the larger part, though attracting the interest and even enthusiasm of an impresario here, an actor-manager there, have not.

The first of these was a piece called *Carrie and Cleopatra*, which was put on, thanks to the tireless interest of that ever-present help in time of trouble, Violet Dean, at the Torch Theatre, one of London's many little theatres of that time, just before the war. Though giving good acting scope to several of the actors, it wasn't very well received. I was not unnaturally disappointed, though undeterred. The result was that on that first memorable assignment to the R.A.F. Bomber Command Station at Oakington it was at first not in the form of short stories that I saw myself expressing the lives and actions of the young pilots there, but in a play. It so happened, however, that before the play could get itself down on paper Terence Rattigan turned up with *Flare Path*, the idea of which wasn't wholly dissimilar to the one I had in mind. I herefore put the idea of the play aside and concentrated, wisely I think, on the stories that were eventually to appear under the pseudonym of Flying Officer X. Not that the idea of the play was dead; on the contrary it continued to be agitated with life and finally became, later in the war, *The Day of Glory*.

Unhappily it proved impossible to produce it until the war was over, a fact that undoubtedly mitigated against any possible commercial success. By that time all fervour for the war had been dissipated and when at last *The Day of Glory* was produced at the Embassy Theatre one could only sense, on the first night, an atmosphere cold and disillusioned. Several parts in the play were also badly miscast, the result being that what I had wanted to say never got put over. The play fared far better on tour, under the auspices of the Arts Council, finding far better acting and far warmer audiences in the provinces than in London, where hard-bitten first night audiences often do as much to kill a play's chances of success as the hostility of critics. *The Day of Glory* is, however, still performed and has even achieved, in Holland, a state of some permanency as an annual event.

I followed this with a dark, Ibsen-like piece called *The Spider Love* (I culled the title from Donne's great lines *But O, self-traitor, I do bring The spider love, which transubstantiates all, And can convert manna to gall*) but its demands on actors are incontestably formidable and it is probably for this reason that it has never been performed. Two other plays have shared the same fate, thus emphasising, if that were necessary, the theatre's eternal uncertainty. The pains and perils of this uncertainty have been well examined and described by my former R.A.F. colleague R. F. Delderfield, who in spite of the phenomenal success of his *Worm's Eye View*, which ran for five and a half years in London, beating even the fantastic pre-war run of

Chu Chin Chow, finally turned his back on the theatre through sheer disenchantment and settled for the less maddening demands of the novel. I can only say that I wholeheartedly share both his views and his disenchantment, so that I fear the Great Bates Play will not, now, ever be written. Nor will this state of affairs break my heart; the theatre is, I realize at last, not for me.

But in the early fifties I had suffered no such disenchantment with the novel. The considerable success of *Love for Lydia* had on the contrary given me fresh heart to set at least another novel in my native Northamptonshire, in whose soil, although I had by now lived in the idyllic pastures of Kent for exactly the same time as I had lived between the valleys of the Nene and the Ouse, my roots still lay deep.

It is a commonplace in art that writers and painters – painters perhaps the more frequently – are often so fascinated by a theme, a scene or a face that they are unable to resist the temptation to do another and even perhaps yet another and another version of it. This was something of the case with the novel I now planned. As a young man, still only in my twenties, I had written my second novel, *Catherine Foster*, very much under the influence of Flaubert. Its theme concerned a woman of passionate nature and imagination married to a small-town bore who could satisfy neither her passion nor her love of music and her appetite for a warmer, freer life. Like many women before her in similar circumstances she takes a lover, enjoys a spell of excruciating happiness and then eventually goes back 'into that obscurity from which she had once come'.

Since writing that book I had had many successes along with some dismal failures brought about largely by my own obtuse stupidities; of these I have written in *The Blossoming World*. But having learned much from these failures I felt I had now matured enough, both in character and technique, to attempt a bolder version of the earlier theme. *Catherine Foster* had been set in a quiet back street of the little Northamptonshire town of Higham Ferrers, which may fairly be called my spiritual birthplace, since most of the golden days of my childhood had been spent in and about it. The new novel, *The Sleepless Moon*, was to be set just round the corner from that quiet street, in the enchanting little chestnut-lined square which to this day is virtually unchanged from the time when I used to go with my grandfather in summer to gather loads of sweet honey pears from the walled garden of a grocer's shop standing in the corner of the square, by the gates of the church. Catherine Foster had been married to a corn merchant; Constance Turner was married to a grocer in the corner shop. 'After all there were no carriages for her wedding. The distance between the church porch and the house on the corner of the square was so short, everyone said, that it was not worth while.'

It was not only carriages, however, that were missing from Constance Turner's marriage; to her bitter surprise the very essence of it was also missing, the very fact of physical love and consummation. To so sensitive a creature such a discovery is little short of tragic; she is driven more and more into herself, imprisoned in solitariness, so that soon she is known as 'the untouchable Mrs T.' Not surprisingly she, too, out of sheer desperation, takes a lover and thereby enjoys a few months of secret idyllic passion. But if the lovers' clandestine meetings are idyllic they are also pierced with pain and the novel moves to its inevitably unhappy climax as surely as any Greek tragedy.

This tragedy of incompatibility is made the more excruciating, I feel, for being set against the calm and serenity of the little town, a town of provincial conventions and gossip, of small intrigues, of church-going on Sundays and fox-hunting in winter: a town in which to such a man as Melford Turner the death of his favourite horse is a greater source of grief than the apparent frigidity of a wife on whom his 'undemonstrative, customary, nightly salutation', a kiss on the forehead, 'a mere brush of dry lips,' has an effect 'as if a great draught of wintry air had solidified inside her, gripping her heart in a freezing neutral shroud'.

All this was far removed from the heat and horrors of *The Purple Plain* and *The Jacaranda Tree;* I was now securely back on my own territory and the result, I confess, did not displease me. It therefore came as a highly discomforting shock to learn that a friend whom I constantly treated as a confidant had reputedly called the novel 'a disgusting book'. This may appear as a criticism both trivial and ludicrous in our contemporary permissive age but at the time it was solemnly and seriously meant. In turn I took it with equal solemnity and seriousness. It was not so much that I was angered; I simply felt crushed by a profound depression; my renewed confidence in myself was suddenly and completely drained away.

When Edward Garnett had lambasted the liver and lights out of me for the *débâcle* I had committed in my early ill-fated novel *The Voyagers* I had simply bounced back next day like a jack-in-the-box, eager to atone for my fatuous misdeeds. Not so with *The Sleepless Moon;* suddenly and quite illogically I was ashamed of the book. I deliberately refrained from reading any notices of it; in my heart I disowned it; and worse still I came to a stubborn and depressing decision: I would never, never write another novel.

I did not then know that David Garnett, an old friend for whose judgement I had the deepest respect, had called *The Sleepless Moon* 'a very great novel'; nor was I to know for some years later, when my vow never to write another novel had achieved an obstinate permanency. Perhaps if I had known of David's judgement at the time the course of my creative output, over the next few years, might have been charted very differently. But the fact is that I did not know and it was fortunate that my native buoyancy again came to my rescue.

The immediate result of that depressive and ill-conceived

judgement on *The Sleepless Moon* was in fact to drive me straight back into the arms of my first love, the short story, and at the same time to induce the *novella* more and more to share the bed with us. As a consequence I wrote much in both media. The discipline so necessary in the execution of the *novella*, the form of 'notorious difficulty', was not only highly challenging but highly exciting too. I have rarely enjoyed writing as much as I did in the next decade, when I produced half a dozen volumes of short stories and almost as many of *novellas*, among them such pieces as *Death of a Huntsman*, *An Aspidistra in Babylon*, *The Golden Oriole* and *Where the Cloud Breaks*, all of which I deem to belong to my best work. The judgement on *The Sleepless Moon* may perhaps be left, therefore, to the department of 'it's an ill wind'. Certainly, on reflection, I am not sorry to have been relieved, for a time at any rate, of the exhausting labours of giving birth to novels. I can only say that I greatly enjoyed, and learned much from, my repeated honeymoons with my first and second loves, the short story and the *novella*.

Moreover these numerous excursions into the shorter fictional forms merely served to prove, if proof were needed, the truth of William Gerhardi's assertion that 'fiction is the natural heir to poetry', a belief shared by Elizabeth Bowen when she claims that 'the short story is at an advantage over the novel and can claim nearer kinship to poetry, because it must be more concentrated, can be more visionary and is not weighted down (as the novel is bound to be) by facts, explanation, or analysis'. Commenting on this Lord David Cecil writes: 'she is right; just because it is as brief as a lyric poem its scope is wider; it can include the visionary and the fantastic as the novel cannot.'

In every sense, then, the aftermath of *The Sleepless Moon* was another phase in my ripening world. Inevitably it led to others, with some of which I shall now proceed to deal.

It is many years now since the short story writer A. E. Coppard first explained to me his contention that we short story writers could learn much from the cinema. I listened with fascination to his discourse on cuts, close-ups, fade-outs and brief swift shots and of how in this way a film was built up to achieve a sharp, pictorial impact. In the same way, Coppard contended, a story should be built up, achieving a comparable visual effect. 'I want to *see* it,' Coppard said. 'I must *see* it.' In other words the short story had to be pictorial rather than discursive or as Miss Bowen rightly says in the passage quoted above 'not weighted down (as the novel is bound to be) by facts, explanation, or analysis'. I was so impressed by the Coppard theory that I instantly resolved to make my writing more and more visual, painting the words rather than writing them, depicting scene and place and people vividly, in pictures, leaving out explanations, letting only essentials do the work. This I have done ever since, thus developing a quality that Edward Garnett had shrewdly detected in *The Two Sisters* – namely that 'the story is implied rather than chronicled'.

It is here worth pointing out that *The Sleepless Moon* is dedicated to David Lean, the film director, who had learned his craft in that graveyard of inessentials, the cutting room. It was not to David Lean, however, that I first owed my association with films, though he was later to buy the rights of several of my stories for that medium. I owed my introduction to films to an American director, Leslie Fenton. It is really wrong, however, to refer to Fenton as an American and I do so only because he had worked solely in America, as a director, for many years. He was in fact English, having steadfastly refused, like Chaplin, to give up his nationality. His devotion to and admiration for England were indeed great, so much so that as soon as the Second World War broke out Fenton immediately shipped himself to England and joined the Royal Navy. In due course he fought in that vicious engagement, the Battle of St Nazaire, where he was badly wounded and finally invalided out.

Even then he remained in London, eager to help England's cause if he could. It was there while contacting the Ministry of Information on some propaganda project or other that he came across the stories of Flying Officer X., for which he at once evinced an enormous admiration. As a result he made it his business to get to know me and then when we met declared, and in no uncertain terms, that the stories were not only admirable in themselves but that unquestionably they ought to be filmed. (That brilliant photographer, Robert Capa, who was later killed in Korea, had already made a similarly emphatic declaration about one of the stories that had come out of Oakington, *The Young Man from Kalgoorlie*, but nothing definite was ever done in that direction). Fenton was more practical. He proposed to make certain of the stories into films himself; if this came about would I write the scripts? I had never attempted a film script in my life and perhaps a little unwisely I said that I would.

One story that had much impressed Fenton was the very first I had ever written at Oakington, *It's Just the Way It Is*, in which the parents of a pilot who had been killed pay a visit to his Wing-Commander, as was the habit of parents, half to satisfy themselves that their son is really dead, half in the touching hope that he may still be alive after all. It was this story that Fenton wanted to film and I not only duly wrote the script for it but even took part in the picture, making my one and only appearance as a film actor in the guise of a dead navigator being carried on a stretcher from a shot-up bomber.

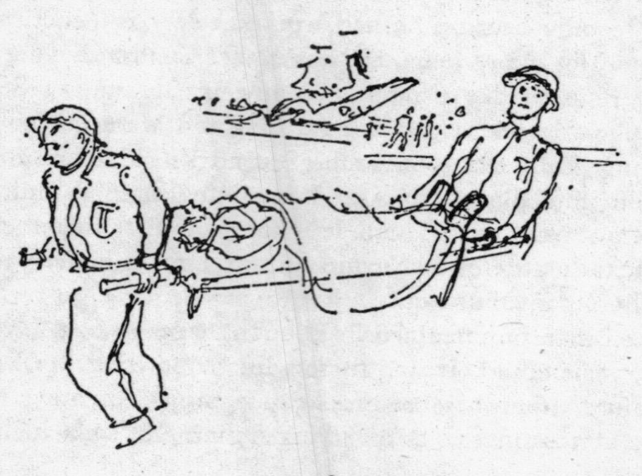

It was during this brief collaboration on the little film that Fenton suggested I must meet Sir Alexander Korda. I knew that Korda and my agent, Laurence Pollinger, had often been in association, and I readily agreed. Accordingly Fenton and I went along one afternoon to Korda's office in Piccadilly, Fenton having explained that Korda was building up a strong pool of writers for a new programme of films and that it was not improbable that he might ask me to be one of them.

But if I had any fond idea that Korda would immediately broach the subject of films and writing for them I was to be swiftly disillusioned. I found Korda a shrewd, cultivated, clever and amusing man and it was utterly in character that afternoon that instead of getting down to the practical business of talking films he immediately launched out on a discourse, hilarious as any Chaplin film, on the subject of farting.

'Ah! you know, Bates,' he said in the strong Hungarian accent he never lost and indeed probably carefully cultivated, 'I adore ze fart. I absolutely adore ze fart. Ze fart is *marvellous*. You know, Bates, what they call it in France? No? *Le piano du pauvre homme*. The poor man's piano. *Marvellous*.'

The eventual result of that inconsequential afternoon was that Korda put me under contract to him at a salary that looked phenomenal enough on paper until you woke up to the stark fact that, thanks to tax, all you got out of every pound was sixpence. There are, however, other desirable dividends in life rather than money and in this case I eagerly reached out simply in order to profit from a new experience. But one other desirable dividend that in due course presented itself was that I was able to meet, through Korda, David Lean.

David as a film director is dedicated to the proposition, as I also am as a writer, that it is the business of the artist to entertain, not to instruct, to give pleasure, not to preach morals. To this end he was extracting, or was about to extract, every ounce of entertainment from *Oliver Twist* and *Great Expectations*, as he was later to extract even more of it from *The Bridge on the River Kwai* and *Doctor Zhivago*.

David is an intense and dedicated man and we instantly got

on well together. He was quick to confess much admiration not only for some of my novels and longer stories such as *Fair Stood the Wind For France*, *The Cruise of the Breadwinner* and *The Purple Plain*, but also for many of the very short ones, the little pictorial sketches in which all is 'implied rather than chronicled', in which there is no time for 'facts, explanation and analysis'. I in turn admired his own methods, a supreme example of which is the dramatic and terrifying cut to the face of the convict in the graveyard in *Great Expectations*, a stroke of arresting shock which tells more in a split second than many a novelist, ambling discursively along, could tell in a page.

Soon David was extending his enthusiasm into more practical form by buying the film rights of *Fair Stood the Wind For France*, *The Cruise of the Breadwinner* and *The Purple Plain*, only one of which, *The Purple Plain*, has ever reached the screen. This fact has never mattered to me; the experience of the association with David was rich enough in itself and the more I saw of him and his methods the more sure I was that Coppard, in his contention that the story writer could learn much from the cinema, was right. This contention obliquely gets the blessing of Lord David Cecil, who in an introduction to a recent anthology of modern short stories has written: 'The "plot" form is a limited form and one which excludes the work of some of the greatest masters of the *genre*, from Chekhov downwards. Anyway, partly under Chekhov's influence and partly from a general loosening up of fictional form, the old convention gradually lost its grip; and by the turn of the century the short-story writer was free to shape his inspiration into what form he pleased. This is why the twentieth century is the great period for the English short story.' Exactly; nor do I think I am exaggerating when I maintain that the cinema has had some part in the evolution of that greatness.

One day, when David and I were having preparatory discussions as to what sort of boat *The Breadwinner* should be when it came to making the film, he suddenly seemed to go

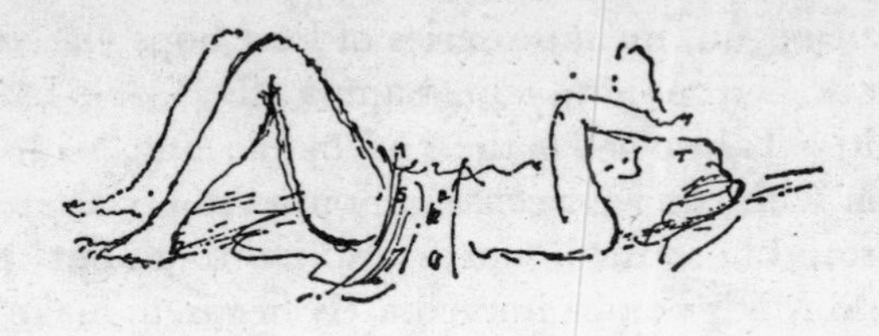

off into a day-dream. When he finally emerged from it he surprised me by asking:

'Have you ever been to Tahiti?'

I confessed I never had.

'Would you like to go?'

I replied that I had always wanted to go to Tahiti. The association with Gauguin and his friends had always fascinated me.

'But why,' I said, 'are you asking me?'

In reply he went on to say that an actor friend of his had just come back from the Friendly Islands, bringing with him some excellent photographs, not only of Tahiti itself but more particularly of the island of Moorea, which lies some eighteen or twenty miles away. The photographs, when produced, showed Moorea to be an island looking very much like a piece of the Dolomites turned tropical. It also looked simple, remote and romantic, with palms restful on the shores of a placid lagoon, palm-thatched huts, high tranquil white clouds.

David asked if I didn't think it looked fascinating and I replied that there was no doubt it did.

'Would you like to go?' he said. 'You caught the atmosphere of Burma so well that I thought you might capture something of the Pacific too. I thought if you could wander around and pick up an idea for a story I'd like to make a film of it. What do you say?'

I decided it was an opportunity too good to miss. I agreed to go. This was simple enough; the problem was to know how to get there. It turned out that a boat from Marseilles took a month, a proposition which had no appeal for either Madge or me. The only possible way was by air and this, since the jet age had not begun, meant a series of long hops via New York, San Francisco, Honolulu, Fiji, Samoa, the Cook Islands and then Tahiti – Tahiti being the end of the line, with no communication with the west coast of South America.

The prospect seemed not only inviting but positively exciting and Madge and I immediately began to make preparations to go.

'It looks,' I said to David, as we pored over the photographs again, 'like a proper Lotus Land.' Perhaps I was thinking at that moment of Pierre Loti, the 19th century French writer who, like Gauguin, had fallen deeply under the spell of Polynesia. Then, recalling the painful surprise India had had in store for me I said on reflection: 'Well, we shall see.'

Lotus Land? Yes. It all depended, of course, on what you meant by Lotus Land.

Westward from New York to San Francisco, that pleasantest of cities washed by the cold waters of the North Pacific; then a long, long haul to Honolulu, with a brief call in the middle of the night at Canton Island, an Anglo-U.S. condominium with a sign-post in the middle of its white barren expanse of rock and sand proclaiming that everywhere in the world was, as I remember it, 12,000 miles away – a proclamation that induced a lowering of the spirits and a chilling sense of isolation; then eventually to Honolulu, to drive from the airport to the hotel through avenues of little stalls selling *leis* made of flowers in every conceivable brilliance of colour, and seeing on the streets girls of such beauty, many of them a cross between Chinese and Polynesian, that they are surely the prettiest in the world, and then out on the ocean itself a great white spouting of whales; and then presently on to Fiji, with Suva, the capital, full of the scent of frangipani and as hotly steaming as Calcutta itself; and then on to Samoa.

'This,' I had said to Madge as we flew on over bluer and bluer waters, 'is the way to travel. Nothing like a flying-boat. Especially the landing. You'll love the landing.'

I began to regret the words as we started to lose height over

Samoa and below us the formerly bluest of seas suddenly became an ugly, sinister charge of white horses. A few minutes later we were landing on a sea like a maelstrom, in a twenty-five mile an hour crosswind, very close to peril.

'Landing?' Madge said. 'I'm glad you said landing. Oh! yes, I loved the landing.'

'Any landing,' I reminded her, 'is a good landing.'

Rain fell in warm, steaming torrents. A number of pregnant Polynesian women moaned with fright as the launch took us precariously from flying-boat to anchorage and then continued to sit huddled in fear as the bus drove us on our long journey across the flooded island.

But even under rain Samoa looked incomparably beautiful. It is an island of great lushness, of wooded mountains and ravines, of many churches of all sizes and denominations (the work of the London Missionary Society), of delightful village greens, all looking as smooth-shaven and green as any in England, all deliciously embroidered with many flowers, all surrounded by big palm-thatched houses looking like circular sea-side band-stands. On one of these greens numbers of small boys were playing cricket, totally oblivious of the torrential rain, using the central rib of a big palm frond as a bat. On another a pretty Samoan girl stood laughingly washing her naked breasts, 'the colour of dark honey', in the rain. All along the sea-coast, a short distance from the shore and joined to it by wooden gangways, stood little huts, on the purpose of which I pondered in vain until suddenly I saw the door of one of them open, to reveal a Samoan woman placidly sitting there on the loo, a sight that woke even the fear-struck pregnant women to laughter.

Apia, above which stands Vailima, the former home of Robert Louis Stevenson, looked utterly dismal under the rain, its harbour showing here and there the gaunt bones of wrecks, its waters half-grey, half-red from soil washed down from the mountains. The waterfront itself looked like something out of Somerset Maugham – indeed it was the perfect setting for his story *Rain* – or Conrad: seedy, shabby, the twilit back-end-of-nowhere, inspiring thoughts of beachcombers getting drunk in bars, except that, as we presently discovered as we wound up at our so-called hotel, there was nothing to get drunk on.

My forethought in buying a few miniature bottles of gin on the flying-boat helped us through an evening dismal with rain, black hordes of flies on the dinner table and some of the most appalling food I have ever been faced with. All night the rain pelted down and we could only pray it would stop by morning.

It did not stop. At breakfast we knew that, with the wind still raging, we were imprisoned for another day. What on earth could we do with ourselves? The answer came from a pleasant Liberian girl working on the island as a schoolteacher. Perhaps we might care to see the school? She assured us it would be interesting.

More in desperation than anything else we accepted her invitation. At the school a big class of small Samoan children sang lustily for us, the chief items of their *repertoire* being, as I remember it, *Rule Britannia* and *London Bridge is Falling Down.* After this we were invited to the staff mid-morning coffee, during which someone inquired if I too was teaching. When I said 'No, writing,' an essay in detective work began. A few moments later someone deduced that I was the author of *The Purple Plain* and a rumble of curiosity reverberated through the teaching staff. This led to the imperative suggestion that we must of course meet the High Commissioner. A meeting must be arranged forthwith.

That evening we sat in the drawing-room at Vailima, the long white timber house standing on the hills above Apia, then the residence of the High Commissioner, formerly the home of R.L.S., the decaying centre of the strangest of *ménages*, where he lived for the last four years of his life. As we sat there

talking with the Commissioner and his wife, two very pleasant people, rain still fell torrentially outside and the air, as in one of Stevenson's own stories, 'smelt strong of wild lime and vanilla'. Throughout the damp, hot evening, in a temperature of ninety degrees or so, the scene was dominated by a portrait of the brooding, sickly, Gauguin-like figure of Stevenson himself, hypnotic, compelling, uncomfortable and by no means unsinister as it stared down from the wall: yet another example of the European artist from the cool north who had found it impossible to resist the enchantments of tropical lands and southern seas.

After another day of black hordes of flies and hopelessly bad food – the only other hotel on the waterfront was reputedly nothing but a whore-house – we flew off at last on the brightest of mornings to the Cook Islands, where big handsome Polynesian girls with long blue-black hair swam in the crystal waters of the calmest of lagoons at Atutaki, or lazed on the brilliant, almost snow-white coral sand.

The fortnightly arrival of the flying-boat at Papeete was evidently always an excuse for a near festival: crowds of gay Polynesian girls on the waterfront wearing purple and pink and white and scarlet *leis*, more *leis* for incoming travellers, a general air of care-free excitement. (I use the word care-free advisedly but will qualify it presently.) A good proportion of the girls, I was assured, were waiting for someone to sleep with, regardless of whatever price they might subsequently have to pay. The girls of Tahiti are in fact very free with their favours, to which may be added that they see no stigma of any kind in having children out of wedlock, indeed rather the reverse, since they are very fond of children and also because unions between Polynesian and Polynesian tend to be unfruitful, whereas the Polynesian female tends to become extremely fertile when mated to French, English, American, New Zealand or Australian men or almost any male except their own. The Friendly Islands would seem, indeed, to be aptly named.

Papeete itself turned out to be a scruffy little port, again half like something out of Maugham or Conrad, half like a French provincial town hopelessly gone to seed. Its shops were mostly Chinese; its bars seemed little more than brothels. Its shabby, seedy air was however greatly heightened by many flowers, most exquisite among them that loveliest of vines, the allamanda, whose butter-pure trumpets trailed with prodigal splendour everywhere. On everything there lay a great air of lassitude, of *mañana*, a feeling of 'why today? – tomorrow will do', so that it took almost all morning to cash a cheque at the old-fashioned French-like bank.

Towards the end of the 19th century a great influx of indentured labour, mostly Indian and Chinese, flooded into the Pacific, with remarkable results to be seen everywhere today. In Fiji, for example, Indians already strongly outnumber Fijians. The Melanesians, physically strong and powerful as they are, have been overtaken by Indians with their renowned merchant skills and a religion which continuously teaches and preaches fertility. These Indians today are a magnificent, prosperous people beside whom Calcutta's pavement-dossing hordes look like scum and even many Fijians look sad and heavy with the indolence which has let them become out-numbered. In Tahiti it is the Chinese who have been notably industrious, so that they are now the shop-keepers, the fisher-men, the landowners, the market-gardeners. Hard-working, skilful, thrifty, they leave the Polynesians as far behind as the Indians have left the Melanesians.

The Polynesians are, in fact, a dying race. Their tendency not to reproduce among themselves is naturally largely responsible for this, but with this goes the sad fact that unions between Polynesian women and outsiders are not only highly fruitful but also productive of children who are very often mentally brilliant. This in turn is another melancholy source of frustration, since the outlook for such brilliance in Papeete is highly limited and the Sorbonne is far, far away. A school-master sadly gave us an example of this, swearing that in a school painting competition ninety per cent of the winning entries, all brilliant, came from descendants of Gauguin.

But if Papeete was shabby, seedy, sad and sunk in apathy, the Pacific was certainly not. It is an Everest among oceans: vast, haunting, restless, dominating. Few areas of the world can give off such a powerful impression of being, in the strangest way, the surviving fragment of a mysterious and long-lost world. Over it broods not only that peculiar fatalistic air of coiled-up violence that is an inevitable part of all tropical atmosphere, but a high-charged feeling that at any moment a vast electric spark may leap across it and set its slumbering dramas burning and quivering. You get the same feeling when a shark explodes from the water, a dramatic slash of sinister power, a feeling that anything may happen here.

Soon, in Papeete, we found ourselves in close friendship with a congenial American doctor. We had in fact met him earlier on the flying-boat, where he had asked me to look after a wooden box for him. He said something about 'precious cargo' and when I inquired what this might be, replied 'Mosquitoes'. They were in fact a particular brand of giant mosquito apparently having the ability, like fleas on the backs of lesser fleas and so *ad infinitum*, to prey on lesser mosquitoes. The American in fact was engaged in research into the disease filariasis, formerly better known as elephantiasis. Filariasis is perhaps the least aesthetic of many unaesthetic tropical diseases, turning the limbs, even of young girls, into hideous elephantine lumps of swollen flesh that are distressing to behold. The disease is carried by mosquitoes, in a cycle as simple as it is sinister. It begins with a coconut falling from a tree. It continues with a rat gnawing a hole in the coconut, then with rain, which falls with fair frequency in Tahiti, filling up the coconut. In the stagnant rainwater mosquitoes breed, subsequently flying off to bite first of all some sufferer from filariasis and then someone who hasn't got filariasis but soon will have. The lymphatic glands having thus been impregnated, the cycle is all ready to begin again via coconut, rat, rain and all.

It was the American doctor's hope that the resident mosquito population might be much reduced, if not wiped out, by his imported giants. In due course he took us along to his research laboratory to see his mosquito menagerie and then to hospital to see some of the mosquito's distressful victims. He had, however, other weapons in his armoury besides the imported giants. These were largely pills and one afternoon he invited me to tour some parts of the island with him, so that I could see for myself another side of his work.

'But not Madge,' he said.

'No? Why not?'

'I don't think this,' he said, 'is for Madge.'

We motored along the black-sanded shore – the beaches in Tahiti are all of black sand, looking very much like a foundry yard – past the sinister fallen coconuts, past the house reputed to have been lived in by Gauguin, past other houses at which the doctor honked on the car-horn in order to give a passing signal to a friend ('No reply. Ah! it's three o'clock. Guess he's in bed with his *vahini*'), until at last we reached a little bay. Some distance inland was a small market-garden growing lettuces, radishes, carrots, water-cress and so on. In a wretched hovel, which stank like the sewer it probably was, a Chinaman and his wife were packing and washing vegetables. The Chinaman's method was to wash his feet and the vegetables in the same water, at the same time. The air was odious with stench; and I now understood why this was not for Madge.

Presently the doctor was speaking to the Chinaman. The Chinaman made gestures of innocent protest. The doctor spoke again. The Chinaman pointed towards the sea.

'What,' I said, 'is it all about?'

'The taking of pills. The artful bastards know a thousand and one tricks to make you believe they've taken them when they never have. They hold them under the tongue, in the cheek, anything. This one hasn't taken his because he's going fishing tonight and he says the pills will make him sick and he'll fall overboard. His wife hasn't taken hers because apparently the stars are not right.'

'Pure superstition.'

'Superstition, pure or otherwise, we have always with us.'

The Chinaman paddled his filthy legs and feet in water containing water-cress. I retched and was nearly sick.

'The Lotus Land,' I said.

'What was that? What did you say?'

'Nothing much. I was merely thinking,' I said, 'of the Lotus Land.'

XII

The casual nature of life in Tahiti was well illustrated a few days later when we were suddenly told by a man who kept one of the town's better bars:

'Oh! by the way, the Larsens are expecting you for the week-end.'

'The Larsens? Who are the Larsens?'

'American couple. They live on Moorea. Dying to meet you.'

I inquired as to how we got to Moorea.

'Schooner. Goes every morning at 9.30. You're expected Saturday. Be down on the waterfront soon after 9.'

On Saturday morning we duly arrived on the waterfront soon after 9. The front was crowded with the usual throng of Tahitians madly doing nothing but there was, as far as I could see, nothing in sight that could be called a schooner. We idled about for half an hour or so, I with growing impatience, until suddenly Madge drew my attention to what seemed tobe a large white ramshackle barrel sawn in half and moored to the quay-side. This was being loaded with cargo, bicycles, casks of wine, people and even a horse, the animal being eventually strapped to the side of the deck. This, it turned out, was our schooner.

We went aboard. Several women passengers, as if in anticipation of terrors to come, appeared already to have given up the ghost and lay immobile on deck or on seats with their heads completely covered with shawls. The horse didn't look particularly tranquil either. Of captain and crew there was no sign but more and more cargo, people, wine and bicycles kept coming aboard.

Ten o'clock came and went but still no crew. By this time the morning was already hotting up and the air was thick and sickening with the smell of engine oil. There is invariably a vast swell on the surface of the Pacific and I began to suffer inwardly for Madge, who isn't the best of sailors. Now and then one of the prostrate covered women would give a stifled groan and the horse, growing more restless, would nervously stamp its hooves on the deck.

When eleven o'clock came I was in a mood to disembark and find ourselves a long cool drink somewhere. At this moment a huge, tipsy-looking Tahitian with one eye stumbled aboard, followed by two disreputable characters in no better state, each carrying a bottle of wine. This, I judged, was our captain and crew and my sympathies were now firmly with the moaning, covered women.

Presently one of the crew opened up a hatchway and disappeared into a black hole below decks. The captain took the wheel in one hand and an uncorked bottle of wine in the other and after a sudden shattering explosion from the black hole below decks we were ready to sail into the hot, blinding white light of the great open Pacific. With a certain trepidation I then remembered that although the journey was a mere eighteen miles or so in distance it was to take four hours or more in time.

The swell on the ocean was vast. The barrel perilously rolled, pitched and ducked. Except for an occasional groan or two the covered women might have been dead. The only persons unperturbed were the captain and crew, who swigged with relish and regularity at the wine bottles, at the same time breaking into loud vinous laughter. This gave One-eye an incongruously leering look, as if he were positively enjoying the tribulations of his wretched passengers. By this time we could see Moorea, jagged against the skyline, and the schooner seemed more than ever like a lump of white, drifting flotsam as it pitched and rolled towards the wall of dark rocks.

About this time I discovered that someone had left a Paris newspaper – which one I now forget – on one of the deck seats. Ever anxious to improve my halting French I seized upon it eagerly and spent the next half hour or so reading columns of those fascinating advertisements, always more beguiling in French than in English, in which lonely persons of both sexes proffer their charms and statistics in a yearning search for a mate. By now most of the women were not dead but horrifically and loudly seasick and I have never been so glad of a newspaper in my life.

Soon, to my undisguised relief, I heard the engine cut out and I looked up to realize that we were drifting in towards an anchorage under the high, palm-clad rocks. When we were finally tied up by a jetty there was an eager rush of passengers to lay hands on great frosty chunks of pink and amber water-melon being sold on the quay. While these were being consumed there was a vigorous unloading of cargo and wine-barrels.

We, having no local currency, were unable to buy any water-melon, but presently one of the crew leapt ashore and came back with two delicious amber hunks, into which we buried our faces eagerly, at the same time staring into the depths of crystal-bright water at vast and brilliant shoals of tropical fish in every sort of colour from dazzling electric blue to vivid yellow, an astonishing fishy kaleidoscope flashing this way and that with ordered speed, the whole thing looking as if freshly painted.

This was the first of three stops at similar anchorages along the coast-line and at each of them the pattern of water-melon, rolling wine-barrels and the kaleidoscope of fish was repeated. We came at last to the entrance to a big lagoon with the inevitable coral reef guarding the entrance and offering a barrier to the Pacific, whose gigantic waves charged it constantly like a massed attack of mad, white-maned fighting horses. There is something fearful about this savage and primeval conflict between ocean wave and coral reef and I never watched it without a certain chill of fright.

After the lash and roar of this ocean conflict the inner reaches of the lagoon were almost deathly quiet. We glided smoothly along between walls of palm and hibiscus and allamanda and frangipani, drifting quietly for perhaps two miles, perhaps more, until we could see at last the head of the lagoon, with houses, a cluster of fishing boats and another anchorage.

As we pulled into this we saw, among the little crowd gathered on the jetty, a middle-aged man and woman waving enthusiastically. Anticipating that these were the Larsens we waved back.

They were indeed the Larsens and soon, on shore, we were being welcomed like long-lost relations, returning prodigals or bosom friends. It was not until some long time later that we learned that the Larsens had not the remotest clue as to our identity. They didn't even know our names. They had simply invited us out of an eager hunger for contact with someone from the world beyond the boundaries of the Lotus Land.

Moorea is one of the most beautiful islands in the world; few places can lay a firmer claim to the word paradise. Not only is this pictorially so but the Larsens, on their estate of 4000 acres, were self-sufficient in everything but wine. From oranges to coffee, bananas to fresh-water shrimps, beef to vanilla, chickens to lemons, timber to fish: theirs could truly be called a land flowing with milk and honey.

Their house was roomy but unpretentious, set in a rambling garden of palms, tree ferns, bananas, hibiscus, frangipani and ginger lilies. We ourselves were assigned to a big bare wooden hut that Madge insists was more like an isolation hospital than a house. My own recollection is that it was hot and uncomfortable and that the constant crowing of jungle cocks kept us awake half the night.

In the morning we breakfasted on coffee so exquisite of flavour and aroma that I was inspired to a chorus of praise for it, even going so far as to say that I felt I was really drinking coffee for the first time in my life. It was purest nectar. The Larsens explained its secret: it came, first of all, from the estate; not a single bean, in the second place, was roasted or ground until it was seven years old – coffee beans apparently having the virtue, like wine or sardines, of improving with age; and last, only the essential quantity needed for each day was roasted and ground at any one time. Certainly, neither before nor since, have I tasted coffee of such ethereal quality.

After breakfast we wandered about the estate. Much of it was hilly, all of it lush. 'The air,' as Stevenson had once written, 'smelt strong of wild lime and vanilla'. This was scarcely surprising, since vanilla, which is an orchid, (*Vanilla planifolia*), was growing everywhere: soft cream lady-slipper flowers of great delicacy giving off their slightly heady scent. During the war synthetic vanilla had largely replaced natural vanilla until it was discovered that the synthetic product might be a possible cause of cancer; as a result natural vanilla was again in demand and that morning on the hillside among giant banana trees *petite* Chinese women were hand-fertilising vanilla flowers, which are self-sterile, doing the required work with a matchstick, their delicate fingers so swift that they could fertilise a possible two thousand flowers a day. The resulting vanilla pod takes about six months to mature and then resembles a tobacco-brown bean which, incidentally, may be usefully kept with your coffee beans to give them a subtle aromatic flavour.

As we watched the Chinese women deftly engaged among the vanilla flowers it suddenly began to rain torrentially. The air steamed; it was as if we were in a warm sticky bath as we ran for shelter in a little wooden hut. The rain ceased as swiftly as it had begun, leaving the jungle of vines and palms and bananas and tree-ferns and bamboo dripping and sparkling. As we walked back down the hillside we stopped to pick oranges from a tree, and to the air that 'smelt strong of wild lime and vanilla' was suddenly added the rich fragrance of the oil of orange peel.

Next morning we walked in an opposite direction, along the shores of the lagoon, on a dry stony track that wound through high palms. We had scarcely started when once again it began to rain torrentially. This time there was no hut in which to shelter and we were obliged to walk on, again as in a warm sticky bath, until we were soaked to the skin. There was nothing to worry about in this. We simply walked on until the rain abruptly stopped and the sun came out, immediately hot and sparkling, the palm fronds dripping a great spattering cascade of silver raindrops. Then we found a stretch of sand on the lagoon shore, in full sun, and there took off our clothes and hung them to dry on a bush while we lay naked in the sun and rolled in the tepid shallow water. This, for an hour or so, was truly the Lotus Land.

The strong attraction which islands have for man is one I find of endless fascination. Men long to possess islands as they long to possess lovers. There are never enough islands, it would seem, to satisfy man's great island appetite. Yet John dos Passos, the American novelist, hit on a singular truth when he described Madeira, his birthplace, as 'very lovely but a prison, a beautiful prison'. What is true of Madeira is even more true of Tahiti and Moorea and as many islands of the Pacific as you care to name. What attracted Stevenson and Loti and Gauguin and his several friends to them? No doubt a means of escape from something – but an escape to what? Dos Passos, it seems to me, had the answer – nothing more than an escape to prison.

The Larsens were another illustration of this. Their beautiful paradise, rich, lush, peaceful, self-sufficient, its infinite natural beauties amazingly and dramatically enhanced every evening by what must be the most spectacular sunsets in the world – it is exactly as if the lid of a giant cauldron is suddenly lifted across the ocean, filling the sky with flame, orange, scarlet, yellow, rose and richest purple until the eyes themselves almost burn too as they try to absorb its powerful intensity – was really a prison which caused one to recall another truth, namely that of Sir John Suckling, who reminded us long ago that 'stone walls do not a prison make, nor iron bars a cage'. No: the paradise of a Lotus lagoon deep in the Pacific can create prison just as successfully – so that when I think of the Larsens it is not so much with a memory of their exquisite coffee, the delicious flavour of fresh-water shrimps or the air strong with 'wild lime and vanilla', as with a picture of them, in the days before flying-boats revolutionized communications, sitting down at breakfast every morning and going through the solemn ritual of opening a newspaper that the monthly boat from Marseilles had brought. That the paper was a month old was of no importance. It was an infinitely precious link from prison to the outside world.

Before we left Moorea one other thing seemed to me to symbolize the illusion that here was paradise. We were again walking along the shore of the lagoon when we came upon a tree, a species of hibiscus. This is not the hibiscus which provides the glorious saucers of pink and scarlet and yellow that Polynesian girls wear in their hair but an altogether taller tree whose bark provides the material from which so-called grass-skirts are made. An interesting characteristic of this hibiscus is that its flowers, more like bells than saucers, begin the day by being white, then turn creamy-yellow by noon and then a sort of cloudy crimson by sunset, when they at last fall off, their brief daily cycle of blossoming finished. Beautiful and ephemeral, that tree has ever since seemed to me to symbolize the Polynesian *malaise*.

The week-end being over, we took the schooner back to Papeete and then, a week later, left Papeete too. I wasn't sad to leave the sadness of Tahiti, a sadness made deeper by an incident of a character I later weaved into a story called *Mrs Eglantine*.

'Every morning Mrs Eglantine sat at the round bamboo bar of the New Pacific Hotel and drank her breakfast. This consisted of two quick large brandies, followed by several slower ones. By noon breakfast had become lunch and by two o'clock the pouches under and above Mrs Eglantine's bleared blue eyes had begun to look like large puffed pink prawns.'

'I suppose you know you've got her name wrong?' my friend the doctor said to me. 'It's really Eglinton. What makes you call her Eglantine?'

'She must have been rather sweet at some time.'

'You think so?' he said. 'What has Eglantine got to do with that?'

'The Sweet-briar,' I said, 'or the Vine, or the twisted Eglantine.'

Mrs Eglantine was in fact a piece of alcoholic flotsam such as Maugham and Conrad were fond of describing. She at least had no illusions about the Paradise and the Lotus Land:

'Swindle. The big myth. The great South-sea bubble. The great South-sea paradise. Not a decent hotel in the place. All the shops owned by Chinks. Everybody bone-lazy. Takes you all day to cash a cheque at the bank. Hot and dirty . . . You've seen the travel posters, haven't you, dear? Those nice white sands and the Polynesian girls with naked bosoms climbing the palms. All a myth, dear. All a bloody swindle. All taken in the Cook Islands, hundreds of miles away.'

Mrs Eglantine had other sources of disillusionment and bitterness. She had come all the way from Australia to marry a Frenchman in Tahiti only to find, on arrival, that the Administration had posted him, in her view deliberately, to New Caledonia. Her dilemma now was that she was either waiting permission to stay on the island, or deportation – she didn't know which. She was bitter too with the French, who didn't like the British, and further embittered by the Governor, who didn't like her. 'Undesirable type, dear. Divorced and drinks too much. Bad combination.'

Eventually it turned out that Mrs Eglantine was to be deported and it happened that she flew out on the same flying-boat as we did. She was much depressed and I bought her customary breakfast for her on the plane. The irony of her going was that she had to be deported to the nearest British possession, which happened to be the Cook Islands, which under a system of partial prohibition were virtually dry. It was hard to know what Mrs Eglantine would have for breakfast.

At Atutaki, after the flying-boat had landed on the lagoon and was being re-fuelled, a group of Polynesian women and girls were singing songs of farewell to a young man about to leave on the plane.

'The songs of Polynesia have a great sadness in them. A few of the women were weeping. Then at the last moment a girl rushed on bare feet along the jetty towards the waiting launch, wringing her hands in sorrow, her long hair flying, bitterly weeping final words of good-bye.

'On the scalding white coral beach, under the palms, there was no sign of Mrs Eglantine. And presently, as the launch moved away, I could no longer hear the songs of sad farewell or the haunting voice of the girl who was weeping. But only, running through my head, haunting too:

' "The Sweet-briar, or the Vine, or the twisted Eglantine".'

XIII

During the war and in the years immediately after it I had travelled much and far. I had seen the squalor, the fatalism and the charm of India, the ruin and grace of Burma, the colonial piracy of the Bahamas, something of the West Indies and America, something of the Middle East, from the Pyramids to the great wondrous towers of Baalbek, much of Europe and a glimpse, an unaffectionate glimpse, of the Far North. But wherever I went, and however far, I was for ever left with one unbreakable, unshakeable conviction: there was, for me, among the wonders, the paradises, the Lotus Lands and all, no place like England. The more my world enlarged and ripened the more English I became.

At the heart of all this lay an odd paradox. Whenever I began to think in terms of a novel I could conceive of no other background than my native Midlands, the valleys of my childhood which I had left many years before. The powerful knot which bound me to them refused to be broken. Ardent lover of the south country and, in particular Kent, though I had become, consistently maintaining that here was some of the loveliest countryside in the land, I felt no kind of urge to place a novel there. Short stories and *novellas*, yes, but never a longer work. To complete the paradox I no longer felt impelled to place a shorter work in the county of my childhood.

Somewhere in the mid-fifties, however, I began restlessly nursing a new idea. I had long been fascinated by a rural junk-yard I used to pass two or three times a week. Its crazy mess of old iron, rusting implements, pigs, horses, geese, turkeys, haystacks and useless junk of every kind sat incongruously next to the most beautiful of bluebell woods, the junk mocking the beauty, the bluebells mocking the junk. Here, it seemed to me, was something that had to be written about. The more I thought about it, however, the farther I seemed to get from any kind of accomplishment.

Here, in fact, was the perfect example of a negative needing a positive to wake it to life. I did not, however, go round consciously searching for a positive; experience teaches that these things happen by accident, unexpectedly. And so it was. One early summer evening Madge and I were driving through a Kentish village twenty-five miles east of us, in apple orchard country, when she suddenly had reason to stop and make a few purchases at the village shop. As I sat waiting for her in the car I noticed, outside the shop, a ramshackle lorry that had been recently painted a violent electric blue. Two or three minutes later there came out of the shop, in high spirits, a remarkable family: father a perky, sprightly character with dark side-burnings, Ma a youngish handsome woman of enormous girth, wearing a bright salmon jumper and shaking with laughter like a jelly, and six children, the eldest of them a beautiful dark-haired girl of twenty or so. All were sucking at colossal multi-coloured ice-creams and at the same time crunching potato crisps. As they piled into the lorry there was an air of gay and uninhibited abandon about it all. Wild laughter rang through the village street and the whole scene might have come out of Merrie England.

This, I suddenly knew, was my positive; here were the inhabitants of my junk-yard. Next morning, in a fever of excitement and laughter, I set the family going in a short story called *The Darling Buds of May*, in which the unconventional natures of Pop, Ma and their children are unashamedly revealed. The eldest and most beautiful girl, unmarried, is revealed as being pregnant, but exactly by whom she doesn't know. Does it matter? Not on your life – 'perfick', says Pop. He, the junkdealer, his pockets stuffed with fat rolls of pound notes, is revealed as never paying income tax. He regards it as sort of immoral even to think of doing so. The entire family is gargantuan of appetite, unenslaved by conventions, blissfully happy. Pop is further revealed as a passionate lover of the countryside, as ardent a worshipper at the bluebell shrine and its nightingales as he is of Ma's seductive, voluptuous

bosoms. He yields to no man in his warm, proud love of England. All is 'perfick'.

Presently it seemed to me a thousand pities to confine such a rich gallery of characters to a short story. In their lusty love of life they cried out for greater space, richer pastures. I accordingly began to expand them into a novel. The Larkin household was then revealed in all its uninhibited glory: two enormous television sets, a Rolls-Royce, a vast glittering cocktail cabinet from which Pop dispenses cocktails of a terrifying potency with such names as Red Bull and Rolls-Royce, a potency that affects Mr Charlton, a visiting tax-man, with dire consequences. His seduction by Mariette being at last complete, he finds himself surrendering completely to the Larkins, the Larkin household and above all the Larkin philosophy, which is all *carpe diem* and the very antithesis of the Welfare State. The Larkins' secret is in fact that they live as many of us would like to live if only we had the guts and nerve to flout the conventions. Pop and Ma demonstrate that they have the capacity by indulging deeply in love and champagne before breakfast, passion in the bluebell wood and encouraging their enchanting daughter to a life of wilful seduction. Ma too has a philosophy all her own. It is what she calls 'lending Pop out'. Thoroughly aware of Pop's attraction for the opposite sex, and *vice versa*, she has no compunction whatever about letting him have an occasional fling with others, whether beautiful or, like the spinster Miss Pilchester, merely hungry and unsatisfied. Result: much Chaucerian fun and infinite happiness.

The Darling Buds of May was instantly a phenomenal success. It went into many languages. Colonials and Americans, having tended to think of the English as cold stuffed-shirts, seized upon its wanton, Chaucerian joys, its flouting of conventions and the Welfare State, with joy and relish. It also became revealed as a healer of the sick, a blower away of the blues. From all quarters came reports of laughter killing depression, of the Larkins working miracles in hospital wards. An American woman wrote to say that one day on looking out of her window she was much startled to see her next-door neighbour writhing on her bed in the throes of apparent agony. On rushing to her aid she found that it was nothing of the kind; she was merely reading *The Darling Buds of May*.

Thus encouraged, I proceeded to a second novel, *A Breath of French Air*, in which the entire Larkin family, new baby and all, set off in the Rolls-Royce for a French holiday, only to suffer certain disillusionments in the matter of French weather, French food ('We shan't get very fat on this') and French sanitary arrangements. The whole thing develops into a wanton Bacchanale. From this I proceeded still further to *When the Green Woods Laugh*, *Oh! to be in England* and finally to *A Little of What you Fancy*, not the least distinctive feature of which is the behaviour of Primrose, the beautiful archseductress who is not only capable of thinking, in true Larkin fashion, through the pores of her skin but also proves she is capable of a double act by openly seducing the local curate with her voluptuous body in a mushroom field, having first softened him up with even more voluptuous quotations on the subject of uninhibited love from Blake and Donne.

The Larkins could, if necessary, be read on two planes: purely for the sheer joy of their enviable way of life, but also as a reflection on the revolution that had overtaken post-war England, a revolution that had nowhere been so marked as in the English countryside. In the early thirties not a single farm worker in my village had a car, many not even a bicycle; today many have two cars, many a cottage inhabited by a family displays four, five, even six cars; few village shops sold anything but mouse-trap cheese, fat bacon, candles, paraffin, tart oranges and boiled sweets; today every one has its deep freeze dispensing scampi, smoked salmon, *spaghetti bolognese* and exotics of every kind. Not that it was either essential or necessary to interpret the books as being in any way a treatise on the revolution; the point was never laboured or forced. The surface delight was no mere coating for a pill; it could be unashamedly enjoyed, as Ma and Pop unashamedly enjoyed their love and champagne and Primrose her seduction by flesh and poetry in the fields, for its own sake.

The comedian in me, which much earlier in my career had produced *My Uncle Silas* and other pieces in lighter vein, is not only capable of laughing at the foibles of others or indulging in the effervescence of comedy; it is also a source of self-criticism; it is a means of preventing myself from taking myself too seriously, of becoming pompous; it even enables me to poke fun at myself and my own short-comings.

It is not to be denied, moreover, that there is something of myself in Pop Larkin: a passionate Englishman, a profound love of Nature, of the sounds and sights of the countryside, of colour, flowers and things sensual; a hatred of pomp, pretension and humbug; a lover of children and family life; an occasional breaker of rules, a flouter of conventions. The only things I don't share with Pop are a business ability to sell junk at a profit of three hundred and more per cent or to avoid the payment of income tax.

Pop is in fact an expression of my own philosophy: the need to go with the stream, never to battle against it. The prolific fruits of this are to be seen in Pop's many children, as they are to be seen in mine. To my four, Ann, Judith, Richard and Jonathan, all now grown up, are now added progeny of their own: Stephen, Jeremy, Andrew, Beverley, Emma, Jonathan, Lydia, Timothy, Catherine and Justin. A handsome cornucopia.

As I write these final words I am looking out over the garden that, forty years ago, was a derelict farmyard; it is now rich in maturity, bright not only with autumn colour but here and there, with a mauve iris or two, a witch hazel, a viburnum in blossom, with a premature touch of spring. Beyond it stand the great turkey oaks, pure molten gold against the most tranquil of blue November skies in the morning sun. These splendid trees are, to me, something more than trees. They stand for England, my England.

In them, indeed, I see the world in ripeness. *Bon fruit*, the French say, *mûrit tard*, or if you prefer English: 'ripeness is all'.